# MEMOIRS OF
# A FEMALE THIEF

# Memoirs of
# a Female Thief

DACIA MARAINI

**NEW ENGLISH LIBRARY**
TIMES MIRROR

Translated by Nina Rootes

Original text © Casa Editrice Valentino Bompiani, Milan, 1972
This translation © Abelard-Schuman Ltd, 1973
First published in Great Britain by Abelard-Schuman Ltd, 1973

*

FIRST NEL PAPERBACK EDITION FEBRUARY 1975

*

*NEL Books are published by*
*New English Library Limited from Barnard's Inn, Holborn, London, E.C.1.*
*Made and printed in Great Britain by Hunt Barnard Printing Ltd., Aylesbury, Bucks.*

45002029 0

# I

My mother was fifteen years old when she gave birth to Eligio, her first son. Then came Orlando, in 1912. By the time I was born, she was twenty-four and had already had several children; some were living, some dead.

They say I was born wrong, half-strangled by the umbilical cord, which was wound round my body like a snake. My mother thought I was dead and my father was on the point of throwing me into the dustbin. Then, they say, I opened my great, gaping hole of a mouth and let out a furious howl. So they realised I was alive; they cut off the snake, washed me and popped me into bed with my six little brothers.

Aunt Nerina says that, as a small child, I was like a monkey – black, hairy, spiteful and always imitating people. But I don't believe it – ever since I can remember I've had a light complexion and gingery-red hair. Still, I must admit I don't remember the time when I was very small. My first memory is of my brother Orlando poking a finger into my left eye, when I was six years old. He said my eyes were as clear and shiny as marbles and he wanted to play with them. He damn near put my eye out for me.

This memory is tied up with another one. They both happened about the same time, but I couldn't say which came first.

One night, I was woken up by some frightening dream, which I've forgotten now. I got up and went to the kitchen to fetch a drink of water. As I passed the door of my parents' bedroom, I heard a little sound, like someone moaning. I put my eye to the keyhole and saw my father, sleeping curled up with his mouth

5

open, and my mother, sitting stark naked on the bed and stroking herself between the legs.

At the time, I thought she was playing, and I didn't change my ideas until years later, when I too started to play that game, and then I understood that it was more than just a game, it was something potent and intoxicating.

I remember my mother well. She had a splendid body. She was sturdy, but with dainty wrists and ankles. She had lots and lots of fair hair which she wore plaited round her head. She was cheerful and energetic but occasionally she was afflicted with fits of gloom, when her troubles weighed her down.

I loved playing, having fun. All day long I was out in the streets playing *bottonella* with my friends. We had heaps of buttons of all colours. The gold ones were the most precious, they were worth a million; black ones came next in value, then red and yellow, then the white ones which were the least valuable. Green buttons were rare and they were said to be unlucky. When we came across one, we put it in the ground and peed on the spot where we'd buried it.

My mother had a favourite dress, black with yellow flowers on it and a row of buttons all down the front. Every time she found the buttons missing, she went mad and gave me a good hiding. Then she bought some new ones and patiently sewed them on. For a few days I would be as good as gold, then I would go and rip them all off again – the thick, yellow buttons were too tempting. When mamma got hold of me, she squeezed me tight between her knees and thumped the living daylights out of me.

I was a bad loser and often got into fights. I tried to find excuses to reclaim the buttons I had lost. 'You pinched them, you rotten thief!' I would shout. Sometimes the little girl took fright and gave them back, sometimes she resisted. Then I walloped her one.

I was very vain about my clothes. If I put on a new belt, I thought I was the cat's whiskers. My playmates and I sat under the trees and talked and admired ourselves: we compared our figures, our feet, the size of our waists. We indulged in fantasies: we were going to be actresses when we grew up. I said I would rather be a ship's captain and spend my life at sea, day and night, riding the tall waves and playing *bottonella* with the sailors.

We rolled up bits of newspaper and pretended to smoke. Then we played our games again, with fags dangling from our lips.

6

Towards evening, my mother would come, grab me by the hair and say, 'You're always playing, you useless layabout! You can't go on like this. Tomorrow, I'm sending you to the tailor to learn a trade!' Every day she said the same thing and sometimes she pulled my hair for good measure.

Once, she really did send me to a tailor to learn how to sew. She took me to a mute who worked in a room all hung about with trousers – they were even dangling from the light-fitting. As soon as I came in, the tailor made signs that I was to sit beside him and handed me some cloth and showed me how to put in the over-stitching. I learned quickly, but inwardly I was fuming. If I'm stuck in this dump, I thought, at least I want to learn how to cut and sew, how to make up garments by myself. But I wasn't allowed to do anything except overstitching, and even then the tailor wasn't satisfied. He was dumb, the silence weighed on me and made me melancholy. So I sang. And while I was singing, bent over my work, the tailor cuffed me on the head.

I went on doing those wretched stitches for six or seven days, then I'd had it. I left. The tailor wouldn't pay me a brass farthing and my mother even had to go and apologise for me.

At home life was chaotic. My brothers were in and out all the time, shouting and squabbling. My mother chucked them out. My father beat them. But they always started fighting again.

One day my mother said to me, 'Listen, your grannie wants to see you – you, your brother Orlando, Balilla and Nello as well; she wants all four of you.'

'What for? To give us a hiding? Or preach us a sermon?'

Our grandmother was very strict, a moralising old bore, in fact. With everybody else she was as sweet as pie, but with us she was cantankerous, I don't know why. She'd say to us, 'Your mother's given you up as a bad job, she doesn't even try to bring you up properly! You're a pack of idle, good-for-nothing rascals!'

My mother hadn't much time to devote to bringing us up because she had to do the work in the house, in the bar and in the small-holding we had. And she had to go fishing as well. She was worn out with child-bearing. She would be breast-feeding one and already pregnant with the next. Babies, babies, every year another one.

Grandma Teresa, in that querulous, crotchety voice of hers, would say, 'Your mother's a heathen, she never takes you to church!' Grannie was a bigot, always beating her breast in church. She'd grab me by the scruff of the neck and say: 'Have you been to early Mass today?' I always said yes, but it was a lie.

Later, mamma would round on us: 'Why do you get me into trouble with that narrow-minded old grandmother of yours, you little wretches? Just because I don't go to church, that's no excuse for you not to go.' To avoid grandma's sermons, we always made out it was mother's fault for not sending us to church, but it wasn't true.

Then grandfather would come with a big stick in his hand and hit me and Orlando on the backside with it. He was known as 'the Colonel'. The other grandchildren, our cousins, were a mealy-mouthed lot and sucked up to grandma: 'How are you, grannie darling? Give us a little kiss.' And they twisted her round their little fingers. I was no good at playing the hypocrite. I loved my grandmother, but I felt more like biting her than kissing her, especially when she grumbled at us in that quavering, spiteful voice of hers.

So that morning, as I was saying, my three brothers and I go to see grandmother. 'Listen,' she says, 'would you like to come and pick water-melons?'

We went in a little donkey-cart, all piled in on top of one another, clippety-clop, clippety-clop all the way to grannie's fields, nearly two miles away. There were some olive trees, ancient and contorted, with black holes in them where ants, spiders and snakes hid. And some vines so loaded with grapes that the bunches touched the ground, like the teats of a bitch that's just pupped. It was a lovely, rich, fertile bit of land.

'Come on,' she says, 'get a move on, we've got to collect all the water-melons. Hurry up!' Meanwhile, she was choosing the ripest ones, tapping them, sniffing them and then handing them to us. We ran and piled them up in the shade of the pergola.

We ran up and down, to and fro, under the broiling sun. 'Christ!' I say after a while, 'she's making us scurry about like ants. When's she going to give us a water-melon to eat, then?'

'Never,' says Orlando, 'not on your Nelly!'

'Right!' I say, 'we'll soon fix that!' Bonk! And I let a melon fall on the ground. 'Oh, grandma, I've dropped a melon!' I exclaim.

'Never mind,' she says, 'we'll eat it later.' So Orlando and I started guzzling that lovely red pulp full of warm juice. How thirsty we were! What with the heat and the sweat, it was a joy to eat that melon.

'Aha, I see!' says my other brother, 'if we drop one, we can eat it!' Bonk! Down goes another one. 'Oh, grannie, I've dropped a melon too! What can we do?'

'All right, all right,' she says, 'put it on one side and we'll eat it later.'

By the end of the day, our bellies were bursting with watermelon. We had split so many that we got sick of them and squirted the juice into the spider's holes.

When it grew dark, we all climbed into the little cart and went home. Grannie counted the melons and said there were very few, so, to take her mind off it, we started a furious fight amongst ourselves.

As soon as he saw me coming in the door, my brother Luciano stuck out his foot and sent me sprawling. I grazed my knee badly. Then father came along and went for him with the strap. But Luciano dodged and the strap caught me. At that moment, I hated my father. It wasn't his fault: he'd meant to thrash Luciano but belted me instead. He gave me a purple bruise on the thigh that didn't fade for a week.

My father was very busy in those days. So he says to my brother Orlando, 'As from tomorrow, you'll feed the pigs, I haven't got time.' In the evening, my father showed him how to fill up the bucket and carry it on a pole resting on his shoulders.

In the morning Orlando took the pig food and off he went. I went out with him. For a long time now, I had been Orlando's shadow, following him everywhere, copying everything he did. As soon as he sees me, he says, 'Piss off, stupid! I don't want you tagging along.' But I followed him all the same. Then I saw that, instead of going up to the small-holding, he went down to the river and chucked all the food into the water. He sat down under a tree, with the empty bucket beside him, and smoked a fag. I go and sit beside him and he says, 'Keep your mouth shut, Teré, or I'll have your guts for garters!'

'What do you think I am, a sneak?' I say, and he lets me have a drag on his cigarette.

Once, twice, he got away with it. After three or four times, father says to him one morning, 'You've been quick! How do you manage it?'

Orlando, bold as brass, answers, 'We had a race to see who'd get home first.'

Then father says, 'And how is it that when I went up there yesterday I found the pig trough as dry as a bone and heard the pigs squealing their heads off?'

'Well,' said Orlando, 'it's obvious. They'd eaten the lot and licked the trough clean.'

My father didn't say a word. But that evening he went to see if Orlando really had taken the grub to the animals. The pigs were squealing. They'd squealed themselves hoarse. Then he realised they hadn't eaten for days. But still he didn't say anything.

Next morning, when Orlando went out with the bucket, he followed him. He saw him throw the food into the river, waited for him on the doorstep of the house and gave him a sound thrashing.

'And you!' he says to me, 'you didn't know a thing about it, eh?'

'Me?' I say, 'what do I know?' But he didn't believe me, and wham! a beating for me too. My legs were black and blue from the strap.

'That'll teach you to aid and abet your brother!' he says.

'But if I'd told, Orlando would have murdered me!' I say. Then my father gave me a punch on the nose that knocked me to the ground. I was about thirteen at this time.

Another thing I couldn't stomach was school. There was a teacher who used to sit up in her high desk knitting all day. She would call a pupil to the blackboard and say, 'Write: ITALY IS A PENINSULA, all in capitals.' Then she'd go on, 'Did you wash your ears this morning? Good. Go and sit down.' And that was the end of the lesson.

Instead of going to school, Orlando and I liked to take the boat and go fishing for octopus, devilfish and sea-urchins. I lost the use of a finger because of these sea-urchins. I picked them up with my fingers instead of using a knife. These prickly creatures have straight, black spines, hard and sharp. One day, as I was grabbing a sea-urchin, a spine went in under my nail. It hurt, it throbbed, but I took no notice. Then it started swelling and turned yellow with pus.

My father took me to a doctor in Anzio, called Verace, who's dead now. He cut my finger open and said, 'If you'd left it any longer, we'd have had to cut off her hand.' Then I had my hand all bandaged up. I ran a high temperature. Mamma fed me, she carried me to the lavatory in her arms. But the finger didn't get any better, so father took me back to Dr Verace. He slit my finger open in a new place. Then he sewed it up, but he was in a hurry and he pulled the thread too tight. To cut a long story short, from that day to this my finger has stayed bent – I can't straighten it out because of that nerve sewn up in haste.

I couldn't write with my finger like that, so I didn't have to go to school. That was a blessing. Orlando and I went collecting sparrows' eggs, him in front, me behind, clambering about on dry, rotten branches. How it was we never fell, I don't know. We prised limpets off the rocks. Then I would throw myself into the water like a fish and we'd race each other at swimming. We dived, too. Orlando was small, smaller than me, blondish, with a big head and a pale face. He looked delicate, but in fact he was robust and athletic.

In the end, father insisted on our going back to school. I passed the second class and stayed on for another year. The same teacher was still there, knitting all day long. She'd call someone up to the blackboard and say, 'Write: ITALY IS BEAUTIFUL, all in capitals!' When the girl had written it, she stood waiting, chalk in hand. The teacher looked up from her knitting and said, 'The "I" of "Italy" is crooked, write it all again!' Meanwhile, we were playing *bottonella* between the desks. When the pupil had finished writing again, teacher said, 'Do you think I can't see you've been putting charcoal on your eyebrows? You look like a gypsy! Go away, you shameless little hussy!'

After a year of this charade, I left school. It suited mamma to keep me at home to help her with the housework. I cleaned, ironed, and tidied up after my brothers. And there was always a new one, smaller than the rest. When I look back on it, I don't know how I managed it all. I would wash ten or a dozen sheets at the pump, and when it was all done, and I was sweating and spattered with soap, I would strip off, duck into the water, splash myself all over and come out as fresh and cool as a fish. I did it every time; I loved the feel of water.

If Eligio didn't find his shirt ironed and his trousers nicely pressed when he came home, he hit me. He was always thumping me. My eldest brother was a selfish character, taciturn and morose. Most likely, if you went to his house as a guest, he'd treat you like a lord, because he's generous, but he's ignorant and

11

boorish. I used to wear short skirts, and the moment he saw me with a bit of knee showing, he would come at me, wham! with his belt, or kick me on the shins. He couldn't bear to see my legs, it got on my nerves. He was an ignoramus, always hunting and shooting or messing about with horses, a country bumpkin in fact. He was tall, well-built, red-headed. Like me. But I'm a bit gingery, he was auburn.

Orlando, the second son, has light, gingery hair like me. For years we were inseparable – wherever he went I went too. Always together. Then he found older friends, sailors, and he didn't want me around any more. With these new friends he went out drinking, he went with women. He never showed his face at home.

Once, my mother went into the barn where we kept the farm implements and found Orlando with his friends and a woman. They had got hold of some whore off the streets and brought her in there. Mamma grabbed her by the hair and gave her a good thrashing. Then, I remember, the hay caught fire, because the sailors hadn't stubbed out their cigarettes properly. Orlando used to steal things from home, too: dresses, underclothes, food. He took them to that woman he and his friends consorted with. I saw her once, by chance. They kept her shut up, but one evening she came out to do a pee and I saw her. She was as skinny as a rake, white-skinned and with hair cropped short like a nun's.

Orlando and Eligio were the most treacherous of my brothers. They were always beating me. Black and blue. A kick from one, a slap from the other, they vied with each other to see who could get in the most blows.

After Orlando came Nello. Then Luciano, who died. Then another one they called Luciano. Then Libero, who was killed by a train. Then Luciano, Luciano the Third. Then Matteo and Balilla. Then Oreste, who's in America now, and then Iride. After the war, my sister Iride married an American N.C.O., and Orlando was so angry that he put hand-grenades all round the church.

Four other brothers died as babies – one month, two months old, or newly born. Luciano, Duilio, Oscar and Benedetto died when they were a few years old. And then there were others, but I don't remember because I was very young. I know that when the last one died they came to disinfect the house because he'd had croup. And there was a male nurse who took Oreste in his arms and said, 'This child is really beautiful, he will be rich one day.'

And it has come true. Oreste is of my mother's stock: blond, brown-eyed, clear-skinned, wth prominent cheekbones. Libero, too, was beautiful; he had dazzling white teeth, almond eyes, shining hair. He was the handsomest of all. He threw himself under a train.

# 2

When my mother died, I didn't grieve for her at all. She had gone to our small-holding in Bruciore to feed the pigs. She was in a hurry. Mamma was always in a hurry because my father was a terror and if he didn't find his lunch ready at the proper time he ripped the cloth off the table and threw everything on the floor.

In the mornings, my father worked on the land or went fishing. He had a deep understanding of those two things: the soil and the sea. At 4 a.m., he and my mother went to the port to wait for the fishing-boats. When the catch was unloaded, he looked it over, chose, bargained and bought. Then he sent my mother to Bruciore to feed the pigs while he went to the market in the piazza to sell the fish.

So, one day my mother came tearing back from Bruciore. It was late, so she immediately set about preparing lunch. She had to take in the washing from the line, serve the people in the bar and cook a meal for us. With all these chores, she didn't have time to change her clothes, though she had been soaked to the skin driving the horse and cart back from the fields. She had been caught in a downpour and now she was dripping water all over the place. 'Oh, Lord,' she said, 'your father will be home any minute and the food's not ready!' And instead of going to change, she started work in her sopping-wet clothes so that father, who was worse than the devil himself, would find his meal ready when he came in.

That evening, she had a temperature. She had caught a cold, her face was red and she was coughing. 'My throat's sore,' she said, 'it's burning.' But she couldn't go to bed because there was too much to do. She neglected herself. And she got bronchitis. Even with a temperature of 102 degrees, she never went to bed. And the bronchitis turned to pneumonia.

In a week, my mother was dead. Only during the last day or two did she go to bed. Verace came. He gave her some cough syrup, drew off a little blood and went away. I knew it was serious because mamma looked at me without recognising me; her mouth was always open as if she was short of air. But I was certain that, after a few days, she would be up and about. But she never got up again.

I was disconcerted when I realised she was dead, but I felt no sorrow. I was still without any feeling. My only thought was that now I would have to do the cooking as well as the washing. And I was right.

After her death, I could no longer do as I liked at home because Aunt Nerina, my mother's sister, came to stay with us and she was strict. She kept us under her thumb and wouldn't give us much to eat. Aunt Nerina wasn't unkind, but she was terrified of my father. She quaked at the sight of him. And she virtually never spoke.

Some months later, Lanky Dora turned up again. She had been with us before, when mamma was alive; she had come to help in the house and in the bar, but my mother had chased her out when she caught her screwing with my father. So she went away, but as soon as she heard about mamma's death, she popped up again, with her curly hair and her goggling eyes and a bag full of clothes in her hand. She dumped herself on us for keeps. Later on, she wrote home to Friuli and told her sister to come down. The three of them set up as a threesome in my house, that is, in my father's house. He kept them. Married one and kept the other. They all slept together, one on each side and father in the middle. They made a monkey out of my father because he was a simple countryman and he'd had nothing to do with women – he'd never made love in his whole life except with my mother, until Lanky Dora came along.

These two women got their hooks into him, dominated him, made him sign everything away – first the bar was sold, then the small-holding, then the house. In the end, there was nothing left and my father died virtually a pauper.

As soon as Lanky Dora arrived, all my brothers left home. The eldest had had an education and my mother had found him a position. Now he lives in Nettuno; he owns property and is well off. The others left because they couldn't stand that creature from Fruili; they got married out of desperation. Iride was at boarding-school and my grandmother paid her fees. She was at the San Biagio College in Rimini. Grandma wanted her to study and become a school-teacher. She studied all right, but when she left school she got a job at the rifle range in Nettuno. There she met an American staff sergeant; they got engaged, married and went to America. Now she is in Florida and she has grown-up daughters. She writes occasionally but I never answer. She writes to Lanky Dora, too, because Dora is always poking her nose into our business, complaining about us, weeping and wailing. She's cunning. She tells her I'm a bad lot, a disgrace to the family and so on and so forth.

They despise me and keep me at arm's length. They're ashamed of me, but I'm ashamed of them too. Just because they have money, they think they're royalty. Well, I've had pots of money through my hands. I could have been richer than they are, but I always blued the lot. They, on the other hand, put money aside, save up, pinch and scrape and when they're old and doddering they buy themselves a fine house so that they can die on a feather-bed. A great consolation!

One of my brothers was so miserable with Dora that he went and got married when he was only seventeen. I couldn't stand her either. One day, I went for her. I hit her in the face with a *zoccolo*, one of those wooden sandals you wear on the beach. I clocked her one, right on the mouth, and split her lip open for her. I did it because she was always slapping and punching me. And she was a sharp-tongued bitch, always insulting and provoking me. 'You're incorrigible!' she would say, 'you're as stubborn as a mule and you obey no rules. You wait, you'll come to a sticky end, my girl!' She needled me. She knew I was nobody's fool and that, as long as I was in the house, she would never get the old man to marry her. She thought to herself, I'll have to get rid of her somehow.

And she had her way. She taunted and tormented me till that day when I split her lip with the wooden sandal. Naturally, she soon started screaming and yelling. She sent for my father, showed him all the blood pouring down, for, instead of washing and drying the wound, she had deliberately opened it up to make

16

it bleed more. 'Look!' she said to him, 'look what your daughter has done to me!'

My father picked up a chair, one of those brown ones with a straw seat and wooden back. Wham! He broke it over my back and all the pegs fell out. 'Get out!' he said to me, 'get out of this house!'

So much the better, I said to myself, at least I'll be free! Because by then I was eighteen and they were still keeping me locked up. I was never allowed out, I couldn't go to the cinema or anywhere. Once, when my father found me on the flying chairs at the fairground, he almost murdered me. I was with a cousin of mine, a girl who loved to dance, swim, run wild like me. We loved having fun; we went fishing, we went to the fair. So my father finds me there on the flying chairs and takes me home without a word. As soon as we get home, he closes the door and grabs me by the hair (at that time, I had long plaits, right down to my waist). First he gives me four slaps across the face, then he crosses my arms behind my back, ties my hands together and chops off my hair with a pair of scissors.

I saw my two lovely braids lying on the floor, under his boots, and he stamped on them in fury. I wanted to cry. But I wouldn't give him the satisfaction, so I kept quiet and I didn't cry. As soon as he untied me, I put on one of my brother's caps and went out. But first, I glanced at myself in the mirror. 'I look just as pretty!' I said, but it wasn't true. I was ugly, cropped. I looked as if I'd had typhus.

The long and the short of it was that, on account of this Lanky Dora, my father said to me, 'Get out, leave this house! The world is yours!' Perhaps his words are true, I said to myself, at last I'll be able to go dancing, or go to the fair when I feel like it. I was raging with a fever to be free, because I had never known what it meant. If I had to go for a walk in the direction of the station, only half a mile from home, they made me take two or three little brothers with me. I was never allowed out in the evenings.

And so, when I pictured all this freedom, I said to myself: Fine! Now I can go and fetch my cousin. Her name was Amelia. She was full of fun and we agreed on everything. There was another girl, called Rosalba, who always came with us. Her father was dead. I attached myself to these two good-time girls and together we ran wild and free. When I told them my father wanted to throw me out, they were delighted, they hugged me. 'Good!' they said, 'now you can do what you like! Let's go down to the beach.' And we spent all day long in the water, fishing for sea-urchins, plucking little octopuses from the rocks.

In the evening, dead tired, I went to Aunt Nerina's to sleep. The first few times she took me in, gave me a bed and something to eat. Then my father kicked up a fuss and she was too scared to help me any more.

'But, Auntie, where am I going to sleep?' I asked her.

'My dear girl!' she says, 'I'd willingly keep you here, but I'm so afraid of your father.' Everyone in Anzio was afraid of my father, he was a fiend, and Aunti Nerina was a widow, alone in the world; she couldn't stand up to him.

My father had brothers and sisters, all dynamic go-ahead people, and later they became rich. But they were misers and lived in a closed family circle. They never went to the cafés in the piazza in case they had to treat someone to a cup of coffee. They all knew I was homeless, but not one of them was willing to take me in. Not even grandma Teresa, who was still alive then. They were all selfish and cautious. At night, having nowhere to lay my head, I was taking shelter in a cupboard under the stairs in a courtyard; they knew, they had been told about it, but they didn't give a bugger.

After a few days, I was chased out of the cupboard and I roamed about, not knowing where to go. That's when I began to realise that it wasn't much fun being turned out of your own home.

There was an old lorry, without wheels, standing up on blocks in a courtyard; it had been abandoned and was falling to bits. I slept underneath it. At least it kept me dry. There was a bakery nearby where they worked at night, and the bakers' voices kept me company. They worked and I slept. Sometimes I heard steps and saw a shadow passing by. I was frightened. But I comforted myself with the thought that the bakers were not far away; if I shouted they would hear me. And they all knew me. I lay there, quiet as a mouse, wrapped in a blanket Aunt Nerina had given me, and as soon as daylight came I crept out. In the mornings, I was so hungry that my head swam. If I couldn't scrounge something to eat somewhere, I went looking for my smallest brother, Balilla. I sent him to Lanky Dora's to steal a bit of bread, a sausage, and bring them to me. 'Don't let her see you,' he said, 'or she'll wallop me.' Balilla was about twelve; only the youngest children were still at home.

I ate what Balilla brought me and it kept me going for the rest of the day. During the daylight hours I felt like a tigress on the prowl; I went fishing, I went to the fair, I went to watch the workmen building a new road. But when it grew dark, I began to feel thoughtful. Sometimes I went into the church to get warm. I sat as near the altar as possible, as that was the warmest spot. The country people looked at me and said, 'What a devout young girl!' But it wasn't true. I went there only for shelter. I never prayed. I sat there with my hands folded and looked at the statue of the Madonna. This Madonna had a long blue cloak and a crown of stars on her head, rosy lips, rosy cheeks and dark eyes. But one of the eyes had a bit of a squint. I spent hours staring at that eye and wondering whether the Virgin really did have a squint!

Most days I spent with Amelia and Rosalba. They didn't have tyrannical fathers, so they could come and go as they pleased. Being the eldest, I was the boss. If I said, 'Let's go and look for octopus,' we went and looked for octopus. If I said, 'Let's hunt for crickets,' we went and hunted for crickets. We caught them and put them in a box with holes in it. Sometimes we pulled off a leg to watch them limping.

One day we happened to find ourselves near a little villa on the seashore. It was a summerhouse, nobody lived there in the winter. There was a persimmon tree growing out of the wall. 'Let's pick some persimmons!' I say, so we jump over the wall and into the garden.

While we're picking the fruit, my cousin says, 'Let's go into the house.'

'But how can we get in? It's locked,' says Rosalba.

'I'll soon fix that,' I say, and give the door a mighty shove with my shoulder. It opens and in we go.

I had never seen such a beautiful house. There were beds with embroidered counterpanes, wardrobes with painted doors, a gleaming kitchen, a divan with flowered cushions. 'Know what we'll do?' I say. 'We'll sleep here, and first we'll make a meal, there's plates and everything in the kitchen.'

'What about food?' says Rosalba.

'We can pinch it,' says Amelia. 'I can nick some oil and pasta from home.'

'Me too,' says Rosalba.

So we made ourselves thoroughly at home. We cooked a generous supper. Rosalba burnt the sauce. We ate huge platefuls of spaghetti smothered in burnt sauce, but to us it tasted delicious. And how we laughed! I don't know what was so funny, but we nearly died of laughter! Then we made up the beds. We folded the counterpanes and laid them neatly aside. We found pillows. They were filled with feathers, as soft as cream. We slithered down between the sheets.

After sleeping out under that lorry for months I felt as grand as the Pope. I tossed and turned in that silken bed. I stroked myself between the legs: I played the game that I secretly called 'mamma's game', and it filled me with a delicious warmth. I didn't want to sleep, I wanted to wallow in the luxury. I propped myself up on one elbow, and my elbow sank in; I put my head down, and my head sank in. I wanted to go on like that, just to feel the pleasure of sinking in. But I fell asleep almost at once.

In the middle of the night the night-watchman arrived. He opened the door, shone the torch in our faces and said, 'What are you doing here?' We jumped up, grabbed our clothes and ran, while he shouted after us: 'Stop, stop!' We thought nothing of it. It was just a childish escapade. However, the watchman reported us to the police.

I was charged and sentenced to two years' imprisonment. But I was on the run and the judgement was given in default. Then there was an amnesty because somebody – some Princess of Savoy, I think – had given birth to a son, and I was let off those two years. Rosalba and my cousin Amelia finished up at a reformatory. They stayed there for a few months and then they were given a judicial pardon as they were minors. And that was the end of it all.

# 3

The son of the station master at Campo di Carne was always hanging about after me. He had known me since I was twelve, before my mother died. This Sisto kept looking at me and smiling. He was good-looking, thin and wiry, with a moustache. But I didn't fancy him. There was something stupid, something degenerate in his face. He was six years older than I.

To tell the truth, I was keen on another boy, Duilio, who worked at the ironmonger's, selling nails and hardware. He was a handsome, curly-headed blond, with a broad, serene face. He was from Nettuno and had come to Anzio to work. I liked him a lot and was in love with him. But my father didn't take to this Duilio. 'Steer clear of that lout,' he says to me. But I took no notice. I always used to stop and talk to him near the fountain.

One day, when I was standing there talking to him, my father came along and started knocking him about. We hadn't even noticed him coming. He raised his hands, which were as hard as iron, and slapped Duilio twice, once on each cheek. We were right in the middle of town and there were people passing by. Duilio didn't say a word or do anything. He was white with mortification. And from that day on he never showed his face again.

I waited and waited for him. Then, when I realised he wasn't coming, I went looking for him. But I stopped half-way there. If he doesn't come, that means he doesn't want me, I said to myself. And I turned back. I was too proud to chase him. And that was that, all over. But Duilio was really a good-looker, tall and fair, and he liked me, I know he did.

One evening, after my father had turned me out of the house, I met Sisto, the station master's son, and he walked along a little way with me. 'How come I haven't seen you around lately?' he says, 'have you been away?'

'No,' I said, 'I'm living with my aunt now.'

So then he started hanging about outside my aunt's front door, trying to catch me. But he never laid eyes on me, because I was sleeping out, under the lorry, only I hadn't told him that. Then one day he waylays me, stands right in front of me and says, 'Now why aren't you living at home with your dad?'

'I had a fight with Lanky Dora. I nearly murdered her, so my father turned me out.'

He says, 'How come I spend hours waiting outside your aunt's front door and never see you coming in or out?'

'Ah, well,' I say, 'I go out very early, while you're still asleep.'

Then he gives me a look, grabs me by the arm and says, 'Come to the signalman's house with me!'

'No, I don't like you and I never have.' But he keeps on about this signalman's house, where he works as a sort of sub-station master, checking the trains in and out. He keeps trying to persuade me to go with him.

After a few times, I begin to think: Maybe I will go there, then at least I won't have to roam the streets like a stray cat. I could have a bath, sleep in a bed. I was sick of being a vagrant, sleeping under the lorry, washing at the pump and having to dry my clothes on me. So I said to myself: 'Right! This time I'll say yes and go to the signalman's house. I'll be able to eat and sleep like a Christian!

I was a naïve little fool; there were so many things I didn't understand. All I wanted was a roof over my head. Sisto liked me, that's a fact, but he was also thinking of the dowry. He knew my father had a bit of land, and my grandmother was well-known in Anzio for her fertile fields. This girl will bring me money, he thought. 'Let's get married,' he kept saying.

I made love with him, just like that, out of curiosity. I didn't enjoy it. 'You never enjoy it the first time,' he says to me. 'Later on, you'll see, you'll get to like it.'

'We'll see,' I say, and meanwhile I'm taking a good look at him and finding certain defects I don't like: he walks rather like an old man, with stooping shoulders. When he laughs, he exposes

22

his gums, which are red and kind of bloodshot. That puts me off.

To be honest, I still fancied Duilio. I was mad about him. And, to put his nose out of joint, I showed myself around the town with this fellow Sisto.

I went to live with him. He took me to the station house at Campo di Carne where his sisters and his father, the station master, lived. As soon as his sisters clapped eyes on me they put a broom in my hands. They made me wash the dishes and scrub the floor, and if I didn't obey their orders, they complained that I didn't know how to do anything right. These sisters were very earnest and very stern. They were pretty girls. Their mother had died when they were children. That older one was a spiteful sourpuss and Agnesina, the younger one, did everything Ines told her to. She would have been kind to me if she hadn't been afraid of her older sister, who was such a bitch that she remained an old maid all her life.

When I went to live with Sisto I was a slip of a girl, just eighteen years old. One day, by sheer chance, I ran into my brother Eligio. I was shopping, dawdling along absent-mindedly looking at the ground. All of a sudden, I feel somebody grab me, and before I have time to see who it is, he lands two punches right in my face. He's an ignorant pig, a peasant, that brother of mine, and thick-headed.

He seizes hold of my hair and punches me on the chest, in the stomach. He's a great bear of a man and I'm small. I try to bite him but can't get at him. Then he lifts up my skirt and kicks me there in front, between the legs, so hard, and with hard shoes on, that I fall down in a dead faint. And he leaves me there, pouring blood from down below.

I was out cold for an hour, and nobody happened to pass by. It was more than two hours before I really recovered my senses. If I had been a different type I would have gone and reported him to the police out of revenge. Instead, I got up, dazed and tottering, and went back to Sisto.

'What's happened?' he asks as soon as he sees me.

'My brother beat me up,' I tell him, and he starts to laugh.

'A good thing, too,' he says, 'that's the proper thing for a brother to do.'

'Why don't we get married?' I say, but he pretends not to hear me and goes out to play cards with his friends. The truth was, he didn't want to marry me till he got the dowry from my father.

We lived some way from my father's house, so Sisto sent his father, the station master, to deliver a message: 'Tell him I'll marry his daughter, but only if he sends me a dozen sheets, a dozen towels, a dozen tablecloths and a bedroom suite – a bed, a wardrobe, a dressing-table, a tallboy and a nice upholstered armchair.'

Meanwhile, I was pregnant.

Sisto's father came from Ciociaria. He was severe and rather gloomy; he never laughed and never looked anybody straight in the eye. He delivered his son's message and waited. My father said to him, 'I haven't got time to think about my daughter now, come back some other time.'

He came back and reported. Sisto was angry. A few days later, he sent his father back to Anzio to see my father again. In the end, my father got fed up with it and said, 'I'm not giving my daughter a thing. She ran away from home so I don't owe her anything.'

Sisto confronted me with this, saying, 'You bloody liar! Your father didn't throw you out, you ran away of your own free will! What did you do that for, you silly bitch? Now I can't marry you, because you've got no dowry and you're dishonoured!'

'It's my father who's the liar,' I say, 'he *did* throw me out.'

'It's not true,' says Sisto, 'your father told my father that he wanted to marry you to a good boy from Naples, but you wouldn't have it, so you ran away.'

It was true about the Neapolitan. But that had happened two years ago. One day, my father brought a man to the house. He was a short, fat little Neapolitan. He says to me, 'Here's a fine husband for you. Marry him within the week and I'll have you off my hands!'

I took one look at this pale, insignificant creature. Then I said to my father, 'If you fancy him so much, marry him yourself!' And I walked out, slamming the door.

But I certainly didn't run away. Two hours later I went home, and I stayed there another two years, till that incident with the *zoccolo*.

Even though I was pregnant, Sisto wasn't keen to marry me.

24

'Your father's unnatural,' he says, 'he ought to give you a dowry, no matter what. If he doesn't, then I won't marry you.' The sisters became sourer than ever with me. They made me get up at five to clean the stairs, wash the sheets and cook. I even had to do the shopping, and, in the afternoons, I was on my knees polishing the floor. It's a wonder I didn't have a miscarriage.

# 4

When I realised I was in labour, I took the bus and went to San Giovanni hospital to have the baby. I ask for a bed at the hospital. 'Wait!' they tell me. I sit down on a bench and wait. People running about all over the place, but nobody taking any notice of me. Two hours go by, three, and I start to feel scared. I feel like a lost soul.

I am a normal woman. I started making love at eighteen, but I was still very naïve. With Duilio, when he stroked me, made a fuss of me, I was on fire, and I loved to kiss and caress him. But I didn't understand anything about sex. I was so innocent that, sitting there at the hospital, I expected the baby to be born out of my arse. Since childhood I had heard women screaming at their kids: 'You rotten little bastard, I shat you out, now I'll eat you up again!' and because of these words I had taken it into my head that babies were born from behind. I was wondering whether it would be painful, and I was worried in case the baby came out while I was doing my business. I didn't want it to fall into the lavatory pan.

Towards evening, still sitting on the bench, I was seized with violent pains. I got up and started pacing up and down. But I didn't say anything because there was a woman dying in a bed nearby and the sister signalled to me to keep quiet.

In the end I couldn't stand it any longer and let out a yell. Then they took notice. They shoved a lot of forms into my hand. 'Fill up these documents,' they said.

'What?' I say, 'I can't even breathe and you talk about documents!'

26

'All right, never mind. Just sign here.' So I scribbled something, cursing all the saints in heaven at the same time, since my father wasn't there to beat me for blaspheming.

It was only right at the last minute that I realised where the baby was going to be born, because there he was, coming out: a great, big, beautiful boy! First the head, which tore my flesh, and then the shoulders. 'Ah, so that's how babies are born!' I said, 'you might have told me before!'

I stayed there six days, in the bed next to the woman who was forever dying and never died. Now and then they brought her baby to her – he was lusty and screaming with hunger – but she didn't recognise him. They said her blood was wrong, poisoned or something, I don't know. She died on the very day I left.

While I was in there, none of the family came to see me. I went in alone and I came out alone. The nurses were always scurrying about, always in a hurry. They wanted me to vacate the bed as they needed it for someone else. I was still losing a lot of blood. On the sixth day they handed me my baby, all swaddled up, and sent me away.

I take the bus, get out and walk the rest of the way. By the time I get home, I'm so weak I can hardly stand up on my two feet. I go in and find them all very chilly, very distant. Up comes Ines, glances at the baby, makes a face and says, 'Pretty!' The other one, Agnesina, doesn't speak, but her eyes are popping out of her head. I can see at once that they're knocked sideways by the fact that my son is so beautiful. He's big, with a white skin and huge eyes. He's always laughing.

Then Agnesina says, 'Look, Sisto, look at your son!' But he takes no interest, pretends to be busy adjusting his railwayman's cap. He doesn't even look up.

In the end, Agnesina picks up the baby and puts him right under his nose, so he has to look at him. He bends his face down as if he's sniffing him and goes: 'Hmmm!' He doesn't say a word.

Next day, although I was very weak and had to breast-feed the baby every three hours, they put me to work. I had to cook, do the washing and ironing. The baby was in a broken-down iron cot I had found amongst some old rubbish. Nobody took care of him, but luckily he was good and never cried.

Later, as he began to grow, they became very fond of him. Sisto, especially, loved that boy with a passion – in fact he was so possessive that he didn't like me to touch the child. Because of this, and the fear that I would take him away, he married me four months later. And perhaps, too, he had grown a little fond of me, who knows?

But my father-in-law had other ideas. He hated me because I had not brought a dowry with me. He wanted to get rid of me and find a woman with money for his son. The fact that we were married made no difference, he wanted me off his back.

He chewed it over, plotted with his friends and came up with a brainwave. His friends were the doctor from Campo di Carne and the local *maresciallo*, the police inspector. They were always boozing together or playing cards. The station master, the doctor and the *maresciallo* were big fish in their own little pool. They were the bosses and they could do what they liked. The three of them put their heads together and agreed: 'This girl hasn't given the father a dowry. Sisto married her against his will. You know what we'll do? We'll make out a certificate saying this woman is insane and we'll put her in the asylum. Since the mother is unfit, the child belongs to the father. And there we are!' And that's what they did.

One day, I was walking in the garden with the child in my arms. I had just finished the washing-up, the sisters were asleep and I wanted to give the baby some fresh air. While I'm strolling up and down like this, I see a Red Cross ambulance; it draws up beside me. A soldier gets out and says, 'Good afternoon. You have to come with us for a medical examination.'

My first thought was that they wanted to send me to a doctor, on orders from my husband, to see whether my milk was good. This came to my mind because, once or twice, when the baby burped, I had heard Ines say, 'The mother's milk is bad.' If this was so, I was quite willing to go, because I knew I was as healthy as a horse and I thought: Good! Let them examine me, they'll soon find out I've got good milk. And if the doctor says so, those idiots will have to believe it. I knew my milk couldn't be bad, or the baby wouldn't be so plump and flourishing, with a lovely pink and white skin. So I said, 'All right, let's go!'

I got into that ambulance without protest, because I was an ingenuous nincompoop. I was still a simple country girl, I didn't understand the ways of the world. Just as I was getting in, someone snatched the baby from my arms. 'Let the signorina take the baby indoors,' he says, 'so he won't catch cold. We'll soon be

28

back, anyway.' And I see my sister-in-law, Ines, who suddenly pops out from behind the ambulance. She takes the baby. It had all been planned. But I didn't suspect anything. I was a dope, a booby.

'Give me the baby,' I say to my sister-in-law, annoyed. 'Where are you taking him?' But I don't even have time to finish speaking before the soldier has pushed me inside, closed the doors and we're off like a shot from a gun. We take the road to Rome. I'm pretty fed up, but I calm myself with the thought: Never mind, the examination won't take long. I'll soon be home again. Be patient, Teresa, put up with it.

While we're travelling towards Rome, this soldier, who has been looking at me with quite a friendly eye, says to me, 'Signora, I must warn you.'

'What about?' I say, still thinking it's to do with my milk.

'I want to advise you, because I am a father myself and you could be my daughter. When you get to this hospital, you must keep calm, and, when the specialist comes, don't cry or laugh.'

'Why ever not?' I ask.

'Because if you cry, they'll think you're mad, and if you laugh, they'll think you're mad. Instead, you must make them understand, very calmly and patiently, that you've been sent there on your husband's orders, and with the complicity of a doctor, who is his friend. Tell me, did the doctor who signed the letter examine you?'

'No, he didn't examine me. Why?'

'Ah,' he says, 'I thought as much. I could see what was going on: it's a plot to take your baby from you and have you locked up.' Stunned, stupefied, I sit there listening to him, but I only half believe it. I can't help thinking he's the one who's mad.

I arrive at the hospital. Everywhere I see bars, locked doors, white overalls, and I hear shouts and screams and I understand that this is no ordinary hospital. They immediately take hold of me and put me in a cot amongst all the madwomen. I'm under observation. Nurses and orderlies dash in and out, locking the door behind them. After a couple of hours, I finally manage to stop one of them and ask, 'Excuse me, nurse, when will the doctor come?'

'Tomorrow,' she says.

Tomorrow comes, but no doctor. I'm stuck there in bed, watching all these crazy women fighting, wandering about restlessly. I feel my heart shrink. My breasts hurt because of the stagnant milk. I get hold of a nurse and ask, 'When is this doctor coming, then?'

'Ah,' she says, 'you're new. It's always the same with new patients, you keep asking when the doctor's coming. Keep quiet and wait! The doctor will come when he feels like coming!'

I wanted to cry, but I didn't dare, because the soldier's words were imprinted on my mind: 'If you cry, they'll keep you in there longer. The calmer the doctor finds you, the sooner he'll send you home.' For this reason I kept calm and quiet. I thought to myself: The doctor's bound to come soon. He'll send me home straight away.

But instead days and days passed and I was still there. My breasts were painful. The milk had turned to stone; my bosoms were hard and feverish. I called the nurse and explained, very calmly and clearly, that I had recently had a baby but had to leave this nursing baby at home. 'Oh, is that how it is?' she says. 'All right, we'll see to it tomorrow.'

Next day, a lady arrived with a little pump and took away my milk. I didn't want to cry but it was so painful that tears started to my eyes of their own accord. 'Ah, yes, I know it hurts,' says this lady who's drawing off the milk, 'but where's your little one?'

'How do I know?' I say, 'they took him away and I've heard nothing since. They've hidden him because they want to get rid of me and keep my baby themselves. My father-in-law wants my husband to leave me and take another woman, a woman of his choosing, one with money. My father-in-law hates me because I didn't bring a dowry with me. It sticks in his craw and he keeps on about it: "You didn't even bring me a shirt!" he says.'

In short, I told this nurse lady the whole story. And at the end she said to me, 'Tell the psychiatrist all this. He'll understand, you know.'

'But when's he coming?' I ask.

'Soon.'

But the psychiatrist never came. The lady with the pump appeared every day and took off my milk. It still hurt. Then one day she said, 'Haven't you got any relations – a mother, brothers or somebody?'

'My mother's dead,' I say, 'and my father threw me out of the house.'

'And your brothers?'

'I've got nine of them.'

'Well, then,' she says, 'write to one of them and tell him to come and get you out.'

'But I haven't even got any writing paper,' I say, 'I haven't got anything here and the nurses just ignore me if I ask for anything.'

'I'll bring you some tomorrow,' she says.

Next day she brought me a postcard. There was the hospital stamp, the space for the address, everything. First she took off the milk, then she said, 'Write the card and I'll post it for you, but don't say anything to the doctor, because it's forbidden. We're not supposed to do it.'

'Don't worry,' I say, 'I've never set eyes on this doctor. God knows when he'll come.'

'Tell your brother to come to Rome at once and speak to the specialist. Then he can sign your papers and you can go home,' she says.

The lady gave me this advice because she could see I wasn't insane. So I wrote to my brother Nello. Well, I don't know if the post was delayed, or what, but a day passed, a week, and not a sign of my brother. I was worried. At night, so that no one would hear me crying – I was still scared of what the soldier had told me – I pulled the sheets over my head to muffle my sobs and in the morning I bathed my eyes, dried them and tried to appear cheerful.

Meanwhile, I enjoyed the company of all the madwomen who talked to themselves, fought, raved and sang. I looked at all these lunatics and said to myself: If I stay here long enough I'll go crackers for sure! When will they let me out? When will I see this doctor?

I watched them going about stark naked, playing with their own shit, shrieking like babies. One evening a woman came up to me. She thought I was her fiancé and she hugged me tight, almost throttling me, till the nurse came and dragged her off and took her away. There was another one who wanted me to sing with her, but I didn't feel like it so she started biting my hand. I had to kick her to make her stop. Yet another one wanted me to eat the meat she had been chewing. She took it out of her mouth and wanted me to take it.

I was in there a month. And I endured all these things. I was

31

depressed and pining for my baby. Yet sometimes it was quite cheerful: the crazy creatures would carry on like actresses on the stage, dancing and singing, as gay as larks. It amused me to see them.

At last, Nello turned up one morning and I told him everything. 'They've taken away my baby, they had me shut up in here with all these nuts and they've never even been to visit me.'

My brother understood. He could see for himself how things stood. He went to look for the doctor. He explained my case to him and the psychiatrist said: 'If you take full responsibility, your sister can leave, but we can't give you a certificate to say whether she's sane or insane because she's still under observation.'

'What?' says Nello, 'she's been here a month and you still don't know whether she's sane or crazy? Well, never mind, I'll take full responsibility, of course.' Then the doctor told him to sign the form and take me away. My brother told him, 'For my sister, I would sign a hundred times over, sir!'

And he did sign. And then he took me to the station at Campo di Carne on his motor-scooter.

When my husband's family saw me coming they got a shock. They had never dreamed anybody would take me out of that place. They were green at the gills. They couldn't make out how I had managed to write a letter to Nello and let him know what was happening.

'So you thought you'd get rid of my sister by sending her to the lunatic asylum!' said my brother. 'You took away her child and sent her off, all alone, to that hell-on-earth! Well, you reckoned without me, didn't you? And now I'm going to take her home with me. There's room enough for my children and for her. Give her back her baby this minute!'

But they were dead cunning. 'First show us the certificate proving she's sane and in her right mind,' they said. 'If you can't show us that, how do we know Teresa is cured? We won't give you the baby.' And they shut the door in our faces.

My brother said, 'Now, let's go to the police station and lay an official charge against them.' And we went, but there again it was the same story: 'Without the certificate stating that the mother is sane, we cannot allow you to take the child.' Nello then offered to take the boy on his own responsibility, but they said no, you

32

could only do that if the child had no father. Otherwise, the father had first claim.

'Well, then, I want to accuse them publicly of having sent my sister to the lunatic asylum on a false certificate and without medical examination,' said my brother.

The police officer looked at him. 'Look,' he said, 'forget about all these denunciations and so forth, they'll bring you nothing but trouble. Besides, you haven't any real proof – it's just your sister's word against the certificate signed by the doctor from Campo di Carne. You're in no position to start litigation. Why don't you go to the mental hospital and get them to sign a certificate for you? That would solve everything.'

Two or three days later Nello went to Rome and asked for a certificate of sanity for me. The people at the hospital told him they were unable to say whether or not I was sane, since I had only been there under observation. They had not had time to make their assessment. So poor Nello came back empty-handed. No certificate.

That evening at supper he said, 'You know what I'm going to do? I'm going to go there and threaten those sons-of-bitches, because it's the only way.'

That same evening he went to Sisto's family and said to them, 'If you don't hand over the little boy within twenty-four hours, I'm coming back with a revolver and I'll shoot the lot of you! I don't care if I go to prison, I want my nephew! And I'm going down to the station to raise hell – I'll tell them the whole story and make a scandal! My sister isn't alone, you know, she's got me! As for you,' he said, turning to my husband, 'just watch your step, because I'm going to get you!'

My husband must have been scared stiff, because he immediately changed his tune. He said sweetly, 'But what's Teresa so excited about? She's too nervous, that girl. Tell her she should calm herself, I love her – we all love her! If she likes, she can come back home, the house is open to her, any time.' He spoke like that out of sheer funk.

Nello said, 'She doesn't need this house. She's with me and she's fine right where she is.'

In fact I stayed with my brother, but without the baby. Every now and then I went to my husband's home to see my son. And whenever I saw the child, I saw Sisto, too, and he never took his eyes off me. He stared at me all the time I was there. I realised I had become fond of him in the short time since our marriage, because I felt that I still wanted him as a husband. And he wanted me too. But he was afraid of his father and sisters. One day he said to me, 'Wait for me at the end of the lane, behind the barn.' And so we made love, furtively, like a couple of kids.

# 5

One day my husband was dismissed from the railway because he'd been dipping into the till. Then he came to me and said, 'Look, I'm moving to Rome. Why don't you come with me? We'll set up home, with the baby and all.'

So we rented a flat in via Santa Maria Maggiore. My husband had no job, nothing to do. However, he had dozens of friends and spent the days with them. At first Sisto's father, the station master, sent us money and food. Then he got sick of it and stopped sending, so I had to go out to work.

I got a job in a shop near Campo di Carne, where they sold wallpaper, because I knew the boss, Mr Alfio. I travelled to and fro by bus every day. Mr Alfio paid me 500 lire a month and I had to serve the customers.

At that time I was about twenty. I was plump and well-shaped, and Alfio the Boss started ogling me. But I avoided him because he was ugly and oily and reeked of medicines. I could feel his eyes on me when I bent down, when I walked up the stairs, when I sat down, when I moved my hands – he never stopped gaping at me.

Then one day he comes up to me and says, 'Here, Teresa, this is for you,' and he gives me a wad of money.

'Whatever for?' I ask, 'I've already had my salary for this month.' Then he comes close to me, catches me round the waist and starts pawing me. I give him such a violent shove that he lands on the floor. He was a big man but I was young and strong.

That evening I go home and say to Sisto, 'Alfio the Boss

assaulted me today. He even gave me some money, but I gave it back to him. I'm never going back to work for that lecherous old pig!'

I was expecting my husband to say, 'I'll go and sort the bastard out!' Instead, he gawps at me open-mouthed and says, 'You'll have to put up with it!'

'What?' I say, 'let him put his filthy hands all over me?'

'You bloody well put up with it till I can get my job back!'

'Not on your life,' I say, 'I can't stick him!'

'You'll have to, otherwise what do we live on?' And with that he stands up and goes out.

So I confided in my friend, Egle. I told her what Sisto had said. 'That husband of yours can't love you very much,' said my friend. 'He sounds like a right ponce to me.'

It was my husband who had introduced me to Egle. When we came to live in Rome he said to me, 'I've got lots of friends here, I'll introduce them to you.' But the only one I ever got to meet was this Egle, a small woman, pretty and as sharp as a needle. When Sisto went out to see his pals, he'd say to me, 'Go and see Egle!' and I'd go. I used to pour my heart out to Egle, tell her everything.

In one particular way, Egle was kinky: she liked to watch people undressing. The first time, I found out by chance, because I caught her with a pair of binoculars spying into the house opposite, where a woman was undressing. She was embarrassed and pretended she had been watching a cat. Later on, though, she became quite brazen about it and one evening she asked me to take off my clothes in front of her.

I did as she asked, because it seemed to me such a trivial thing and it didn't cost me anything. I took off my sweater and skirt.

'Shall I go on?' I asked.

'Go on,' she said, 'we're both women, aren't we?'

After that, I often did it, but I must say she never laid a finger on me. She was content to watch me, that was all. And I let her watch. When I took off my knickers she swallowed hard a couple of times. Nothing more. Then I'd get into bed and say good-night.

It was Egle who revealed to me that Sisto liked to go with tarts. I was a simpleton; I didn't understand anything. I hadn't even cottoned on to the fact that Egle let out rooms by the hour. She knew all the thieves and prostitutes, and Sisto knew them too. But I didn't know it at the time. I was dim. I walked around with my head in the clouds.

This Egle started taking me round the bars and trattorias. I had never been in such places before and I was delighted, curious about everything, wonderstruck.

My husband kept company with all these whores and thieves. He would say to me, 'Go to Egle's, spend the night with her, I'm busy.'

'What have you got to be so busy about?' I'd reply. 'You don't work.'

'That's my business.'

However, I didn't go back to my job. I dropped Alfio the Boss and never even asked for my superannuation. This immediately caused ructions with Sisto. 'If you don't work, I can't support you,' he said.

'And how do you get by without working?' I asked.

'I can always manage,' he said, 'I have friends everywhere, they'll always give me a bite to eat, but I can't look after you. Go to Egle, go where you like, but you're not staying in my house unless you work!'

So I went to Egle, and she fed me and gave me a bed. In exchange, she made me wash the floors, clean the windows, do the laundry; she was a fanatic about cleanliness. I had to make the beds, wash the dishes, clean and scrub; I was her slave. She fed me, but I certainly earned my keep.

I said to her, 'How I would love to have a home of my own, just for me and my husband!' I didn't hanker after luxuries. Sisto, on the other hand, was greedy and vicious, only I didn't know it then. Before me, he had had a Frenchwoman; at night they slept together like husband and wife, but in the daytime he sent her out on the streets to pick up men. I only came to know these things years later.

Meanwhile, since I had no way of keeping my child in Rome, he had been taken back to my husband's sisters. I went to see him as often as I could. They looked down their noses at me. They said I was hopeless, because I didn't know how to iron collars and cuffs without creasing them. *They*, of course, were perfect.

It's true I wasn't much good at these things. I got through the work – washed, ironed and cooked – in a slap-happy way; I wasn't fastidious like they were. And because of this they called me a clumsy clot, a lazy slut. The truth of the matter was, they still had it in for me because I hadn't brought a dowry. Besides, I didn't know how to speak properly. I had no education, I was just an ignorant country girl.

A few months later, my husband was reinstated by the railway. He was pardoned because his father returned the money he had stolen. Sisto came to me at once and said, 'Come on, we're going to the station at Ciampino. Pick up the baby and let's go.'

So we went to Ciampino – no, it was Isernia. We went to Ciampino a little later. There were four of us living in the station house: Sisto, me, our son Maceo and Rita. I had met this Rita at Egle's house. She was a skinny girl with bright blue eyes and long, long hands. I liked her at once and we became friends. I took her everywhere with me because I felt sorry for her: she couldn't bear staying at home because her stepmother was cruel to her. I knew what it was like having a stepmother on your back. Rita, who came from Rieti, was unmarried and lived alone with his stepmother. They hated each other. As I had taken my baby back, I thought to myself: Good, I'll offer her a home and she can help me with the baby. I was pleased. I considered her a friend.

In the mornings I went out shopping. I'd spend three hours out in the streets, looking in the shop windows at all the food and going to Upim, the department store. I didn't buy anything because I didn't have any money, but I liked to window-shop. Rita took care of Maceo while I was out. I'd come home to find the table laid. I put the pasta on to cook, prepared the sauce and as soon as Sisto came in we sat down to eat. Life was peaceful and I was satisfied.

One night I happen to wake up, feeling cold. I think to myself: I'll go and fetch another blanket. I look towards my husband, but he isn't there. I think perhaps he's gone for a blanket, because it's bitterly cold.

Out I go and find him and Rita making love on the kitchen table. I was wild with jealousy and instantly started beating the pair of them. I grab a chair and hit them with that, then I get hold of the scissors and make as if to slash their faces. There were these long pointed scissors in the station First Aid box, so I get hold of these and think: I'll really scare them now! In fact, my husband was so terrified that, from that night on, he never slept peacefully again.

Rita left. I turned her out. But then I found out that they were seeing each other in Rome. He would tell me he had to go to the Ministry on business for the railway. A pack of lies, but like a fool I believed him. While he was with her I was sitting at home, pining for him to come back so that we could spend a little time together.

A year or so later he got the sack again from the railway. This time, they tell him, it's for keeps. He's been in too much trouble. He told me that he had let a friend talk him into pinching some copper wire. This friend knew where there were some rolls of copper wire in an unguarded place. So if they could steal it, they could sell it at a good price. Sisto let himself be persuaded, out of weakness, and they went there one night in a van. While they were loading up the copper wire, the police arrived.

My husband dropped everything and ran. The other fellow was caught and he talked. He said it was Sisto's idea to steal the wire, so he was arrested, too. He denied all blame, said it was nothing to do with him, but it was no use. The 500 pounds of copper wire belonged to the railway, so of course he lost his job.

'Now what'll we do?' I said. I believe this was in 1939. Everyone was talking about war.

'Let the war come!' said Sisto, 'it'll get my debts and all my troubles off my back . . . and I hope they blow all the railways in Italy sky high!' Luckily he found a job a few months later. Meanwhile his sisters took care of Maceo. Whenever we had no money we had to hand him over to them.

Some time later, God knows how, he managed to get his job on the railways back again. They sent him to Prima Porta, to Roma-Nord. So he started earning a living again. We rented a house in that district. I was happy. I was with Sisto and my baby; I had a home; everything was fine.

One evening Sisto says, 'Put on your best dress, we're going to have dinner at a friend's house tonight, there's a party.'

'What's this party all of a sudden?'

'Get dressed,' he says, 'and let's go.' He was gay and affectionate.

*She* was there at the party, too, that Rita. In fact, I found out later that it was their engagement party. He'd sworn to me it was all over between them. I was a bit suspicious when I saw her, but

I thought: I could be wrong. After all, he's sworn, so it must be true.

It was very lively in the house. We sat down to table and everybody kept plying me with food and drink. I ate like a horse – I was hungry. I drank a lot of wine, but the faster I drank it up, the faster they poured it out. I was half-sloshed. Everybody was laughing, boozing and singing – it was a smashing party.

All of a sudden I look around, and no Sisto. 'Where's my husband?' I ask.

'Gone to the lavatory,' someone says. So I have another drink. Then I look around again and see that Rita's missing too.

'Where's Rita?' I ask.

'In the lavatory,' they say. So then, drunk as I was, I stood up and tottered to the lavatory.

Neither of them was in there. They had gone. Left me alone. That very evening, Sisto went to live with her. He deserted me.

I had to give up the house because I couldn't pay the rent. For a time I went to my brother Nello in Anzio. I had to sell everything I possessed. I even had to pawn my shoes to pay the fare.

# 6

I wasn't too happy at Nello's. The house was small, there were all
the children, and his wife didn't take kindly to me. The war was
on – that meant lean times for everybody. Every day the sirens
sounded and we were all supposed to run to the shelters. There
was a siren in Anzio that howled like a love-sick cat. But we
didn't go to the shelter. Why would anyone want to drop
bombs there, by the sea?

I didn't see a single bomb during my three years there at the
seaside, with my son, my nephews and my sister-in-law who
looked at me in an old-fashioned way all the time. I helped Nello
to sell fish, I went to the market with him and kept busy so that
my sister-in-law couldn't say I was living there on charity. My
job was to clean the fish for the customers. If a lady came and
asked for four pounds of anchovies, I washed and weighed them.
Then another would ask for a mullet, a scorpion-fish, a black
umber. I rinsed them and scaled them with four swift strokes of
the knife (I became an expert); then I slit the belly open with
the point of the blade, pulled out the entrails and wrapped the
fish. If there was some fish left over, we ate it ourselves; if not,
we fried up the innards with a little oil. They tasted good but
they were a bit indigestible.

At first everything went well. Then came the hard times. The
men went off to the war. The women had no money. Nobody
bought fish any more. Nello was in despair. He worked like a
black to earn a mere pittance. We could sell only the cheapest
fish, sardines, garfish, calamari, cockles. They didn't need much
cleaning and scaling, so my sister-in-law looked at me more and

more sourly, and Nello became more and more nervous.

I slept in a rickety little bed with a hot-water bottle between my feet. When I couldn't get to sleep, I played 'mamma's game' and caressed myself. I was twenty-two, bursting with good health and I felt the need of a man. There was a fellow who fancied me but I couldn't work up any enthusiasm – he was no oil painting and besides, he was bossy.

Sisto had joined up as a soldier. He was in Cefalu in Sicily. Then he was posted to Termini Imerese. He wrote me cheerful letters, said he was fine, basking in the sun, making out all right in the army. He'd got himself transferred to the kitchens, and he was making money out of the soldiers' rations; he had even managed to save a bit.

One day he wrote and asked me if I would like to visit him: 'Come down here, take a dip in the sea and get yourself a nice sun-tan, it's lovely here.' I couldn't make up my mind whether to go or not. My son was still very small, I didn't know who to leave him with. It went against the grain to leave him with his aunts again, but I did want to go to Sicily and see Sisto. He wrote that he and Rita had quarrelled, that they had split up for good.

I found out later that actually Rita had run off with a Sicilian. She went away and then came back, but Sisto said he didn't want anything to do with her any more, it was over. And I wanted to go back to him. I thought: Well, he's sorry for what he's done, he's a soldier now and he's saved some money. I was attached to this husband of mine. Not really in love, but certainly fond of him.

I thought to myself: 'I'll leave the baby with Ines and go down to Sicily for a bit of sun and sea.' The problem was, I was no longer on speaking terms with Nello's wife, so I called an old woman I knew, a certain Baldina, and asked her to go and ask Ines if she would keep the baby for a while. Baldina came back and reported: 'Ines says she's delighted to have Maceo, she says send him quickly, she'll feed him and even give him lessons. She also says you're not fit to be a mother and the further your son is from you the better.'

'What! Baldina, how can you come and tell me all this rubbish? Take the baby to Ines, then, and if she says one word about me, stop up your ears. That woman is a viper and she always will be.'

So Baldina took Maceo to Ines and I left for Sicily. The train journey took days, because the line had been broken by bombs.

I found my husband thinner, better-looking. He hugged and kissed me and said, 'It's all finished with Rita, for ever. You are my wife and I want you. How is my son, Maceo?' He was kind, affectionate, warm, and my heart melted towards him.

But things were in a bad way there. Food was scarce, four or five times a day we had to shelter from the air raids, houses collapsed, everything went up in flames. But we couldn't move because you needed a permit to travel north and we didn't have one. The Germans were in Messina and they were blockading everything there.

One day we went into a café, a miserable dump set up in a shed with a corrugated iron roof, and we ran into Rita with a blond, moustachioed Sicilian fellow. She carried it off coolly, but Sisto turned as white as a sheet. 'Let's sit down and eat,' I said, 'anyway, what do you care? You told me it was all over between you.' But he wouldn't eat. He sat there like a ramrod, staring at her. So then Rita, out of annoyance or fright, I don't know which, gets up and walks out. Thank the Lord for that, I think, but, before I have time to turn my head, Sisto dashes out after her. He leaves me alone, sitting there like a twit.

I went straight out and saw them standing face to face, arguing. I threw myself at them and started hitting out in all directions. As soon as she realised what was happening, Rita ran off. Sisto was white, shaking all over. 'Go on then, you rat!' I said, 'go to her!'

'No,' he said, 'I want to be with you.'

'But you're wild with jealousy over her!'

'It's not true!' But I could see he was jealous and when a man is jealous it means he's in love.

At that very moment, a terrific air raid started. We ran. Sisto grabbed my arm and took me to a shelter. This time, I thought, I'll die for sure. Oh, dear God! Goodbye, my son! Because I could see the ground heaving, splitting open, and the fire spreading everywhere. Sisto gave me courage, he held me tight. I wasn't even thinking of Rita any more. I was scared of dying there, underground, like a mole.

Our pensione was destroyed in that raid, too. Sisto and I didn't even have a roof over our heads. Luckily, my husband had a friend, a certain Captain Cacato. This captain had brought his mistress with him from Rome. She was a beautiful woman with a long black pigtail that hung down and bumped on her behind.

The captain had found a farmhouse outside Marsala. He offered us a bed there, so we moved into this house in the middle of the fields. There were five other soldiers, and this signora with her captain. They had one room to themselves and we had another. The soldiers slept downstairs in a big room strewn with hay. During the day the soldiers were out and we two women kept each other company. She too had come from central Italy to be with her man and she sympathised with me. She said: 'You were drawn here by love, the same as me, but we're fools, because we'll end up being killed by the bombs, and once you're dead, who's going to wake you up again?'

Meanwhile, it was rumoured that Mussolini had been captured. First we heard that they'd caught him and were going to shoot him, then that he'd escaped. Finally came the news that a German had stabbed Mussolini to death out of jealousy over women, and that the King had run away, taking the royal treasury with him. Then the soldiers split into two factions: some on one side, some on the other. They said there was no more army, no more king, nobody knew whether the war was still on or not, nobody knew whom they were supposed to be fighting for or against. Sisto said, 'Let's get out of here and go back to Rome, I'm pissed off with this war.' But we didn't have a visa to cross the Straits of Messina.

Nevertheless, we left the farmhouse and said goodbye to the captain and his lady, who, in her nervousness, had wound her plait up as tight as a bit of string. We took one road, then another. But bombs were dropping whichever way we went. And we kept running.

We slept in the fields, concealing ourselves because my husband was a deserter. He was very worried: 'If the Germans catch me, they'll shoot me as a deserter; if the Americans catch me, they'll shoot me as an enemy. What can I do?'

At night we saw the German patrols passing with rifles and machine-guns. We lay in the grass, not daring to breathe. Or we'd be huddled inside a cave, dead quiet. I was so afraid that I forgot to feel hunger. But I was always shivering with cold. The more I covered myself up, the colder I felt. I had a fever. 'You've got malaria!' said Sisto. And he was right. But there was no medicine to be had. In any case, we had to keep going, we couldn't stop. Some of the time I leaned on Sisto. Some of the

44

time I stretched out and slept on the ground, but all the time we were travelling north.

One evening, on the road, a lorry full of American soldiers stopped. 'Oh. Christ! We're sunk,' said Sisto. But they were good Joes, they smiled at us. They spoke to us in broken Italian.

'Where you go?' they said.

'To Messina,' said Sisto.

'Get in, get in!' they said, 'but at Messina you get out, huh? Because Germans . . . lookie-lookie . . . we can't. . . . ' So we got in.

Messina was a pile of rubble. It was filthy and it stank. People were sleeping in tents or on boats. There were dead and wounded everywhere. Those who could had run away, so the city was half-deserted. We reached the port and asked if there was any way of getting over to the mainland. But there was nothing. They were bombing the sea as well as the land; it was boiling with bombs – as soon as the spray from one subsided, another one landed. Because of this, no ships were sailing; not a fly could get across that strait.

After several days of sleeping out and living on dry figs, we met a fellow who said you could get across if you had money. 'How?' Sisto wanted to know.

'If you get on this ferry and hide amongst the crates, you'll be all right.' So we agreed. But we had to pay through the nose for it. Fortunately, my husband had some money and also a gold watch, which he had to sacrifice as well.

Anyway, we got on board this ferry. It was loaded to the gun'ls with big crates, and laid over the crates were dozens and dozens of branches. We squeezed in somehow and settled down amongst the crates. The boat set sail.

When we were out in mid-channel, the bombing started. Boom! Bo-bo-bo-boom! They were falling very close. Water spouts shot up all around us. But they never hit us.

At last we reached the other side. We thanked them and got off the boat, stiff, numb and soaking wet. As we were walking away, my husband said, 'You know what was in those crates? Ammunition, bombs, all kinds of explosives.'

'*Now* he tells me, the idiot!'

'Well, what good would it have done if I'd told you before?'

'You'd never have got me on that old mouse-trap with all that ammunition,' I said.

'Exactly, but as it is, here we are, safe and sound, thanks to our Heavenly Father,' said Sisto.

'You made me risk my life, you were in such a hurry!' I said.

We had got off the boat at Radicona, in Calabria. There were no trains. They'd all been blown up, burnt out, the lines were all broken. There were dead bodies lying on the ground and nobody troubled to pick them up. As you walked along, you saw dead men without heads, without arms, with their guts hanging out and you just stepped over them. People had got used to them, they didn't even look any more. Sisto said, 'We'll go north.'

'How, on foot?'

'Yes, on foot.'

And that's how it was: we set out for Rome on Shanks's pony.

At a certain point along the road there was an air raid; the bombs fell so fast you didn't have time to collect your wits in between them. People were running, screaming, falling down. I found myself amongst a group of women. Everybody'd got separated, I couldn't see Sisto anywhere. Never mind, I thought, I'll find him later. I crouch down in a ditch. One squadron goes over, then another. Each wave drops about twenty bombs.

Finally, it seems to be over. I get up, look around for Sisto. He's not there, he's vanished. I look for him everywhere, turning back along the road and searching among the dead. I think: He must be dead, that husband of mine must be dead. But he wasn't among the bodies. Then I think: Perhaps he's been blown to smithereens, so that I wouldn't even recognise him. Now what shall I do? Well, I couldn't stay there, weeping over him, so I joined the crowd of refugees walking towards Rome.

We walked on for miles and miles till we came to a railway, then we took the train. And when the lines were cut again, we got out and walked for umpteen more miles till we came to another bit of railway that was intact and working. We slept under the trees, wrapped up in newspapers. Thank God it was summer.

In Calabria I was taken ill again. The fever came back. I was shaking like someone who's been bitten by a tarantula, and I couldn't stand up. They carried me into a farmer's cottage, gave me a blanket and left me there. I told the people that I'd caught malaria in Sicily, where I'd just come from, and that my husband was dead. They looked after me till my temperature came down.

I lay in that bed, which wasn't a bed but a mattress on the

floor, and I thought: God knows what's become of that wretched husband of mine! And I imagined the most horrible things, picturing his death and how he was blown up by the bombs. I wondered if he'd suffered or been killed outright. I was sorry that he was dead.

A week later I was finally rid of the fever. I thanked the farmer and his family, said my goodbyes and set out again on the road to Rome. There were still people walking to the capital. I joined the throng. Every so often a dive-bomber came down and machine-gunned the crowd. We all threw ourselves flat on the ground, in ditches, in the fields.

On one of these occasions I heard the plane coming down, threw myself flat at the edge of the road, rolled down an embankment and finished up in a pit full of water. I was in it up to my neck. The mud came up to my eyebrows and my mouth was full of dirt. It took four of them to haul me out. I dried my dress in the sun and it became a grey crust. My shoes I had lost in the slime at the bottom of the pit. I was in a wretched state. I was spitting and coughing all the time. My feet hardened up because of walking barefoot, and in time the soles became like leather.

And that's how I arrived in Rome: barefoot, covered in mud, filthy. People asked why I wasn't wearing shoes. I was ashamed to say I hadn't the money to buy a pair, so I said: 'I've made a vow to the Madonna.' In that pit I had also lost my case, with photographs of my mother and my brothers, Sisto's shirts, my two spare dresses and everything else.

First of all I went to my sister-in-law to see my baby. That bitch Ines didn't even want to open the door. So I sat down on the doorstep and swore I wouldn't budge till I'd seen my son. In the end they let me see him; he was blond and beautiful, and he'd grown so much he seemed like a different child. I hugged him and hugged him, I was so happy. 'Poor child!' I said, 'your Daddy's been killed in this cruel war!' And I even cried a little.

Suddenly, two months later, my husband turned up. 'How on earth . . . ? I'd given you up for dead!' I said.

'I was on the point of death, I can tell you, they kept me in hospital for a month.'

But later on I found out it was all lies. He had gone off to Catanzaro with a Sicilian woman he had run into during the

47

bombing, and they had set up house together. A month or two later this Sicilian woman arrived. She told me she was pregnant by him. I think her name was Irma, I don't remember now. Anyway, Sisto didn't want her and she went off with another bloke, a friend of Sisto's called Redbeard. She was a good-looking girl, this Irma. She always looked a bit puzzled, a bit suspicious. She had a large bottom, large tits and two tiny feet, so tiny that you wondered how she could balance on them.

I thought Sisto had sent her away for my sake, but not a bit of it: it was for Rita. He was still thinking of her and soon after we were reunited he started seeing that wretched woman again, secretly.

In the meantime I went down with malaria again. I go to the hospital and they tell me: 'There's no quinine left, so you may as well go home.' But I couldn't even walk. 'You'll have to go,' they say, 'there isn't a bed for you.' And they throw me out.

Outside, in the entrance, I bump into the nurse from the mental hospital, the one who used to pump out my milk. We hug and kiss each other. Then she says, 'I'll get rid of that fever for you.' She took me home with her, made me lie down and gave me an injection of some black stuff that looked like ink. I fainted immediately. I had fainted only once before in my life.

The nurse slaps my face, she keeps slapping me. At last I come round. I can hear her shouting, 'Teresa, Teresa!' She's in a panic, terrified. I open my eyes to see her red in the face and breathless; she's still pinching and slapping me and putting her fingers into my mouth.

'All right, give over, that's enough,' I say, 'I'm fine now.' And in fact, the fever passed off and from that day to this has never come back.

# 7

Sisto and I were living together, but it couldn't last because he was seeing Rita. Every day he became more and more withdrawn from me. One morning I saw them together, arm-in-arm in front of the house. That made me really angry. I didn't say anything. I went in, threw a few things into a case and left.

I went to Egle and told her the whole story. 'Don't worry,' she says, 'I'll help you.' And she introduces me to some friends of hers, a certain Lilia and another girl called Gemma.

These two women had already been in prison. I didn't know that. I was still innocent, scatterbrained. The first one had been nicked for bag-snatching, the other for breaking and entering. They were professionals, they made their living at it.

I didn't understand a thing: I thought they were good girls. They were generous, always treating me to coffee and cigarettes. I learned to smoke: up till then I hadn't known how to, I watched them carefully and held the fag the way they did it, between the index and middle fingers, casually, as if I'd been doing it all my life. They were kind to me, considerate. They took me to a smashing trattoria, a big place, nicely decorated. And they paid. They paid for everything I ate. Seeing how kind they were, I attached myself to them. I was with them constantly. And they took me out on a job.

Gemma lived with her mother, and Lilia lived there too because she had no parents. Then they took me to their place to sleep. They gave me food and a bed, they took me to the cinema, to the music hall, and they always paid.

One day Gemma said, 'Listen, my mother acts as housekeeper

in a villa in Parioli. She's supposed to keep an eye on the place – every now and then she has to go and give it an airing and clean up a bit. She's got the keys. I'll steal the keys from mother, we'll open up, then we'll break the locks so that it looks like an outside job. There's millions of lire worth of stuff there, gold, old coins, silver. The owners are on holiday in Switzerland.' It was July or August. 'There's three million worth in there, we'll steal the lot and divide it up – one million lire each!'

I was gullible, a noodle. Gemma said. 'We'll buy you a car, we'll have one each and drive around all over the place.'

I was crazy about cars, so I let myself be persuaded, tempted like a silly kid. 'Ooh!' I said, 'will we buy cars? What make do you fancy?'

I was twenty-eight years old, but as innocent as a new-born babe. I hadn't lived. Those two gave me a rude awakening all right. First it was all sweetness and light, then prison.

A fellow named Luigi – but everybody called him Tango – was supposed to come with us. He was a friend of theirs and he had a van. I was a bit taken aback when I saw this Tango – he had an ugly, brutish face like a murderer. Gemma said quickly, 'What's up? You're not backing out? Think of the lovely car you'll be able to buy, the clothes . . . you'll be dripping in diamonds from head to foot.'

Dazzled, all agog, I said, 'All right, then, let's go to this villa!'

Tango says to me, 'You go inside, then we'll come along about five or six o'clock and you can let the stuff down out of the window. When you hear this whistle, you'll know it's us.'

'Why me?' I asked, 'why must it be me who goes inside?'

'Because you're the slimmest and the most agile.'

It wasn't a villa, as it turned out, it was a block of flats. They'd given me some keys and I opened the door to this apartment with them. I went in and started looking around. It was a big place, full of cupboards. I hunted, searched, rummaged: no gold coins and no millions. There was some silver, all right, and some animals made of transparent stone, but I didn't know if they were valuable or not. There were some enamelled goblets. I took all this stuff and put it into a bag, then I put the bag near the window that overlooked the street. And I waited.

I wait and wait, still no sign of them. There's a bed fit for a prince in the bedroom, so I go and lie down for a bit. And promptly fall asleep. I think I must have slept two or three hours.

50

I'm not sure. The ringing of the phone wakes me up. I'm just going to answer it when I think better of it. They'd told me not to answer the door or anything, and not to make a sound. So I didn't answer. And it rang and it rang and it rang. Later they told me it was them, to explain about the delay. I wondered if it was them, but thought I'd better do as I was told, so I didn't answer. I just stayed there, waiting.

Suddenly, I feel an urgent desire to go to the toilet. I go out of the bedroom and into the bathroom, which is all done up with orange-coloured glass. The windows, made of this opaque, orange glass, give on to the stair-well. Just as I'm about to sit on the W.C., I see a shadow beyond the windows. There's someone coming up the stairs. I get up quickly and go back into the bedroom.

But I'm busting for a pee. It gives me stomach-ache, so I hunt everywhere for a chamber-pot. I discover a cut-crystal jug and I do it in there. Then I put the jug on the table and start to laugh when I think of the owner's face when he finds that jug full of piss!

It was eleven o'clock at night and still they hadn't come. I was getting fed up. I thought to myself: 'I'll leave now. Nobody's coming, they've forgotten all about me.

Slowly and cautiously I opened the shutter. The street was empty. I took the bag full of loot and gingerly let myself out of the window. I didn't make a noise.

A moment later, they arrived. They said that, earlier, they'd been whistling for hours. 'What?' I said. 'You tell me you're coming at five, and you turn up at eleven! How the hell did I know you'd be so late?'

The told me that while Tango was standing there whistling, the police had arrived. The night-watchman had seen the shutter half-open and had realised there was someone inside. He'd called the police. So they arrived and nicked Tango and took him in. He said he was courting a maid who lived in the house and that he was whistling to her, but it wouldn't wash.

The two women were arrested a couple of days later. They didn't get me because I was in hiding. Then Rina, Tango's sister, grassed. She told them where I was and they caught me.

I was in the UNRRA stores in Monte Sacro. A friend of mine was working there and she hid me. After I'd been hiding there for several days, I went out one morning for a coffee, and I noticed there was a policeman in the doorway looking at me. I didn't know it, but they had a description of me. They had been told: 'Look out for such-and-such a redhead.' I had, in fact, recently dyed my hair; it was meant to be copper but it turned out scarlet – I looked like a red pepper.

The policeman sees this redhead and yells 'Stop!' and I start to run. And everybody starts running after me. 'There she is! Grab her!' they shout, and one woman starts screaming. 'She's stolen my handbag and jewels!' which isn't true at all, just to make the passers-by stop me, so I'll get arrested.

I run till I can't run any more, then I slip through the front door of that big hotel up there, at the Batteria Nomentana. I go down a staircase leading to the basement, an enormous room where they put all the broken chairs and rubbish from the hotel. I see a great big wardrobe, filthy dirty and falling to bits, but spacious, so I creep in there.

Through the wardrobe doors I could hear the cleaners squabbling loudly. Then I hear footsteps: boom-boom-boom-boom-boom. Someone coming in. A voice says, 'Have you seen a woman down here? A redhead, she got away.'

'No, no, nobody's come in here,' says a deep voice. 'we've been working here all the time, we'd have seen her if she'd come in.'

I hear the *carabinieri* stamping about for a bit, then they go out. I hear the cleaners start fighting and gossiping again as they work. I hear sounds from the street. When I realise they've gone, I kicked the door open and step out. I can't bear it another minute: I'm dying for air.

I go out through the front entrance, hop over a wall and go down into a big field where they're playing football. I look back to see if anyone's following me and catch sight of a policeman; he starts making signs, so I take to my heels and run. Then I pause for a moment to get my breath back. I walk and walk till I come out on to a street where there's a bus just pulling away from the kerb. I jump on the bus and get out at the station. Then I walk towards Piazza Vittorio.

That's where they caught me. I was just going into a delicatessen to buy a roll with *mortadella*, because I was hungry, when I heard someone shout, 'There she is!' I started to run, but they nabbed me just as I was turning the corner out of Piazza Vittorio.

In jail, I met up with my friends again. They had told the police I was an accomplice; they had blown the gaff.

First of all they took my photograph, with a flashlight: profile, full face; I felt like a film star. 'Turn your head!' they said, 'this way, that way!' I thought I was really somebody with all that red hair!

After the photographs they said, 'Give me your hand.'

'What for? Are you going to tell my fortune, like a gypsy? Do you want to see if I'm fated to be a thief?'

I gave him my hand. He took hold of it, pulled my thumb out and inked it. Then: 'Press here!' They were taking my finger-prints.

'How long does the torture last?' I asked. I was getting bored with it, I wanted to go. But he made me give him all ten fingers in turn. Then I said, 'Where can I wash please, Captain?' I was all stained with ink.

'Haven't you got a handkerchief?'

'No,' I said, 'they've taken away all my things. I've got nothing but the dress I stand up in.'

'Wipe your fingers on your dress, then,' he said, 'you won't need it now, anyway.'

And they gave me a shapeless, grey overall which stank of bleach, and shut me in a tiny, cramped cell. The first few hours I was quiet, I just paced up and down saying to myself: Well, things have turned out badly, but be patient.

But when night came, I felt like a lost soul. It was the first time I had been in the nick. I felt suffocated. I wanted to be free. I had always been as free as the birds of the air – I may not have had anything to eat but bread and tomatoes at times, but I had been free. I couldn't bear being shut up in there.

They gave me one year and nine months. Gemma and Lilia were sentenced to four years because they had previous records.

# 8

I was locked up in there for months and nobody came to visit me or bring me a parcel. Not one visitor. Not my brothers, nor my husband, nor my girl-friends. Nobody. Sisto was with that Rita and didn't give a hoot about me. My Brother Orlando was also inside, because he was a Communist: he had stolen 500 pounds of flour and a demijohn of oil from the Germans at the Observatory. He had managed to get away with it, but then someone from Anzio denounced him for the killing of a German sergeant and the Jerries beat him up and put him in the nick on a double charge.

Now it happened that, while I was inside, the Americans entered Rome. I heard the news. And these Americans liberated Orlando, who immediately stole a tommy-gun, a revolver and a pair of shoes from them. But they didn't charge him because he had been a resistance fighter.

During this period my sister Iride got engaged to an American N.C.O. and on the day of the wedding Orlando placed eighteen anti-tank bombs all round the church of Sant'Antonio in Anzio. But just as he was setting them off, he was seen by a certain De Lellis, a *carabiniere,* and the bombs were quickly defused.

Orlando kept writing to me in prison, telling me he was dealing with the Americans, trading in cigarettes, coffee, chocolate. And everything was going fine. Till one day he ran across a negro who tried to rape his wife, Celestina, at gun-point. Then Orlando pretended he didn't mind. He said to this American, 'Go ahead, I don't give a damn for Celestina.' The negro was fooled, he put down the rifle and Orlando instantly seized hold of it and killed the man with two neat shots in the head.

Even that time they didn't catch him, because he and Celestina ran away and hid in the woods at Frosinone. But later on his wife became the mistress of the Commissioner for Public Security at Frosinone, and no sooner was she in bed with him than she found a means of betraying Orlando: she denounced him for the theft of some bed-linen. And so my brother finished up in Regina Coeli prison. I couldn't count on him for any help.

Nello, the only one of my brothers who might have helped me, was away at the war. I always got on well with Nello. He helped me, put me up, gave me money. He owned fishing-boats and traded in fish. He was always singing. He had a beautiful tenor voice, and everybody loved him. He was the only decent member of the whole family, the only one who really loved me. But his wife couldn't stand the sight of me.

All my brothers have taken themselves wives. They all married little maid-servants who now consider themselves to be ladies; they talk posh and look down their noses. They hate me. 'Your sister,' they say, 'is making a monkey out of you.' They are in trade, they own shops, and they give themselves the airs of society ladies. These little servant-girls have gone up in the world, but they're mean, treacherous gossips!

I wrote to my husband and asked him to come to my rescue. He didn't even answer the letter. Maybe he tore it up, I don't know. Anyway, there I was, languishing in the clink, freezing to death. And I was hungry. In those days it was still the Delle Mantellate prison; it was transformed, years later, into Rebibbia. This was about 1944. There was nothing there, the cells were crumbling to bits, you perished from the cold, there were no showers, no toilets, it was hell-upon-earth. I was everlastingly hungry. The nuns looked at me in an old-fashioned way because I complained.

Most of the nuns who were there in my day are still there. Sister Carmine, nicknamed Saint Carmine of the Iron Hands, was notorious, forever hitting somebody with those hard hands of hers. Nowadays she has to be a bit more careful, because things have changed in the prison and the prisoners aren't as submissive as they were.

Then there was Sister Amalia. She was a good soul, always in tears. She was old, perhaps she's dead by now. She gave you a slap and then started to cry. She was kind. Another one, Big

55

Isabel the Spaniard, was a strong woman with muscular arms; she could dig the soil like a man. She only feels at home with murderesses; she's an aggressive brute. Once upon a time, when she could get hold of you, she would give you a wallop on the head that kept you in order for a week, but now that the winds of change are blowing she tries to ingratiate herself with the prisoners.

There was Sister Biancospino, too. She was always kind and good-natured. She read a lot of books, wrote beautifully and helped the convicts to write letters home. She never raised her voice to us. Unfortunately, they sent her away because of quarrels with the other nuns. They didn't like her, they said she was too soft with the prisoners.

Then there's that crafty Sister Michelina; Sister Quinta, who smiles and smiles while secretly putting in the poison; Sister Innocenza who is sweetness itself as long as you keep giving her presents; Sister Lella of the Angels, who passes judgement and sentence and carries on like a dictator. Some are dead, others have been transferred. But most of them are still there, keeping a tight rein on things, and, even though they can't be so free with their hands nowadays, they're still the bosses.

On one occasion in 1945, when I made a protest there at the Mantellate prison, Sister Carmine ordered them to put me in a straitjacket, tie me to my bed and beat me up. As a result of this I lost an incisor tooth. In those days the beds were just iron springs in a frame that folded in two and had a projecting hook in the middle. As I was grappling with the guards, who were trying to get me into the straitjacket, this hook knocked my tooth out. They never managed to get the jacket on me because I fought like a wild beast; I twisted right and left like an eel and wriggled out of their hands. Then, out of anger, one of them bashed my face against the bed-frame. I heard a crack. My mouth filled with blood. Then the tooth seemed to tighten up again, but eventually, when I bit hard on a fishbone or a crust of bread, I could feel it wobbling in the gum and in the end it fell out of its own accord.

Treatment of prisoners in the Mantellate at that time was terrible. They gave you very little to eat, the walls were streaming with water, there were no sheets, no toilets. You had to do your business in a bucket and then go and throw it down a communal hole. Many women developed tuberculosis because of the cold and the damp.

They got chest diseases because of the hunger they endured. Many got pleurisy. Anyone who did not have friends outside to help her was in a bad way. For myself, the Lord alone knows how I didn't get tuberculosis, because no one ever sent me parcels, I had to survive on the stuff the prison dished out. Perhaps it's because I've got strong lungs. But I suffered from hunger – black, raging, ravenous hunger.

Suddenly, after a few months, they transferred me to Frosinone because I fought with those friends of mine, Gemma and Lilia. I found out that they loved each other like husband and wife. I discovered it because of being shut up in there with them.

I said to myself: Now I understand why those two were always together! Now I see why they used to send me away sometimes when they were discussing something; they would go off on their own and I'd get upset and try to push in between them, try to listen, because I considered myself their friend. And, instead, it was all a matter of love between those two, a love that cut me out.

But apart from that, we fought because I accused them of having grassed. I said: 'You come to me with your fine promises: "We'll buy you a car, share out the lolly!" Then you take me on a job, put me up to it and, the moment you're nicked, turn round and denounce me!

'I, on the other hand, denied everything. Said I didn't know a thing. I said it at once to the *carabinieri*, then to the judge, to everyone. I told them I didn't know you or anything. You shouldn't have talked, you should have denied all knowledge of it, like I did.'

'No,' they said, 'we told the facts as they really are, because the other participants in the job ought to take the rap, too, like we have to.'

'What?' I say. 'You were always telling me what to do, teaching me, yet you don't even know the first rule, which is: deny everything!'

An old crone who had been listening, a certain Pierina Lanza, who was very experienced at robbing apartments, intervened: 'You got hold of this girl, promised her a car, took her on the job with you, led her astray – because she'd never done a job before – and now you have the nerve to argue with her; If the facts are as she says they are, you should leave Teresa out of it, it's got nothing to do with her. Why do you accuse her now? Listen, try to put the blame on only one of you, that way all three of you will get lighter sentences. The trial's coming up soon, withdraw your statements, put the blame on just one of you and the others will go free.'

'Keep your nose out of my business!' said Gemma.

Then Pierina came up to me and said, 'Watch out for that Sardinian woman, she's the worst. She's wicked and selfish, she'll try to put it all on you because she's pig-headed and has no decent feelings.'

'In any case, I'm going to deny everything,' I said.

'That's the way,' said Pierina, 'always deny the charge and you'll be all right.'

In fact, at the Tribunal, I denied everything. 'Which one of you was inside the apartment?' asks the judge.

Gemma points at me and says, 'Her.'

'No, my lord,' I pipe up, 'I wasn't there at all.'

Then the judge asks Tango, 'Well, who was inside, then?'

Tango, who hates Lilia, points to her. And the judge does his nut and wishes us all to the devil. I got one year, nine months and ten days. Lilia, Gemma and Tango got four years.

I served the whole sentence, the year, the nine months and even the ten days. It seemed like an eternity. Each day lasted a month, each month a year.

Every morning I got up and made my bed, at the gallop, and woe betide you if you didn't tuck the blanket in neatly, you'd have to go without your supper. Then we went down to the refectory where they gave us a little *ersatz* coffee that left your mouth black and tasting foul.

Then I'd hang about till midday with nothing to do. At noon, they gave me a small loaf, like an army bread ration, and a mess-tin full of pasta and beans, mixed together. The moment I took a mouthful I felt like spitting it out again, but I got it all down somehow, because of the hunger-pangs that were gnawing a hole in my stomach. I'd swallow it all down and then my liver would start to hurt, but there was nothing I could do about it. Quite often they put a lump of rancid fat in the middle of the pasta; it stank like rotten meat. But, so as not to faint from weakness, I held my nose and gulped this muck down.

In the evening they gave us a mess-tin full of hot water. They called it soup but it bore not the slightest resemblance to soup. There was a scrap of potato in it, a sliver of onion and a morsel of left-over beans, mixed and mushed up in this deluge of water, this evil-tasting sewer-water.

Yet that soup in the evening was eagerly-awaited, because it was boiling hot and scalded your guts. But it didn't appease your hunger; on the contrary, it stimulated your appetite, and all night long I tossed and turned in my bed, thinking: Oh! what wouldn't I give for a nice juicy steak! Once a week they gave us a bit of boiled meat. It was sour, God knows what kind of sauce they put on it – some kind of pickle; it was tart, it made your teeth stick together.

Quite a few of the prisoners received parcels from home. Sometimes one of them would give me an apple. But if the other poor benighted devils noticed, they would say, 'One for me, too!' So the person who'd given it to me, not wanting to upset the others, stopped giving me things. Then I had to content myself with watching the lucky ones who got parcels. I'd see them opening them and unwrapping the stuff: lovely cheeses, bread rolls as white as milk, big juicy pears, dried fish, grapes, all first-class quality. There I was, sighing and yearning, with my eyes coming out on stalks.

Anyway, I had a big fight with Gemma and Lilia. I shouted at them, 'You lousy bitches, you've ruined me! Specially you . . . ' I said, turning to Gemma, 'you're a stinking cow! You seduced me with your fine talk, and after all, there was nothing in that flat – no gold coins, no millions!'

I took it out on Gemma because she was the boss, the one who made decisions. She was the stronger of the two. And she fought back, she raised her hands to me. So then I grabbed her by the hair and started kicking her. As a punishment, I was sent to Frosinone.

# 9

Being in Frosinone was worse than the torments of the damned. The mountain air gave me a colossal appetite. I was always as ravenous as a wolf. And there was even less to eat there than at the Mantellate prison.

Because of this devouring hunger I was always gloomy and depressed, always idle. Now and again my companions took pity on me and came to my rescue with a fag, a bit of bread dipped in oil, the head of a dried fish. And I was invigorated. The moment I appeased my appetite a little, I was gay and companionable again. And I'd start singing and dancing and we'd indulge in horse-play to pass the time.

We didn't work at Frosinone. There was only enough work for three or four convicts: the cooking, the cleaning, the accounts. There was no work for us. We sat around with folded hands. I deliberately avoided moving about so as not to work up an appetite.

If you knew how to do embroidery, they sent you along to Sister Santa Croce and she gave you a thimble and a needle and thread. But I don't know how to embroider, the stitches come out all crooked. I never was much good at sewing.

At long last, a parcel arrived for me, too. My brother Orlando had sent it to me from Regina Coeli prison. I don't know how he managed it but he sent me a box containing soap, pasta, American flour, Piedmontese biscuits, thing like that, whatever he could lay hands on, because he, too, was alone and abandoned. I remember there was a packet of *Nazionali* fags, too. They handed me this parcel; it was quite small. I started unwrapping it, saying to myself: Well, there's not much of it, but at least I'll have something to eat! I was feverish with delight over that parcel. And, as I unwrapped it, I was a bit disappointed, because I'd hoped for more, but part of me was happy and laughing, too. I soon finished the cigarettes. But I made the biscuits last over a month, by eating half at a time.

At Frosinone the only food they had ever heard of was beans. Every day they gave us beans, beans and pasta, beans and bread. Never anything else. I asked them once: 'Don't you ever change the menu in this convent?'

'Teresa, you're always grumbling!' said the wardress, and, as a punishment, she gave me a half-portion of beans instead of a whole one, the miserable pig!

There were two wardresses. One was the boss and she ordered everybody about. She was a thirty-year-old spinster, tall, nasty and with a face like an executioner. She had two strong, massive arms on her, like a wrestler. The other one was tiny, skinny and she looked like a mouse.

There were thirty to thirty-five of us. Twelve to a cell. Three cells. The two of them had to keep an eye on all of us. One would be coming, the other going. You'd think they'd never be able to cope, but on the contrary they were quick and crafty, you couldn't get away with anything; wherever you went, there they were, with their eyes on you.

Down below, on the ground floor, was the men's prison. There were many more of them than of us, so they were very cramped, and they spent their time fighting and complaining.

The most famous amongst them was a certain Giglioli who had murdered his wife with a pick-axe. On the day of the Festival of Prisoners, Giglioli, in a black suit, sat down at the harmonium and played. He played well.

They made us wear black, too: black stockings, black overall, a black veil over our heads. 'Who's dead?' I asked.

'It's the Festival of Prisoners, a day of solemn ritual,' they told me.

They took us all out into the courtyard in front of the prison church. It was July or August, and murderously hot. I said to myself: I don't give a bugger about their Festival, I'm not standing in this sun. But there was no way out of it; we were obliged to stand there, sweltering in all that black clothing.

I wonder what Giglioli was thinking about while he was playing the 'Ave Maria'? Two tears oozed out of his eyes, then two more, till he was bathed in tears. And the women prisoners cried too. I thought to myself: Holy Mary, Mother of God! It's like a blooming funeral! Everybody in black, weeping their eyes out, under the broiling sun.

My head was throbbing fit to burst. When would the Mass come to an end? *They,* the guards, the governor, the priests, were all under the canopy, nice and cool. We had to stand melting and sweating in the sun. It was murder!

I was really miserable in Frosinone. Fortunately there were some kind, generous people there. Gypsies, tough and independent, but good-hearted. When they had something to eat, they'd call me over: 'Here, Teresa, take this bit of bread; here's an anchovy for you, a cigarette.' And by way of thanks I made them laugh, I danced and sang songs when I was in a good humour, to cheer them up.

One day, as a result of those everlasting beans, I got an attack of colic. For a few days I was in bed, locked in my cell. We had those bunk beds, made of wood, with a pelmet and a white curtain for the sake of decency.

The doctor came along. I had diarrhoea and kept vomiting. It was a serious attack, brought on by that monotonous diet of beans.

'Put her on a light diet!' says the doctor, and I think: The Lord be praised, at least they won't give me beans now! It'll be a change, something different. And, in fact, at noon they gave me a bowl of soup, mostly water, with a little oil and vermicelli in it. I ask what is to follow. 'That's it, that's your lot!' they say. And that, indeed, was it, the 'light diet lunch'.

After a few days I started to feel better, the colic was passing off. But I still stayed in bed. I couldn't face leaving that warm nest, standing up and going out into the cold with the others. When they went out into the fresh air, I stayed behind, locked in, rolled up in my blankets.

There I lay, rolled up in those rags in the warm. And I sang to myself, softly, softly: ' . . . under the eaves of the ancient tower . . . flits the little swallow. . . . '

All of a sudden the door flies open and in comes the wardress: 'Teresa Numa, who gave you permission to sing?' She looks like Jesus Christ, tall, thin as a rake with a harsh, raucous voice. 'Numa,' she says, 'if you don't shut up, I'll take you off the light diet!' She was a sour-faced bitch, a country bumpkin from Molise.

'Right,' I say, 'take me off the light diet! You can stick it up your arse for all I care!'

This ogress forces me to my feet, and at once, bonk! a bop on the head. Then she sends me down to the refectory to eat pasta and beans with the rest of them. She takes me off the light diet. 'But what the hell has singing got to do with diet?' I ask.

So once again it was stewed beans, bean soup, bean mash, and the worst of it was they were dried beans, which don't agree with me. I ate them grudgingly and afterwards the wind rolled round my stomach like thunder, grumbling and rumbling.

One morning they say to me, 'Teresa Numa, get ready, you're leaving!' Certain that they're sending me home, I wash everything, chuck away the disgusting old rags I've been wearing, and it's goodbye to all my friends, hugs and kisses all round. 'Now I'm going home,' I say, 'and the first thing I'm going to do is eat a steak as big as a sheet of newspaper!'

And they all say, 'Lucky you, Teresa! All the best!'

Instead, I come out of Frosinone and they send me to the regional prison of Ceccano. They send convicts who have only got a few months left to serve to Ceccano.

It was like Heaven on earth there: we ate soup made with oil and never saw so much as half a bean, and on Sundays they gave us a handsome slice of tender meat. Oh, it was marvellous, I soon put on weight and felt fit again. Even my rheumatic pains went away.

At Ceccano there was only one wardress, Donna Rosaria, with her husband. There were no nuns and no *marescialli*. Those two, the husband and wife, were kind and considerate people.

Years later, there was a scandal and they were denounced in the newspapers. It seems they had been letting wives of convicts go into the cells. They charged a certain sum of money, then left them alone together to do their thing. To my mind, it was a kindness, and the prisoners got their money's worth. They should never have been condemned! If I had had a man at that time, I would willingly have paid a thousand lire for the chance to make love. But I didn't have a man, and, come to that, I didn't have any money, either.

# IO

I served my one year, nine months and ten days and came out at last. I found myself outside, alone, adrift, not knowing where to go. I had gone in without a lire and without a lire I came out.

Now where do I go? I say to myself. I start walking towards Rome. Half way along the road I hear a bus stop just behind me. I turn round. The driver leans out. 'Do you want to get in?' he says.

'I haven't any money.'

'Never mind,' he says, 'get in.'

And that's how I got to Rome.

I got off the bus at Porta Maggiore and started walking towards Piazza Vittorio. I thought I would go and look for my friends. I was walking along like this when I noticed a man following me. I was twenty-nine years old, I was pretty, a healthy country girl with a good bosom. I slowed down a little and he slowed down too. I felt a bit confused, after being inside for so long. This fellow says to me, 'Are you alone? Do you mind if I walk a little way with you?' I take a good look at him: he's neither young nor old, around forty, quite good-looking, bald, with a handlebar moustache. A bit ridiculous. I think to myself: I'll tell him to piss off, he's a nuisance and I don't like the look of him.

Then he says, 'May I invite you for a cup of coffee?' And suddenly I really fancy a scalding hot coffee. So we walk towards a bar, and on the way he asks me, 'You're not from Rome, are you?'

'No,' I say, 'I'm from Anzio.' I didn't tell him I'd just come out of Ceccano.

'Could we see each other this evening?' he asks.

'Visiting a relative of mine,' I say.

'Could we see each other this evening?' he asks.

I'm thinking: My word, he wants a lot for one cup of coffee! But, just to keep him quiet, I answer, 'Yes, certainly, this evening will be fine. Where shall we meet?'

'At the station, at nine o'clock.'

At last we get to this bar. He orders two coffees and while I'm drinking mine, which is like manna from heaven, he keeps yakking and yakking, till my head's spinning with words. I keep saying 'Yes, yes,' but my mind's on other things. I'm wondering where I'm going to sleep that night, with no money. I wanted to go to Anzio, but how was I to get there without a ticket?

Meanwhile, my eye lights on a plate of brioches, nicely puffed-up and brown on top. Let's hope he'll offer me one, I think! But not on your life, he keeps chattering on and laughing, oblivious. In the end, I pluck up courage and say, 'I wonder if I might have one of those brioches?'

'Er, no,' he says, 'I'm so sorry, but I haven't got any more money.' So I have to do without my brioche.

Well, I think, there's nothing more to be got out of this geezer, I may as well take off. But I couldn't get rid of him. He kept chuntering on, and laughing, and I couldn't get away. I hope Handlebars will offer me a fag, at least! I'm dying for a cigarette.

At a certain point, aha! he pulls out a cigarette, lights it and takes a drag. One for him, one for me, now he'll offer me one! And I'm waiting for it, gasping. But no, it's the last one, he tells me as he's crumpling up the empty packet.

So then I cut in and say, 'Well, I must be off now. Goodbye!'

'Till this evening, then?' he says.

'Yes, this evening!' I say, but to myself I add: You'll have a long wait, you ugly old baldpate, you mean, bullshitting Handlebars, you!

I left him and walked towards the Aquarium, where the buses for Anzio started. Now, I thought, I'll go to my brother Nello, he's the only one in the family who really cares for me.

I went to the bus terminus and asked if I could travel to Anzio on credit. Maybe, they said, we'll see. I spent three hours trying to persuade that clot of a driver and in the end he said no and swore at me. Then I started walking. I'm bound to get there sooner or later, I thought.

On the road, a lorry stopped and let me get up at the back amongst a lot of sheep. It was cold; I huddled down amongst the sheep and went to sleep. A few hours later I was in Anzio. I thanked the driver, got down and went to Nello's house.

It was a big house on the beach. All windows, like a hotel. It was almost dark when I arrived. The lights were on. I wonder what Nello's up to at this moment? I thought.

When he saw me, my brother threw his arms round my neck. He was happy to see me, but I thought he was looking thinner, not so handsome. 'What's wrong?' I said, 'aren't you well?'

He took me to see his wife, who was in bed. Then he told me she had been ill in bed for four months. I asked what was the matter with her. 'I don't know,' he said, 'it may be hereditary, or the consequences of a miscarriage she had, but she's got T.B. I took her to the hospital and spent a fortune on treatment, but then she wanted to come home, so I have to take care of her, and the children, and the fish business and all. I didn't even have time to come and visit you in prison, my poor, dear sister, though I grieved for you in there.'

'Listen,' I said, 'I want to get my baby back.'

'Go and get him, then,' said Nello, 'your father-in-law's got him.' So I collected the baby and set up home with him in Nello's house.

Nello's wife was twenty-six years old. There was nothing left of her, just skin and bone, and she kept spitting blood. There was nothing her husband could do for her, no cure. Nello had drained himself dry, spent his last lira trying to cure this woman. They didn't have any insurance or anything. At night he went fishing and in the morning he sold the fish, then he had to come home and look after the family. It was a dog's life and he was worn out with it.

Luckily, the house was large. There was a bed, and in fact a whole room, for me. But there was this bed-ridden sister-in-law, and the kids, filthy and neglected, crawling all over the floor, playing with their own poop.

I took a couple of pounds of soda and started to clean up. I scrubbed till my hands were raw. I disinfected everything with salt, with bleach, with vinegar.

Then I began cooking separate food for the children, because

66

they had been eating the mother's left-overs. The mother had neglected herself, she had had an abortion, she'd lost a lot of blood, then she had worn herself out with constant work, and that's why she was tubercular. Or so she said. But later on I heard that all her family were like that – they had passed the disease on from father to son for centuries.

After I had cleaned and thoroughly disinfected the house, and made it beautiful and sweet-smelling; after I had washed all the children's clothes, fixed up the bathroom, darned the socks, scrubbed and mended the pots and pans and everything else – my sister-in-law suddenly went and died on me.

Just a few days earlier I had run into a friend of mine in the piazza. She was a Neapolitan girl called Lina. I asked her what she was doing and she told me she'd got the sack from her job as a maid only the day before. 'Come and help me clean the house,' I said. 'We can whitewash the walls and put up some pretty wall-paper, I want to make the sitting-room look nice.'

So this girl came to help me. And when my sister-in-law died, she helped me wash and dress the body. Then she helped me with the disinfecting of the house and took care of the children. I became very fond of her. I didn't realise she'd set her cap at my brother.

Nello suffered a great deal over his wife's death. He cried, he gave up eating. He looked pale. But after two or three months he began to revive.

The Neapolitan girl and I slept in the same room, in little narrow twin beds. One night I wake up and see that her bed is empty. Where can she be? Maybe in the bathroom. I get up and go to the bathroom but she isn't there. Nor is she in the kitchen.

I look at the door of my brother's room and see that the light is on, so I think to myself: Aha, so that's where she is, the ungrateful hussy! Has she no respect for the dead? And all that affection she showed me was just eye-wash!

That Lina was in there with my brother. What they were up to, I'm sure I don't know! I went back to bed, but I was too upset to sleep. In the morning, when Lina came back to our room, I faced her with it. 'Do you think that's the proper way to behave? Aren't there any other men in the world? Do you *have* to take up with my brother?'

Then she says, 'But you're crazy, I never touched your brother. I've been in the bathroom.'

67

'You're the one who's crazy,' I say, 'I went to the bathroom and you weren't there. The light was on in my brother's room. You were in there with him.'

'You must have been dopey with sleep,' she says. 'I tell you, I was in the bathroom.'

'Listen, you idiot,' I say, 'I was awake, more wide awake than you, and now I know how you carry on in other people's houses.' She was trying to make a complete monkey out of me.

In the end, I told her she'd have to go. I'd taken her in, enjoyed her company, treated her like a sister, but now she was making love with my brother, she couldn't stay here any longer.

'But what's it to you?' she says. 'Are you jealous of your own brother?'

'Of course not,' I say. 'I'm not his wife, you know! But it makes me sick to think of my brother making love to my friend, behind my back, before his wife is cold in her grave.'

'I see,' she says. 'You want to make your brother miserable! But he's still young, virile; you can't stop him taking himself a wife! And if he *does* take a wife, then we'll see who's boss around here!'

'If you think you're going to make love to my brother, here in this house, while I'm around, you're making a big mistake. I'll kick you out, and him too, because of the children. I don't want them to see such things, when their poor mother's only just died.'

There was a lot of weeping and wailing and gnashing of teeth. But she didn't go. She stayed in Nello's house. She told him I'd been bossing her about, hitting her, ill-treating the children and so on, a load of old cobblers. But she convinced him. Oh, these men! They're like babies; the moment they lay eyes on a woman they go gaga.

My brother said to me, 'I'm not turning you out of the house, but I can't send Lina away because she's got nowhere to go, and anyway I love her. I'm thinking of marrying her.'

Well, I've got my pride, and besides I was nervous and upset, so I grabbed a case and left. I shot out of that house like a scalded cat. And I never went back.

I took my little son back to my sisters-in-law, asking them to keep him till I could fix up a job for myself in Rome, then I'd come and take him away.

# II

I took the bus to Rome. When I got there I started racking my brains: where could I go, where would I sleep that night? I had 3000 lire which my brother had given me, and that was all. All because of Nello, I was forced to set out again on the road to Calvary, roaming about like a stray cat. He didn't want me any more, because he'd gone and fallen in love with that wretched Neapolitan girl. It is my fate to run foul of these wicked, conniving women.

I rented a room near the Aquarium. I paid the old landlady 150 lire a day, I remember. It seemed such a lot of money then! This was about 1946–7.

I still didn't know many people in Rome. There was Egle, but she had moved. She'd made a bit of money by letting out rooms, and now she'd taken a larger and more comfortable apartment. I went the rounds, meeting new people, making friends.

One day I met a friend of my husband's, a beautiful girl with dark hair. She said, 'Come with me, I'll introduce you to my friends.' And she took me to the Bar Bengasi in Via Gioberti. It was the hang-out where all the girls who were on the game used to meet.

I sat down amongst them. This friend told me she had seen Sisto again, that he had changed, settled down, and no longer went with whores. While we were talking, I could hear the others asking who I was and what I did. They wanted to know my name and where I came from. I told them, 'I'm from Anzio. I've been in the nick for a year for housebreaking.' And we soon made friends; they bought me drinks and gave me cigarettes.

Each of these girls had her own man. They were well-dressed, they had gold wrist-watches, gold rings. They wore coats with fur collars, high-heeled shoes; their hair was beautifully done. To me, they looked like princesses, and I was a poor wretch beside them: I had on an old black dress and shoes that had been re-soled thirty times. I felt inferior.

The boy-friend of one of these women said to me, 'Ah, you're from Anzio and your name is Numa? I knew your brother. We were inside together for many years. He always wore a red scarf round his neck, because he's a Communist, and he was always singing at the top of his voice, it was killing! Well, well, so you're Orlando Numa's sister! Good. I'll take you around, introduce you to my girl-friends.'

I met some women through him. 'These girls aren't on the game,' he says. 'We steal wallets with them. If you'd like to come along with us, wait at the No. 12 bus stop and we'll give you something. All you have to do is take the wallets off us when we pass them to you. But if somebody spots you, we all split up and run. We'll all meet here at the bar in the evening.'

'Yes, all right,' I said, but I was afraid. I kept saying yes, and every day I went to the Bar Bengasi, drank coffee, smoked a fag and talked to these bag-snatchers. I made a show of being at ease, afraid of nothing, ready for action. But in fact I kept putting it off because I was scared. 'I'll come tomorrow,' I'd say, but then I'd invent some excuse – I was ill or too busy. I couldn't face the thought of going back to prison.

These girls found me a cheaper pensione, one where I even had hot water. It was a place where whores lived. They slept in the daytime because at night they were working. And when they were out, at night, I heard a great coming and going of couples, for the landlady let out their rooms by the hour.

The girls said to me, 'Why don't you get in on the game? We earn good money, we make a living, and look at you, wasting your time! You're still young, you've got a good body, you could make as much as we do.'

'Listen,' I said, 'I like to be on the move, running and jump-ing, stealing things, making them disappear like magic with quick, skilful hands. But when it comes to men . . . no, I can't! If I like a man, that's fine, but if I don't happen to fancy him. I'll probably punch him on the nose.'

'What a song and dance!' they said. 'Look, these men pay

good money. All you have to do is shut your eyes, grit your teeth and then take the money. It only lasts a few minutes. What do you care?'

'If you want me to pinch something, right! I'm with you,' I said, 'but if I've got to suck up to some bloke I don't even know, nothing doing! I can't help it. I only go with a man who pleases me, and that's that.'

In fact, I got to know all the thieves and pick-pockets in the neighbourhood, and we went out on jobs together; swift, deft, professional, we never got caught.

I was forced to it because I was penniless and I had been living on credit for two weeks already. I said, 'I'll come with you tomorrow for sure.' And I actually went with them next day.

The first time they take me to a villa near Castelgandolfo.

'What do we have to do?' I ask.

'We're going to steal a car.'

'But isn't there anyone in the villa?' I ask.

'Yes, but we'll be very quiet, they won't even hear.'

So we stole the car, a beaten-up little thing, but it still went very well. We used it to drive to Frascati and rob a trattoria. After the burglary we abandoned the car in the street and each of us made his way home separately on the tram.

That evening we met at the Bar Bengasi. 'Well, now,' I said, 'how much do I get?'

They said, 'You get least of all because you're a beginner and you don't know much yet.' And that's how it was. The three of them took equal shares while I took a half-share.

We stole the money out of the tills in various trattorias. Our boss, Amedeo, told us what to do and we had to obey his orders. He said, 'You, Teresa, go in with Giovanni and sit at a table, just as if you were ordinary customers. Order a beer, or a couple of sandwiches. Meanwhile, I'll sit at another table and pretend to be alone. You two make out you're lovers, or husband and wife, and hold hands. You don't know me, I'm on my own.'

And that's what we did. We went into a trattoria, a first-class place with good food, at about half-past two to three, when there weren't many people about. We ate our food, paid, and waited for the opportune moment. When we saw the owner go out into the kitchen, I made a sign to Amedeo and he moved. If the owner unexpectedly started coming back, I held up one finger to warn our boss to wait. Then, when I saw that the owner was really involved in the kitchen, arguing with the cook or replenishing the dishes, I made him a sign. He got up without making a sound and tiptoed over to the counter, whipped the money out of the till and went out.

After a couple of minutes, we went out too. We always made sure of paying in advance. We said goodbye and left. Outside, we ran round the corner, where Amedeo was waiting with the car and we took off like a rocket.

Sometimes we got a good haul, sometimes very little. Whatever we got, we split three ways. As a beginner, I collected only a half-share, but I was happy to see some money coming in.

In one day we could work two or three trattorias like this. We went to Ciampino, to Tivoli, to the Castelli Romani. We were a good team and we worked well together.

Whenever I had a little money in hand, I went to the Bar Bengasi and treated the girls to coffee, repaying their kindness to me when I was skint. I played the Lady Bountiful, buying coffees, cakes, cigarettes. Then I was broke again, and for two or three days didn't show my face.

One morning, I go meet Amedeo and he says to me, 'We're going on a different job today. In any case, we've squeezed all the trattorias round here dry by now.'

'What kind of job?' I ask.

'It's a textile warehouse. We'll have to get a shutter off its hinges, but it should be quite easy, it's old and half-rotten. Then we load the bolts of material on to the van and go and sell them. There's just one danger, though. The night-watchman. If you see him, you and Giovanni must pretend to be making love. You must be in each other's arms, leaning against the wall.'

His girl-friend Clara was listening. She was very much in love with Amedeo but she never came on the jobs with us. She was a prostitute, on the beat. She wasn't too fond of me, because I was always with Amedeo; she was suspicious and jealous and kept a beady eye on me.

Amedeo went on: 'Take my advice, if the police stop you, you don't know a thing, you've never seen me in your life and you don't even know Giovanni's name, get it?'

'But if they find me hugging and kissing Giovanni?' I said.

'You tell them you just picked him up in the street, you took a fancy to him and you're flirting,' said Amedeo. He was always giving me lessons like this, teaching me how to behave. 'And if you don't do as I say, I'll kill you,' he would say. He was very masterful and sometimes threatened us, but he wasn't mean or wicked. I got on well with him. He was a fair leader.

Well then, that day – it was a Monday, I remember – we went to do this textiles job. The previous evening we had stolen a van, brand new and sky-blue. We stopped in front of the warehouse. Amedeo tried to spring the padlock, but no luck. Then he made a hole in the shutter with a hammer and chisel. Giovanni went in and started passing the rolls of stuff out to Amedeo, who loaded them on to the van. Everything went swiftly, smoothly, in silence. The street was empty, not a soul about. I was on the look-out at the corner.

As they were loading the last two rolls, with the motor already running, ready for the get-away, the fuzz arrived. This patrol car just happened to be passing and they saw us.

'What are you doing?' they ask.

'Well,' I say, 'I met a bloke and he wanted to go to bed with me. We were talking, but I couldn't make up my mind. In the end, I didn't go with him.'

'What's this fellow's name?'

'I don't know. I don't know him, I just picked him up in the street.'

'What? You're lying!'

'No, sir, officer, it's the truth, I swear it.'

Meanwhile, Giovanni and Amedeo had split. And they left me in the hands of those bloodsuckers who, seeing the hole in the shutter, discovering the robbery and not finding the thieves, took me in as a suspected accomplice.

At two o'clock in the morning, I find myself once more at the Commissariat of Police. 'You know we've got them, locked up in there?' they tell me. 'They've grassed, they told us your name – Teresa.'

'That's right,' I say, 'my name's Teresa. I told that bloke my name as soon as we met, but I don't know them, I don't know who they are.'

'Look, we know perfectly well that you know them. You must tell us their names.'

'If you've nicked them,' I say, 'why don't you ask them their names yourselves?'

Then they blew their tops. The Vice-Commissioner, a bald geezer with his eyes all boggy with sleep, started yelling. Then he said to me, 'You won't walk out of here a free woman, I'll see to that!'

At first they were all right, but then they got rough and tortured me to try and find out the names. I kept saying, 'I don't know anything.'

'Liar!' they said, 'give us their names and we'll let you go at once.' But I wouldn't talk.

Then they got hold of me, pushed me and knocked me to the ground.

'You ugly bitch!' one of them said, hauling me to my feet by my collar and bashing me against the wall. 'You lousy, rotten whore!'

He was big and tall, his hands were like blocks of wood. He pounded me to a pulp, but still I wouldn't say anything. Finally, they got fed up. They took me and shut me up in a little black closet without a window.

There were big, hairy rats running all over me. I had to stamp up and down to keep them off. It was the Sette Sale jail, at Colle Oppio.

In the morning they came to fetch me. 'Well now, have you thought it over? Do you know these men?'

'No,' I said, 'I don't know them from Adam.'

'If you don't give us their names,' they said, 'you'll go behind bars for a year!'

Then I invented a couple of names. 'I think they were called Franco and Nicola.'

'Surnames!'

'I don't know their surnames,' I said, and they shoved me back into that dark, airless hole.

They left me there for four days, in the pitch dark, amongst the rats. When they brought my meals, it was a battle: those filthy vermin tried to get the food out of my hands. They crawled up my arms, over my chest. So I stood on the table, with my body well away from the wall, and ate as fast as I could, stamping my feet, boom, boom! on the wooden top to frighten them off.

Every now and then they hauled me out and asked the same everlasting question. No response. 'In any case,' I said, 'you've got no evidence against me, you'll have to let me go.' But they were obstinate pigs, and the more I denied it the more they insisted.

At the end of four days they got sick of it. They sent me away, broken and battered, half dead from hunger and exhaustion, full of fleas. I was chilled to the marrow and filthy dirty. My skin was black with dirt and I stank worse than a sow. Luckily they returned my handbag to me with the money intact: my last 500 lire.

The light made me dizzy when I came out after enduring four days of darkness. My eyes burned, I couldn't keep them open. I sat down on the parapet of the bridge for a while, overlooking some gardens. People thought I was blind, because I looked at things without seeing them. I stayed there for about an hour. Then I said to myself: Now where? I know, I'll go to the public baths, before this stink makes me faint.

I went to the baths in the station. I was tottering like a drunk. In there, everything was clean and fragrant. I paid. They gave me a lovely bathroom and I thought I was in Paradise. White tiles, hot water, steam, clean towels, carnation-scented soap, the lot.

I took off my dress, my knickers, my bra. I washed my body, my hair. I rubbed that cake of soap over my whole body with ritual solemnity. I washed my underclothes, wrung them out and put them on again, sopping wet. I hadn't realised that, with all this washing, a couple of hours had gone by. Then I heard a voice: 'Are you all right, signorina? You're not ill?'

'No thank you, I'm fine. Just washing!'

'Hurry up, please, there are people waiting!'

But I paid no attention. I cleaned out the bath, filled it up and plunged in again.

It was so lovely in the water that I thought: I'll spend the night in here, and if they don't like it, they can lump it! But that attendant kept hammering at the door and in the end I had to come out, dripping wet, with my wet clothes on my back. I walked very fast in the sunshine so as to dry myself.

# 12

I went back to the Bar Bengasi and asked for Amedeo and Giovanni. Nobody knew where they were. 'They owe me some money for that job we did at the textile warehouse,' I said.

'Ah, but those two have split, God knows where they are! You may as well forget about the bread.'

'What!' I said, 'do you mean I've put up with four days' interrogation, all amongst the rats, for their sakes, and they don't even give me one lira? Where did they sell the stuff?'

Nobody knew anything about it. They'd vanished with the money and I had given my services as look-out, free, gratis and for nothing.

At that time, I didn't know where to lay my head. I hadn't a lira and they wouldn't let me stay at the pensione. 'Pay up or out you go!' they said.

'I'll pay you, I'll pay,' I said. But how? I went around, looking for someone who was planning a job, but there was nothing doing.

One morning I ran into Edera, a woman I had known a few years earlier. She sold cigarettes on the black market. She came from the Abruzzi, but she had been living in Rome for years. 'Why don't you come to Perugia with me,' she said, "we're going to pick up a consignment of cigarettes.' So I went along.

We couldn't get hold of any cigarettes, but we managed to buy some oil. And we start selling this oil. Edera fed me and she gave me a bed, but no money. She treated me like her slave.

We travelled on buses. We'd collect the oil in some barn somewhere and take it to Rome. Then we sold it door-to-door. We travelled all over the place on these country buses, and we walked, and walked, and walked! I wore out two pairs of shoes in a month.

Occasionally we managed to get hold of cigarettes instead of oil. Edera and I would go into a store and meet the black marketeers; then we'd carry the fags to Rome in straw bags. I carried two bags, she carried one.

When we got a good price, she'd give me a little something. There wasn't much money in it. She always diddled me, saying she had used the money to buy up more stock, and that the cost of living was very high and we could barely manage as it was. I had to put up with it, but I was pissed off. I was just waiting for a chance to leave her. I couldn't stand her bossiness. 'Do this, do that!' she'd say, ordering me around as if she were a great lady. And I had to obey, or else I didn't get anything to eat.

One day, when I was shopping in Piazza Vittoria, I met a girl who was on the game. Well, she was and she wasn't, because she only pretended to go with men so that she could steal their wallets.

Her name is Dina, she's from Civitavecchia. She's intelligent and as sharp as a razor. She's a pretty little blonde, dainty and slim. 'What are you doing?' she asks me.

'Working with an old bag, selling oil. She's mean, she won't give me a lira.'

Dina says, 'Are you any good at nicking wallets?'

'No,' I say.

'Come with me and I'll teach you,' she says. 'You know what to do? Get hold of a man, make out you're going to give him a bit, kiss him, embrace him, and when he's all steamed up, you slip out his wallet.'

'But I'm no good at that, I couldn't do it,' I say.

'Just watch me and you'll soon get the knack. When I get hold of his wallet, I'll pass it to you.'

'All right,' I say, 'I'm a quick learner.' I was delighted to leave that old trout, and Dina and I soon became bosom pals.

On the very first evening, Dina said, 'You know, I think we'd better lay off the wallets in Rome for the time being. A friend of mine was nicked yesterday and they're looking for me, too. Why don't we go to Genoa? There's rich pickings to be had there, nice fat wallets.'

'Listen,' I said, 'when you've got these men in tow and they

77

want to go with you, how do you get rid of them?'

'Don't you worry,' she said, 'I'll do the work. You just stick by me and we'll go halves on everything.'

'All right,' I said, 'I trust you.' And in fact I did trust her, because that Dina was a crafty little devil, very intelligent, artful.

We took the train to Genoa. Somehow, Dina managed to borrow the fare. We got out and looked around us. It was a beautiful city. I hadn't been there before. It was full of rich people, hurrying about, wearing splendid woollen overcoats. Just what we were looking for.

We started strolling up the main street, one blonde and one redhead, making ourselves conspicuous. We were both wearing pink coats and high-heeled shoes. Naturally, the men were soon following us.

Dina had an expert eye. She soon rejected anybody without money. Those who had money she could spot from two miles away, then she'd slow down to let them catch us up, or even move towards them without appearing to do so. When they had taken the bait, she smiled alluringly at them; she was irresistible, so sweet and shy.

After we had been walking for a while, we found our man: middle-aged, with a great big conk and a velvet collar. He caught us up and turned round. Dina shot him a furtive glance. He stopped, turned back. Dina pretended not to have noticed and she walked on. I followed a little way behind, doing whatever she did. I was learning.

We went on like this for another two hundred paces, shilly-shallying. Then Dina took action: she stopped, waited for him, then slipped her arm through his. The man was a bit annoyed when he saw that I was glued to her side. 'Couldn't we be alone?' he said, and Dina said, 'Good heavens, if my mother knew I went out alone, without my cousin, she'd kill me!'

So he had to put up with it. Then he said, 'But where can we go? I feel like a little kiss-and-cuddle.'

Dina said instantly, 'Let's go to the cinema.'

Inside the cinema we sat down in this order: Dina in the middle, the bloke on one side and me on the other. Then she started touching him up. She hugged him, squeezed him and in the meantime slipped his wallet out of his pocket. As soon as she'd got her hands on it she passed it to me secretly in the dark. All the time she's talking to Big Conk: 'You're so sweet, give me a little kiss! Shall we see each other this evening? But don't come round to my cousin's place, you'll ruin my reputation!'

Holding the wallet, or rather with it tucked into my sweater, next to my skin, I stand up and say, 'Excuse me a moment, I'm going to the Ladies.' And out I go.

I wait for her outside the cinema, quaking. Two minutes later she comes out. As soon as she appears we start to run, kicking our legs up till they nearly reach our ears. We run, change tack, jump on a tram, vanish.

At last, safe and alone in a quiet street, we open the wallet. Twenty thousand lire. 'What did I tell you?' says Dina, 'I knew that fellow had money.'

'But how did you know?'

She says, 'I just know, by smell. I don't often make a mistake.'

'But what did you say to Big Conk in the cinema?'

'After you'd been gone a minute or two, I said: "I must go and see what my cousin's up to, she may be feeling ill. I'll be back in a minute." So I got up, very casually, and came out.

'And now,' she says, 'let's go to a good restaurant, then we'll find somewhere to sleep. We can get by for a few days now.'

We slipped into the first fancy-looking restaurant we came to and ordered a fantastic dinner: risotto, mushrooms, ices, and whipped cream. We drank beer and coffee. We ate till we were bursting.

Then we went to look for a pensione, but they were either full up or so bleak-looking that our hearts shrank and we went away. In the end, we wound up in a terribly expensive hotel near the hill. We were tired, couldn't walk another step.

They gave us a lovely room with a balcony. I looked out; you could see the whole city lit up beneath you. 'Look, Dina!' I said, 'Genoa's a beautiful place!' But she was too sleepy to care.

'Shut the window, you idiot, it's cold!' she said. And so ended our first day in Genoa.

We didn't put our noses out of doors for two or three days. Then, as soon as the money was all gone, we started again. Sometimes the wallets were empty or had only a couple of hundred lire in them. Then it was back to square one.

Dina was talented, her hands moved so lightly that nobody felt them. She showed me how to do it, too, she gave me careful instructions. But I never became as skilful at it as she was. She was a cool customer, but when I put my hand on the wallet to slip it out, my heart pounded like a drum.

She teased me in that drawling, Civitavecchia accent of hers: 'What's the maaatter? Does it give you the jim-jams? Christ, how you're treeeeembling! Get on with it! Your heart will jump out of your moooooouth! Gerrrr off!'

She was completely unemotional. Young, younger than me in fact, and totally impassive. She never trembled; she was calm, shrewd, sure of herself. I tried to copy her, to be like marble. But I never achieved her cold-bloodedness and my hands were like lead compared to hers: Dina's hands were like two little spiders.

We found a pensione in Genoa where the rooms were cheap and quite clean. There was a wash-basin and even an iron bidet on little wheels, so that you could move it round the room. Curtains with yellow flowers hung at the window.

Every four days the landlady waylaid us and said, 'Well, are you going to pay me or aren't you?' She was a nosy old hag and she was always rummaging through our things. She begrudged us clean towels and served our food up half-cold. She was spiteful and took pleasure in her spite.

On the first day we had struck it rich with that fat wallet, but then for ten days or so we had a run of bad luck. We couldn't pay our bill at the pensione. And, as we were not what the landlady called 'good, solvent girls', she stopped giving us sugar and was stingy with the hot water. She became sour-faced and insolent.

'Let's move,' I said to Dina, 'this isn't the only pensione in Genoa, you know.' It was called the Pensione Strauss.

Dina said, 'How will we pay?'

'We won't,' I said, 'we'll leave without paying.'

Next morning we got hold of one of those cheap cardboard suitcases and filled it with bricks that we pinched from a nearby building site. We put the case outside the front door. Then we took our stuff, tied it up in a bundle and threw it out of the window.

Dina went out first, picked up the bundle and went off. A little later I went down, empty-handed. 'Good morning, signora!' I said to the landlady, and joined Dina round the corner. We cleared off fast, the pair of us, saving ourselves a week's board and lodging and leaving a pile of bricks behind for Signora Strauss of Genoa.

The same evening we moved into another pensione, the Portofiorito. I was tired, I wanted to go to bed, but Dina said, 'Let's take a little turn first, see what turns up.'

'It's cold,' I said, 'besides, I'm sleepy.'

'Let's go out,' she said, 'I've got a feeling our luck's in to-night.' So out we went.

It was bitterly cold outside. I had only a light-weight overcoat, I was perished with the cold. 'Let's go back,' I say.

'Wait,' says Dina, 'let's see if we can pull off something a little better this evening.' Round and round we go, wearing our feet out, in that cold wind that slashes your face.

Then a fellow comes up to us, a good-looking boy with dark hair. 'Signorine!' he says, 'are you alone? Allow me to escort you somewhere!' Dina gives him one searching look, scowls, and sweeps on.

'Maybe that one had bread!' I say, 'sometimes these shabby-looking boys are loaded with the stuff.'

'No,' she says, 'you keep your mouth shut, you don't understand a thing; that geezer was penniless.'

We walk on. My feet and hands are frozen. My nose has gone dead. 'Is it worth it?' I say, 'all this suffering for a blooming wallet!'

We keep walking towards the city centre, feeling pretty depressed. We stop near a posh restaurant. People are going in in couples, all the men have their wives with them. Nothing doing.

Finally, we see a smart-looking man coming towards us, elegant and well-dressed, in a camel-hair coat with a wide belt. He doesn't say a dickie bird. Just stares at us and smiles.

Dina nudges me. 'This is it!' she says. I stick close to her, ready to do whatever she says. She walks away quickly, then slows down. I am still glued to her. Every few steps, Dina turns round to make sure the camel is still following.

After a long chase, Dina finally lets him catch up. She speaks to him: 'We're students from Rome, here on holiday. We don't know anyone in Genoa, we're feeling a bit lost.'

The camel bows, very courteously. He slips his hand through Dina's arm and we all begin walking together. It seemed odd to me that he didn't speak. Was he a mute? Well, so much the better – he wouldn't be able to call the police.

He wanted to go into a bar, but Dina led him on towards a cinema. At last we heard his voice: it was like a baby's. 'Oh, I've already seen this film,' he said. What now? I thought. I hope we're not going to walk any more, I'm so cold I could weep.

But Dina, who is much more enterprising than me, just said, 'It doesn't matter, we won't even look at the film. Let's go in, we can cuddle up together in the warm.'

The fellow agreed, he was delighted. He went to the box office, paid and we went in. They were showing a western with dozens of dead bodies, blood spurting all over the place, heads rolling, horses spilling their guts – a right massacre.

Thank the Lord we're inside, in the warm, I think to myself. I hope Dina will take her time, I don't want to go out into the cold again. But instead, a few minutes after we've sat down, I feel her hand touch my elbow. I grab the wallet, slip it under my coat, get up and go to the Ladies.

I've hardly got the door open when I see Dina coming after me. 'Run, hurry up!' she says.

'What's up? Has he found out you robbed him?'

'No, no, everything's fine, but so cold, let's run!'

We started running, down one street, up another, twisting and turning, until we reached a lonely spot were there was nobody about. Finally, under a street lamp, we pulled out the wallet.

It was heavy, crammed to bursting. 'Look at that! What did I tell you?' says Dina. We open it up. Inside, there's one hundred lire and a wad of photographs of naked women. The stinking turd!

We threw away the wallet and went back to the Portofiorito. Our hunger was sharpened by frustration. We were tired and breathless from running. We had been looking forward to a sumptuous dinner, and instead . . . nothing.

We went into the dining-room at the Portofiorito. It was late, the waiters had already cleared the tables. Dina made a fuss: 'But we pay full pensione,' she said, 'we're entitled to an evening meal.'

'I'm sorry, the kitchen is closed,' said the manageress. After a lot of argy-bargy, we managed to wangle a slice of cold beef, which tasted like cardboard, and a bit of stale bread out of them. We ate it, such as it was, and went up to bed.

In the morning, we got up rested and refreshed. On our way out, we noticed that there was no one at the reception desk. 'Signora, signora!' we called, but nobody came. Our documents were lying there on the desk, within easy reach, and there was a key on top of them. We grabbed them and split, as fast as we could. 'You know something,' says Dina, 'I hate this bloody Genoa!'

That same evening we took a train to Milan. It was cold and foggy there. We went straight into a pensione near the station; it was called the Commercio.

'Have you got a room?' I asked the manager, a little fellow with a paunch like a water-melon.

'For two such pretty young ladies,' he says, 'there is most certainly a room,' and he starts making sheep's eyes at Dina.

She flirted with him and played the gracious lady. 'We would like a spacious room please, one that doesn't overlook the street!' She was such a good actress, that Dina, no wonder everybody fell for it. And this twit was tying himself in knots to try and please her.

He took us up to a room. To be honest, it was a bit small, but clean. If you opened the door of the wardrobe, you couldn't get by, you had to climb over the bed to get to the window. But it was all right by us, all the same.

# 13

So we carried on with this dog's life, sometimes getting hold of a well-stuffed wallet, sometimes an empty one, according to the luck of the game.

When things went well, we'd go to a good restaurant: hors d'oeuvres, fish, meat, dessert and coffee; we ate like fighting cocks. When we were out of luck, we trailed back to the pensione and ate the soup smelling of greasy saucepans that was the speciality of the Commercio, and a bit of charred and shrivelled meat.

One day Dina says to me: 'Listen, I'm fed up with doing all the dirty work; it's time you learned to pinch wallets. We'll go out today and you do the job; I'll wait outside.'

'All right, I'll have a go,' I say, 'but I'm scared.'

'Don't worry,' she says, 'cuddle up to him, nice and close, kiss his ear, that always drives men wild, and meanwhile slip your hand into his pocket, do you understand?'

We didn't go out till fairly late that afternoon, when it was already getting dark. It was cold but there was no wind. It wasn't too bad. I was still going about in that light-weight overcoat I'd worn in Rome, because I hadn't managed to scrape up enough money for a new one.

We walk towards the centre, and stroll round the cathedral square, the piazza del Duomo. I look up at the stone spires, all lacy and white. Dina says, 'Never mind gaping up there, keep your eyes on the ground – churches don't have wallets.'

Immediately I start peering at the passers-by; to me they all looked wealthy: fur collars, crocodile handbags, beaver hats.

'There's good pickings here!' I say.

'Don't you believe it,' she says, 'it's all show.' Dina liked to be Miss Know-All, but she could make mistakes too – just lately, she had made a lot. I told her so, and she lost her temper.

'Is it my fault if men walk about with their wallets empty?' she says. 'I can tell a rich man by his face, but I can't tell whether he's got money actually in his pocket or not.'

While we're arguing, a man goes by and gives us the old glad eye. Dina pinches me and says, 'There's our boy, get after him!'

I am not a good actress like she is, but I screw up my courage, turn round, smile invitingly. He turns round, too, and stops. He turns back. 'Now what do I do?' I whisper and Dina says, 'Be gracious, but shy. It'll be all right, you'll see.'

I simper and smirk, but it's no good, I'm an obvious phoney. I'm dying to laugh and itching to punch him on the nose, because he's a nasty-looking bit of work: face all crooked, sallow skin, and he's got a little hat perched right on top of his nut.

Dina was pushing me forward and kicking me on the shins. At last this geezer opened his mouth. 'Are you alone?' he asks.

'Yes,' I say, 'we're not Milanese, we don't know the city.'

'May I have the pleasure of showing you around, if you're free?'

'Oh, yes,' I say.

And he starts trotting us round Milan. Dina keeps digging me in the ribs. I was supposed to suggest he should take us to the cinema, but I couldn't get around to it. We kept walking round and round like idiots. He's saying, 'This is the Cathedral, and that's the statue of the Madonna up there. Lovely, isn't it?' And me: 'Oh, yes, lovely!' Dina's furious!

Luckily, at a certain moment, we happen to find ourselves outside a cinema where they're showing a famous love story. 'Ooh,' I say, 'I would like to see this film. Shall we go in?'

'All right,' he says.

'But my friend must come with us, I can't leave her alone.'

'As you wish,' he says.

He buys tickets for us both, and pays through the nose for them, because it's a first-class cinema.

I really wanted to see this film. I thought to myself: later on, towards the end, I'll get his wallet. But it was impossible. Dina kept twisting my arm. And the fellow wanted to touch me up. 'Look,' I said, 'don't go too far or my friend will be shocked.'

I wouldn't let him touch me. But I touched him. I stroked his neck, his shoulders, and put my hand between his legs. Then I shut my eyes and said to myself: now I'll kiss his ear, like Dina told me to, this is the moment to do it.

Dina was quivering because I was so slow about it, and so clumsy. But I was terrified the bloke would notice that I was scrabbling about in his pockets. Besides, the Lord alone knows why men have to have so many pockets. This fellow had two in his jacket on the outside, two inside and two in his trousers. I was in a right old fix.

Dina always knew instantly where to find the wallet. I didn't. Later, she told me she watched carefully while they were paying for the tickets at the box office. I would never have thought of that.

Anyway, there I am, poking into all these pockets. I was so anxious that I was streaming with sweat, bathed in it. At last I felt something hard between my fingers. The wallet. I gritted my teeth and very nearly bit off his ear in the process. Luckily, he took it to be a sign of passion. With his ear-lobe still between my teeth, I slid out the wallet and passed it to Dina, under the arm-rest. I was so pleased at my success that I kissed that idiot in earnest, for sheer joy. I gave him two smacking kisses on the cheeks and two on the mouth and he was in seventh heaven. He was an ugly little man, with ears that flapped in the wind. I thought to myself: Mamma mia, what a twit he is!

Dina gets up and goes to the toilet. I stay with him a little longer, whispering sweet nothings in his ear. I put my hand between his thighs. Then, after about three minutes, I say to him: 'Excuse me, I'm going to see what's happened to my friend. I hope she's not ill.'

I stand up and go out. The moment I'm outside, I start to run so hard that even Dina can't keep up with me.

We stop in a deserted street. Pull out the wallet. There are 230,000 lire in it. We share it out at once: 115,000 each. 'You see?' I say, 'I did it, all by myself!' I was proud of myself, I felt I had really accomplished something. Admittedly, I took my time working up to it.

Dina scolded me: 'Ach, you stupid thing, you make a balls of everything!' But it was by listening to her insults and reproaches that I learned to be as crafty as she was.

That evening we had a sumptuous dinner to celebrate. We ate tripe, cod in a cream sauce, lobster, *dolce di ricotta*, coffee, wine and beer. We were so bloated with food that we could scarcely get up from the table.

We went back to the Commercio half-stoned. The manager came to meet us, all smiles. 'Ah!' he says, 'you are gay tonight! Life is treating you well, eh? May I offer you a drink? Vermouth, grappa? I'll bring it up to your room, we'll have a little drink together, a toast to your health.'

I belched right in his face. Dina, who never loses her cool, says: 'How sweet of you! Thank you. But we must go to sleep now because we have to be up early in the morning. We'll see you tomorrow, then! Goodnight.' And she leaves him standing there like a fool. She's so clever with men. She pretends to be afraid of them. She leads them on, promises them the earth and never keeps her word.

There was one man she really loved: his name was Domenico, but he was known as Mimí. But they didn't see each other very often because he was a thief too and he was always travelling around on business. They worked different stamping-grounds.

We slept all next morning. Then we went shopping to get ourselves new outfits. Dina bought a red leather handbag and a pair of pink high-heels. I bought a sky-blue coat lined with fur, it was lovely and warm. The fur lining was nylon, but it kept me warm just the same. It was a lighter shade of blue than the coat. Then we bought gloves, stockings, underwear. We went to a posh hairdresser and had our hair set.

Next day and the day following that, we lived on capital. We stayed in bed, reading the newspapers, doing our nails, chatting, eating almond cakes.

When we went out, we put on all our new finery and looked really elegant, we got all sorts of admiring looks. We ate, we drank, we were happy.

After a few days, though, the money was all gone. 'We'll go hunting again tonight,' said Dina, 'it's your turn.'

'No,' I said, 'it's yours.' We squabbled over it for a bit, then decided it was up to me.

She said, 'Now, remember your name's not Teresa, it's Luisa.'

'Why?'

She says, 'Because it will be harder for them to recognise you afterwards. You must always have a professional name. You're Luisa, and you come from Frascati or Aprilia or somewhere or other – you decide. Never give anyone your real name and address.'

That evening, we got our hooks into an old fellow from the country. The old fathead thought he was going to have it off with the pair of us.

Dina kept well away from him, but she couldn't treat him too badly because we hoped he'd turn out to be the goose that lays the golden egg. As before, I told him to keep his hands to himself: 'If you touch me, I'll scream.' But, in compensation, I touched him up. I ran my hands all over his behind to see where he had stuffed his wallet. Then his chest: I slipped my hands inside his jacket. I couldn't find that blasted wallet. Yet I had seen him slip it into his jacket after he had paid at the box office. He must have shifted it when we came in, I thought, perhaps when he tipped the usherette.

Meanwhile, he stretched out a hand towards Dina's knees. She blew her top at me and I blew mine at him. At one point I said to him, 'If you don't keep your paws off my friend, I'll walk out and leave you flat.' Then he behaved himself for a while.

While I was kissing his grubby old ear, which nearly made me throw up, I at last discovered his wallet, the old boy was wriggling about on his seat and trying to put his hands up my skirt. I held him off.

While I'm burbling sweet words into his ear, I'm yanking away at his wallet. But, partly because he was fat and the pocket was stretched tight, and partly because the wallet was full, I couldn't get it out.

Well, suddenly this old fellow notices what I'm up to and starts saying, 'Ach, you bitch! You were trying to rob me!'

'I was just joking,' I say, but he keeps on.

'I'll take you straight to the police station.' I try to soften him up with kisses. Meanwhile, I realise that Dina has split. She's smelled danger and gone, leaving me to it.

I didn't know what to do. He starts raising his voice. People are turning round to see what's going on. I was all embarrassed: Help! I thought, what do I do now? Then Dina's words came

88

into my mind: The best method of defence is attack. So I attacked. I started yelling louder than him: 'You filthy, slobbering, lecherous old bastard! You put your dirty hands on me, you tried to take advantage!'

The people around us were inquisitive. Some sided with me and started glaring at the old man. Then the usherette came along with a torch in her hand. The old man got scared. He stood up and went out.

After that scare, Dina did all the work for several days. Her hands were so light she was never caught in the act. But she was unlucky. All the wallets turned out to be empty.

Meanwhile, the proprietor of the Commercio was demanding payment. He let Dina know that either we must pay up or she must go to bed with him, but things could not go on as they were. He was becoming a pest. At night he lay in wait for us, brought drinks up to our room, tried to paw us.

'What are we going to do about him,' I said to Dina, 'he's getting on my tits.'

'I've promised to go to bed with him, and if I don't keep my word, he'll chuck us out,' said Dina. 'We've got to leave.'

'When?' I said.

'Tonight.'

It was one in the morning when we got back to the Commercio. The last wallet had been a flop and we hadn't a lire in the world. As usual, there was the proprietor in the doorway, all smiles, with the bottle ready.

So Dina goes up and whispers in his ear: 'Come up later on when my friend's asleep, and we'll make love.'

'What time?' he asks.

'About three or four.'

'And if she doesn't go to sleep?'

'If she doesn't go to sleep, I'll send her out for a walk. I want to be alone with you,' says Dina, and that makes him very happy. He pours us a drink, flirts and simpers at us, with his great fat belly rumbling and growling as if it's full of wild cats.

As soon as we got upstairs, we arranged our usual system. Dina climbs out of the window with our stuff. Luckily we're on the first floor. Then I go downstairs and out, passing in front of the proprietor who is half-asleep but on the watch.

'I can't sleep,' I say to him, 'so I'm going out for some air.'

He says, 'Have a pleasant walk, signorina!' Now, I think, he'll dash upstairs. And in fact, the moment I was out of the door, I saw him starting up the stairs. So I ran, rejoined Dina and we split like the wind.

That same day we left for Rome on the proceeds of a wallet containing 20,000 lire that Dina had whipped off some poor devil 6 foot 6 inches tall in a crowded cinema.

# 14

In Rome I ran into a woman I know. We met in a shop on the via Nazionale, up near the station. Her name's Marisa, but they call her La Spagnola, though she's no more Spanish than I am. She was a beautiful woman with black hair, a swarthy skin and a husky voice.

She was buying a three-quarter-length jacket. 'Carluccio's spoken to me about you,' she said. 'Are you still with Dina?'

'Yes.'

'Listen,' she said, 'why don't we all go to Florence together? I hear there's plenty of work up there, you get wallets like you've never seen in your life, they're bursting with money and the men walk about with them half-falling out of their pockets, just *asking* to be taken.'

'All right,' I said, 'I'll have a word with Dina.'

So I told Dina about these wallets that jump out of men's pockets like flying fish, right there in the streets of Florence, and she said yes at once. 'In any case,' she said, 'we're bitched in Rome, we're too well-known, it's dangerous.' We took a train to Florence, the two of us together with La Spagnola.

No sooner do we arrive in Florence than we read in the papers that there's been a big raid on the Banca Commerciale and the place is crawling with fuzz, the entire police force is combing the city.

We immediately take another train, to Liguria, and from there we go to Nervi, by the sea. We get out and start looking for a hotel.

There were two, one called the Internazionale and one called the Minerva. They were both lovely. 'Which is it to be?' says Dina.

''The Minerva,' says La Spagnola. 'I like the look of it better.' Anyway, that's where we went, to the Minerva. We handed in our identity papers (false!).

In the basement of this hotel there was a night-club called La Marinella. It was a smashing place, with a dance-floor, beautifully decorated with shells and fishing-nets hung on the walls and greenish lighting; you thought you were down at the bottom of the sea.

Dina said, 'Oh, I'd really love to go dancing tonight. Let's put on our glad rags, go to the hairdresser, have our nails done, get all made up and perfumed, then we'll go to the Marinella and see what happens.'

So we washed, tarted ourselves up and went down to the night-club. Dina had put on a green dress, I was wearing black and La Spagnola had had her hair done up like a Japanese girl. She's a good-looking woman, as I said a little taller than me, with jet black hair.

Well then, we go down and sit at a table in the corner. There's a red candle on the table, a clean cloth and shining glasses. We order orange juice.

After a while, the place begins to fill up with lawyers, shop-keepers, people of all kinds. Seeing us sitting there alone, some of the men came and asked us to dance. I don't know how to dance, I've never learned.

'I can't dance,' I said. But these fellows insisted. 'Look,' I said, 'dance with my friend, I can't, it makes me dizzy.' So they danced with Dina or La Spagnola.

In the end, Dina brings one of these men to our table, makes him sit down and drink with us. She pretends she's drunk too. She calls out to the waiter, 'Another whisky, please!'

'What if this geezer doesn't cough up, if he's skint?' I say.

'Trust me,' she says, 'I'll play this one my way. Go on up to our room, I'll join you later.'

This fellow she'd got hold of was quite old, with fair hair and a soppy face. 'Go on, go on,' she said, 'I'll be up later.' The pair of them, him drunk and her pretending to be drunk, said good-bye to us and started dancing again.

La Spagnola and I went up to our room. All three of us were to sleep in the same room; there was a big bed and a little one.

92

We shut the door and undressed. Then we waited.

A bit later I said, 'I'm going to the lavatory.' I put on my coat and went out. As I was going along the corridor, I heard a loud snoring. I looked around and saw a half-open door. There's someone inside, asleep, snoring: bzzzz, bzzzz. I give the door a little push. I see a great fat body, all bloated and slack, dressed only in vest and pants, sprawled out on the bed.

On the bedside table I spy a watch, a big leather bag like a doctor's and a pair of gold cuff-links.

Back I go at once to call La Spagnola. 'Come quick,' I say, 'there's a job to be done.' She comes with me and peers through the door at the sleeping man.

'Let's go in,' she says.

'Hang on,' I say, 'they've got our documents in the hotel desk.'

'What do you care?' she says, 'the names are false. My identity card is a fake, too. Let's get cracking!'

We go in. Grab the gold watch, the bag, the cuff-links, and hop it, quick. We go back to our room and lock the door. Meanwhile, Dina's appeared. 'I did his wallet,' she says, 'he didn't even notice. There's 40,000 lire in it.'

'And what did you do with Blondie?' asks La Spagnola.

'I left him in front of his house, face down on the pavement. He's dead drunk. Here, let's have a share-out.'

'Wait a minute,' I say, 'we've been busy too: look at this little lot!' And I show her the loot. But the bag was padlocked. We got at it with scissors, penknife, the heels of our shoes, and managed to spring the lock, which fortunately wasn't very strong. We opened it up; inside there were banknotes, nothing but banknotes, brand, spanking new as if they'd just come from the mint.

'Shit! Just look at that!' I said. We were thunderstruck. We'd never had a stroke of luck like that before. I seized a bundle of notes at once and stuffed them down my bosom.

'No, let's leave them in the bag,' said Dina, 'the first thing is to get out of this hotel, immediately.'

'What about our papers?' I said, 'we can't go around without papers and they're the only ones we've got.'

'I'll see to it, you two go out with the bag and wait for me round the corner.'

She went to the night porter, told him we'd had an urgent call from our employers in Rome and had to leave at once, and so on and so forth, a whole load of crap, and got him to give her our papers; she paid the bill out of the 40,000 lire from Blondie's wallet and sailed out, smiling and serene.

A minute later, we were at the station. We took the first train that happened to come in and landed up next morning at Voghera. Not knowing where to go, we went into a restaurant to eat and have a little rest, though it was barely 11 a.m.

We ate and drank our fill and then paid with money out of the bag. A moment or two later, the waiter came and said, 'Excuse me, signorine, I'm very sorry, but this money is no good.'

'What do you mean, no good?' I said. 'Can't you see this is brand new money, straight from the bank?'

'Exactly,' he says, 'it's brand new because it's false.'

And, in fact, it was all counterfeit money. But I didn't want to believe it. 'What do you mean, false?' I said. 'Let's go to the bank, and then we'll see who's false! Obviously you don't understand anything about money. Come along, we'll go to the bank.'

Dina laughed her head off, she was delighted that our job had turned out to be a flop. The more she laughed, the angrier I got and the more I argued with that stupid waiter.

Well, anyway, we finished up at the bank. The cashier looked at it, inspected it, felt it, then said, 'Listen, signorine, I shall have to retain this money because it's forged.' Then he wanted to know where we were going.

'To Rome.'

'Very well,' he says, 'if it turns out that they're not forged, you can withdraw them from our branch in Rome.'

'Tell me,' I say, 'are these false, too?' And I show him the two or three notes I'm holding in my hand.

'I'm afraid so,' he says.

I had another bundle in the bag, but I didn't give him those; 700,000 lire in all. I was thinking: The waiter said they were forged and now the cashier says they're forged, so they *must* be fakes! I was so angry I could cheerfully have torn up the lot.

'Let's go back to Rome,' says Dina, 'there's nothing to keep us here. The money's false and we haven't got a bean.' She was enjoying putting us down. 'These things never happen to me,' she says, 'I've never nicked a wallet with false money in it, never.'

I said, 'Wait, we may be able to spend it all the same.'

So we went into a goldsmith's and bought gold watches,

chains, rings, all sorts of things, just so as to spend the money. We paid with the forged bills and they accepted them, no problems. Then we went to a leather goods shop: we bought handbags, belts, suitcases. The money changed hands without a hitch. We were happy. 'You see?' I said, and Dina never made a murmur, because she too enjoyed spending the money and buying nice things.

Next day, we bought three tickets and travelled to Rome. We arrived there looking so elegant you'd have thought we were tourists. New cases, new shoes, rings, bracelets – everybody looked at us.

At the Bar Bengasi in via Gioberti they all said, 'Hi, how are you? Wow! You girls have made some bread!' All the thieves came over to pay us their respects. We were well-received, too, in via Cartagine, where there's a dancing club called the Romanella. It's a thieves' hang-out, we all knew each other there. I felt at home in the place because these thieves were a warm-hearted lot; if they had a little money in their pockets they treated you to drinks, they competed with each other as to who should pay. And when they didn't have any money, nobody minded.

As soon as we got back to Rome, La Spagnola left us, as she had to go away with a boy-friend. She was in love with a fellow in the Air Force, a pilot. With him, she made out she was a respectable woman, but he was only after her money. He took money off her. Air Force or no Air Force, this fellow was a pimp. He was an N.C.O., very smart, always dressed to the nines, and very affable, but his eyes were only on the money. When they went to a restaurant or an hotel, she was always the one who paid.

Dina said to her, 'That boy-friend of yours, that Bruno, I can see he's just a ponce. All he wants is to take money off you, and you don't even notice.'

'No,' says La Spagnola, 'it's not true! Bruno is a serious young man, he's in the Air Force.'

And Dina says, 'Air Force my arse, he's a pimp!'

They had a row about it: 'You're the one who's a pimp!'

'And you're a stupid bitch, you're off your bleeding head with love!' They came to blows. But it was hopeless, La Spagnola was madly in love with this Air Force pilot and nobody could get him out of her head.

When the bread ran out, Dina and I went back to doing wallets. Sometimes we had a good run, two or three wallets with

95

money in them. Then there were times when in two whole weeks we never managed to scrape up one lira. Those were the lean times.

One day we bumped into a bloke whose wallet we had done a few months earlier. We met him between via Gioberti and via Manin. He was a farmer who came to Rome to buy and sell pigs.

This fellow saw us in the street, one blonde and one redhead, and our faces were photographed in his mind for ever. He grabs us and says, 'Now I'll call the police and turn you two in!'

Dina gives a mighty wrench and manages to free herself. But I'm still attached to him, he's holding me with nails like a vulture's talons. 'Now, you come along to the police station with me,' he says.

'Me?' I say. 'Look, you're making a mistake, I've never laid eyes on you in my life! You're off your bloody head!'

'No,' he says, 'you stole my wallet while you were pretending to make love to me. Afterwards, I went to look for it and it had gone.'

This bumpkin starts yelling and kicking up a rumpus. A small crowd gathers round us in the street. 'You're a nut!' I shout at him, 'I'll have you put away in the nut-house! Who the hell do you think you are, anyway? I never saw you before!'

I insulted him, denied his accusations, but it was true: I had taken his wallet. I had slipped it out of his pocket while I was nibbling his ear, that foul-tasting ear all smeared with brilliantine.

He was determined to take me to the copper-shop. I thought I was done for. Dina had got clean away and the people were beginning to give me nasty looks. I was about to give up when I saw Dina coming back. Thank the Lord, I said to myself, she'll get me out of this mess somehow! She's so blooming crafty!

And, in fact, she marches straight up to this bloke and bangs him on the head with her handbag. She starts screaming, loudly, convincingly: 'You stinking misbegotten crackpot! I'll charge you with slander! What evidence have you got, anyway? Can you prove what you're saying? How dare you, you ugly, revolting little peasant! I'll lay a complaint against you, I'll have you put on a charge!' And meanwhile she's kicking him, punching him, walloping him with her handbag.

Stunned by the blows and taken by surprise, the man lets go

of me. I start to run immediately. Dina's close behind me and we're off like two streaks of lightning.

We ran and ran and finished up in a garage. It was raining. 'Let's rest for a moment, I'm done in,' I said.

Dina laughed. 'Did you see that clodhopper's face?' she said.

'You were great,' I said, 'I was just about to let them arrest me.'

'You must always attack, make a show of strength,' she said. 'If he yells, you yell louder; if he threatens you, you threaten him fifty times worse.'

When the rain eased up a little we came out of the garage and walked towards the pensione Margherita where we lived. As we are walking along, a friend of mine from Anzio suddenly pops up.

'Hallo, Teresa! Have you heard about your brother?'

'Heard what?'

'Why, your brother Libero,' he says, 'do you mean you haven't heard? I'm sorry, it's bad news. Listen, go to Anzio, go at once, it's urgent. Your brother fell under a train.'

'Oh, my God! Dina, Dina!' I start screaming, 'something terrible's happened, I must go to Anzio straight away!'

# 15

Dina and I left for Anzio that same afternoon. Accursed journey! I couldn't keep still for a moment. The seat scorched my behind.

All of a sudden, my love for my brother Libero came flooding back, though I'd almost forgotten him. But how could he have died? How could the accident have happened? I wondered.

Libero was twenty-six. It wasn't long since he'd returned from India, where he had suffered a good deal. He had been a prisoner of war for seven years. He had been ill, he had endured hunger.

One day, out there in India, they said to him and to three of his friends, 'Dig, dig your graves, we're going to bury you alive because you're Fascists.'

They decided on the punishment and threw them into the holes, alive. Those English soldiers were burying my brother too. His body was already half-covered with earth. At that moment a captain came along and said, 'No, he's a good chap, let him go.'

They pulled him out, but they made him stay there, stark naked, to watch his friends who were dying, buried alive. He was already ill, he had kidney stones. He was half-starved in that concentration camp, and all his teeth had gone rotten. The business of the graves brought on heart trouble. I was thinking of all these things while that train crawled along like a snail. I said to myself: That poor brother of mine didn't have much luck in this world, fortune did not smile on him!

When I reached Anzio, I found all my brothers, weeping, friends weeping, too. My brother Nello came up and embraced me. 'Oh, God!' he said, 'Libero's been killed by a train.'

'I know,' I said.

'But did you know he did it on purpose, he committed suicide?'

'No,' I said, 'I didn't know that.'

'Come and look at our brother, now that they've stitched him up and he looks whole again.'

The train had sliced him into four. He was torn to pieces. They had sewn the bits together for the funeral. He was swathed in bandages, he looked like a mummy. His face was white, solemn; his forehead was stained with black blotches.

I looked at him and thought to myself: I grew up with Libero, he was the best of my brothers. At the age of twenty, he went off to the war. When I got married, he was the only one who'd give me the money to pay for the licence. My father wouldn't give me a lira, so Libero came out to meet me and give me the cash. He was good, and now he is dead. It's a poxy, dungheap of a world we live in!

That night, Dina and I slept at Nello's house; he was always generous and hospitable towards me. He said, 'There's always a place for you in my home.' He put up two little beds, one for Dina, one for me. The children were there, and Lina, who was now the lady of the house. She and I made our peace. All the same, I left after only two days.

Dina was anxious to get back to Rome, where Mimí was waiting for her. I stayed behind, but I went to sleep at my father's house, with Lanky Dora. I wanted to find out why Libero had thrown himself under the train.

Lanky Dora told me the story: 'You know, Teresa, he shut himself up in the house and sent someone to fetch his fiancée, the girl he had before he went off to India.'

'But who was this girl?' I asked.

'Oh, a young girl from round here. When he came back, he found she was married to somebody else. Anyway, as I was saying, he sent for her, then they both shut themselves up in his room and he said to her: "Here are your photographs, I'm returning them to you now that you're married." Perhaps he had had a great passion for that girl, I don't know. In any case, he was off his head, you couldn't reason with him any more.'

But I knew this wasn't true. I ferreted around and found out the truth. My brother was a very sad man when he got back from

India. He went back to work, but he had to hand over all his earnings to Lanky Dora. He sold fish and all the money went into Lanky Dora's pocket. There was no satisfaction to him in working.

They had put him into a gloomy, empty room, with no furniture or anything, just the bed, like a hospital. It was a new house because the old one had been bombed. So he didn't even have the consolation of being in the house where he had grown up. He was in great need of many things, especially someone who would love him, and instead he came home to Lanky Dora who made him sweat his guts out for her. She used to run us down by saying: 'You see, they left your poor father alone, nobody wanted to take care of the smallholding, so he had to sell it. It was your brothers' fault, they all went off and left him alone, because they hated me, although I'd done them no harm . . . ' yakety-yak, yakety-yak, and so on and so forth. In other words, she confused him with a load of old cobblers.

Then he went to see my brother, Eligio, and Eligio said to him, 'Your father's a disgrace, he's married that woman and brought the sister-in-law to live with him, too. They all sleep together. Your sister Teresa ran away from home, she's in prison, and so is your other brother, Orlando. He committed a robbery and murdered a German. Iride has married an American. Everything's gone to pot.'

At home, Dora accused him of not working hard enough. Father was ill, cranky, gone soft in the head, there was no family any more, nor the comfort of his fiancée's love. All these things depressed Libero and he took his own life.

My father was a crude, primitive type who governed us by blows and beatings. But when he saw his son lying dead he was deeply upset. He cried. Lanky Dora was with him, she didn't know what to say. She watched him cry. And I watched him, too, because it was the first time I had ever seen him weep; he hadn't even shed a tear for my mother.

That evening, I ate with them in that frigid house and I felt sad. After a few days I'd had all I could take. I said goodbye and went back to Rome.

In the city I couldn't find a living soul. Dina had gone away with Mimí. La Spagnola was also on her travels. My other friends, all thieves, were nowhere to be seen. I was penniless and without a friend to stand me a cup of coffee. Something Nello used to say came into my mind: 'Better an honest servant than a thief!'

So I looked for a place as a servant. I soon found one – there's always a demand for servants, especially if they'll work for a small wage. And I, without references, and with my prison record stamped on my identity card, could not ask for much.

I happened on a family who were fruitsellers, husband, wife and three children. And the mother-in-law lived with them, too. I was paid 6000 lire a month. And I had to spend my life washing.

The lady of the house was a good woman, but she was never at home. It was the mother-in-law who gave the orders. She was always breathing down my neck, she would never allow me to go out. She made me wash everything: I put on my apron and I washed – I washed the floors, the walls, the doors, the dishes, the clothes, the sheets.

And the windows, every day I had to wash the windows. Wash this! Wash that! And I washed. My food was rationed. They ate meat, I got soup and cheese. I thought to myself: What a funny thing, they are fruitsellers, yet you never set eyes on a bit of fruit in this house! I was longing for a bellyful of fruit, because I come from a fruit-growing family. But in that house they never ate fruit, I don't know why. Perhaps they didn't like it. It was always cheese, those little portions of processed cheese wrapped in silver paper. Cheese and bread, bread and cheese.

I was never allowed out. 'What do you want to go out for?' they said, 'you've got everything you could possibly wish for here!' And they gave me some more washing to do. And I washed it. And there was always more. I wondered about Dina: what was that crazy little blonde up to now?

At mealtimes they set before me two little triangles of cheese and a piece of bread. 'But what time do we eat in this house?' I asked.

'Where do you think you are, in a hotel?' they said. And I had to lump it.

I stuck if for three weeks, then, one morning, after eating the last portion of cheese, I left. I never went back. I didn't even ask them for the money they owed me for those three weeks. All that eternal washing had made me seasick.

# 16

Back to the Bar Bengasi, and there I find all my friends again. They offer me drinks, fags, coffee. 'Teresa, where've you been? What've you been doing?' they ask me.

'In Anzio, my brother died.'

'I'm sorry to hear that, Teresa, have a coffee.'

They were generous and thoughtful.

In the Bar Bengasi I meet Dina again too, she's looking as lovely as ever and she's gay and cheerful. 'What have you been up to?' she says.

'Nothing,' I tell her, 'I'm broke. I went into domestic service with a family of friutsellers who never eat fruit. Nothing but bread and cheese.'

'Why don't we go to Civitavecchia and see my sister?' she says. 'I've got a brother-in-law they call "The Prince", he sells fish in the port. Let's go and see him . . . he'll lend us some bread.'

'What's this prince going to say when he sees us in this poverty-stricken state?' I ask.

'Don't worry, he'll give us a big welcome, you'll see, he's a good sort.'

'But how can we get there without money?'

'We'll stand on the via Aurelia and hitch-hike.'

No sooner said than done, and off we go. We station ourselves on the Aurelia on the way out of the city. One car passes, three cars, twenty cars, and not one stops.

After standing there for four hours we were getting tired and losing faith. 'This is a rotten idea,' I said, 'nobody's going to stop for us.'

'Wait, somebody will,' said Dina.

About one o'clock, along comes a van at last and the driver brakes. 'Where are you going?'

'Civitavecchia.'

'I'm going to Livorno, or rather, to Siena, get in!' And we get in.

This bloke starts telling us what a beautiful city Siena is, how nice the people are, and so forth and so on – this Siena's no end of a place! Dina says, 'I'd like to go to Siena, I've never been there.' And he gives us his home address and makes us promise to look him up if we ever happen to be there.

We stopped at Civitavecchia, said our goodbyes, thanked him and got out. We presented ourselves at Dina's sister's house. This peasant woman looked down her nose at us. 'What have you come here for?' she said.

The Prince was not at home. Dina explained to her sister that we were down-and-out, we needed her help. But she said she hadn't got any money. Then she said, 'Go on, clear off, I don't want anybody in the house.' And she chucked us out. Didn't even offer us a bite of supper.

'Now what?' I said, 'back to Rome?'

'Yes, let's go back,' said Dina, and we went and stood on the Aurelia again.

A car pulls up, but it's going to Siena, not Rome. 'OK,' I say, 'let's go to Siena, we can look up that fellow who gave us a lift in his van. He was so kind.'

Then I remember that my son Macco is on holiday near there, at Acquapendente, or Acquaviva; I wasn't sure, some place near Siena.

'Shall we go and see my son?' I say.

'What if your relations throw you out?' she says.

'I don't care. As long as I can have a look at him.'

This was in 1951. My son was fifteen, I was thirty-four. I thought to myself: God knows what he'll think of me after all these years! My sisters-in-law never let me see him.

From Siena we had to walk over a mile on foot up to this village in the mountains. We asked for the Panella family. Nobody knew them. It was only by chance that I remembered the name – they were distant relatives of my husband's.

We knocked at a door. They opened it. 'Do you know anyone called Panella?' 'No, nobody.' And they slammed the door in our faces. We tried another door. They didn't know anything either. I kept saying, 'They're a family from Rome, on holiday, with a boy called Maceo who looks like such-and-such.' 'No, there's nobody here like that.' They were shifty and suspicious.

We were tired out from knocking on so many doors. 'You know what, I'm hungry!' says Dina. I was hungry too. I would have liked to go with the search, but it would soon be dark and we had nowhere to sleep and no money to buy food. 'All right,' I said, 'let's go.' But I was aching to see my son again, I couldn't help it.

We went back to the highway. Car after car passed but nobody stopped. We sat down on the ground, worn out, our feet aching. Cars flashed past like arrows, they didn't even see us. 'We're like two needles in a haystack here,' I said, 'let's get up on that hillock there.'

As soon as we were up there, a car stopped. It was a little estate car. 'Where are you going?'

'Towards Rome.'

'Well, I'm going to Livorno. If that suits you, jump in; if not, nothing doing.' We got in and the car started up.

While we're in this car, the driver, a yokel who's sitting there bolt upright with his cap over his eyes, never saying a word, starts ogling our legs. Then Dina says, 'Listen, you don't happen to have anything to eat, do you? We haven't had supper.'

Now, I think to myself, this oaf's going to chuck us out of the car. I would have died sooner than ask such a thing, but Dina doesn't give a hoot for anybody, she's a tough nut.

The bumpkin thinks it over for a moment, then says, 'All right, I'll buy you a meal. We'll stop and have dinner in a trattoria.' Aha, so he thought he was on to a good thing! In fact, he immediately started taking liberties, he stretched out one hand and touched Dina's knee.

'Keep your hands to yourself,' she said, but quite kindly. 'We'll talk about that later.' Her words were convincing, plausible. And the fellow instantly obeyed.

We went into a transport café. There were lots of people eating and drinking. We ordered spaghetti, steaks, fried potatoes, salad, fruit and coffee. We had a good blow-out. Meanwhile, Dina flirted with him, saying, 'Later on, we'll have a good time, eh, darling?'

When we've finished eating, the yokel says, 'They have beds in

104

this place too. Shall we spend the night here?'

'Yes,' says Dina, 'that's a good idea.' I am wondering how she plans to get rid of him.

They gave us the keys and we go upstairs. Just outside the bedroom door, Dina suddenly turns on him: 'Did you think I was going to go with you? Did you think you could buy me for a plate of spaghetti? Piss off quick or I'll split your skull for you. I'll call the police and have you arrested.'

I laughed. What a spitfire, what a little Jezebel that Dina is! She's so smart! She'd already squashed this fellow flat. But he kept trying. And the more he argued, the louder Dina shouted and insulted him. She was like a tigress. In the end, he backed down and went away.

We slept in that place for three or four hours. Then while it was still dark, we got up and jumped out of the window to avoid paying.

We went back to the main road. There was just a glimmer of daylight in the sky. No cars about. We started walking so as not to freeze to death.

Finally a lorry with a trailer as long as a whole train stopped for us. We got in. The driver's dropping with sleep and so are we. 'Talk to me,' he says 'tell me a story to keep me awake.' And Dina and I take it in turns to tell him jokes to keep him from nodding off, but what torture! In the end, all three of us fell asleep and only by a hair's breadth escaped plunging into a ravine. The scare woke us up, good and proper, and from then on it was plain sailing.

We reached Livorno about midday. We started looking for lodgings, but there was no room anywhere. Two o'clock came and still we hadn't found a place.

Tired, scruffy and hungry, we sat down on the steps of a church. Our feet were so sore we couldn't walk another step. 'Let's get our breath back for a minute, then see what we can find,' I said. Dina was down in the mouth, gloomy and dispirited.

As we're sitting on these steps a friend of ours goes by, a thief from Rome. 'What are you doing here?' he says. He was bright and cheerful.

'Things are bad,' I said, 'we haven't got one lira and we're at our wits' end.'

'Come to Florence with me,' he said, 'there's a pensione there with a smashing proprietress. She knows all the thieves and the girls on the game, she's a very reasonable woman. She'll give you credit and you can pay her later on, when you've had a lucky strike.'

'Let's go to Florence,' says Dina, 'I'm fed up with this rotten Livorno!'

And so we went. He took us to this pensione in Florence, a thieves' hangout, people we knew. They gave us a room and we went straight to sleep.

Next morning, we got up, washed and freshened up, and went out on the hunt. Nothing turned up; the whole day went by and still we were empty-handed.

In the evening we went back to the pensione and ran into two friends of ours from the Bar Bengasi; they were dippers, pick-pockets. I said, 'Could you lend us something, we're on our beam ends.'

They said, 'We're out of luck, too, we haven't got a lira to scratch our arses with.'

We went back to our room and got into bed, having eaten nothing and drunk nothing. Where else could we go but bed? 'Now we're in it,' I said, 'we're really right in it! What the bloody hell did we leave Rome for?'

Then Dina says, 'Have you noticed those chests in the passage, where the landlady keeps the sheets? We'll nick a few of those, the nice linen ones, and go and flog them.'

'But where?'

'We'll ask the dippers, they're sure to know of a fence some-where,' she says.

So that's what we did. We took three pairs of fine-quality sheets, hand-embroidered and trimmed with lace. We got the address of a fence and paid him a visit.

He lived in a filthy little alleyway, on the first floor. He opened the door, looked at the sheets and asked, 'Pinched?'

'Yes,' said Dina, 'how much will you give us?'

'I don't want them. I don't deal in this sort of stuff,' he said. Dina insisted. In the end he gave us a few thousand lire and sent us away.

With this we paid our bill at the pensione. The landlady was all hot and bothered over the theft. With so many thieves in the house she didn't know who to accuse! But she didn't make too much fuss, she didn't want to stir it up because she sometimes made a good thing out of it, too: she bought things at very low prices, gold ornaments and so on, and sold them off God knows where.

Next evening we got a good haul. Dina nicked a wallet with 40,000 lire. The fellow we robbed was young, good-looking, very cheery, and he drove around in an Alfa-Romeo. He took us to the cinema in this car. During the drive I nicked a brand-new pair of gloves off him, pigskin lined with fur. They fitted me a treat.

With this money we bought two tickets and went home, to Rome. Every now and then we had to go back because Dina felt homesick for her Domenico. I didn't have anyone. I went back to Rome just to keep her company. But for me, Rome, or any other city – it was all the same.

## 17

'Tomorrow, we'll go to Pisa,' said Dina. 'I've never been there, but I hear people go around with their wallets stuffed with money!' However, we didn't leave the next day because the evening before we'd got hold of a pretty good wallet near the station.

'We don't have to work for a few days now,' said Dina. So we enjoy ourselves on the money, she in bed with her Domenico and me gadding about, going to the Bar Bengasi, seeing friends.

When it was all gone I said to her, 'Well, what do we do now? Shall we go to Pisa?'

'Yes,' she said, 'we'll go tomorrow.' But we never went.

One evening I happened to go to a club, the Occhipinti in via Palermo, with some burglar friends of mine. I can't dance so I just sat there drinking and watching the others having a good time.

It was gay, the music was smashing. But my head was aching and I was in a rather thoughtful mood. In front of me, there was a fellow dancing and giving me the eye. He was handsome, tall and slim. He kept laughing. And he never took his eyes off me. He stared and stared, and I stared back. He was a beautiful dancer. He whirled around, stood on tiptoe, spun like a top. But he seemed to be dancing just for me. He didn't even deign to glance at his partner. He spun round and round, but he always ended up facing me.

Presently he stopped dancing and came over to me. 'Would you like to dance?' he said.

'I can't dance,' I said.

'Just follow me, I'll lead you.'

'No,' I said, 'sit down here with me. All my friends are busy dancing. We can have a little chat.'

So we chatted. I was instantly attracted to him. And he to me. We made a date for the following evening at the Bar Genio in via Merulana and then we said goodbye.

I kept the date. He was sitting there, waiting for me. He was wearing a dark suit. 'Shall we have dinner together?' he said.

'If you like,' I said. I liked him, I liked him a lot, but I didn't let him know it. I played it cool.

I didn't want to give myself away, but already I was wildly infatuated with him. I asked him how old he was .'Twenty-six,' he says, 'and you?' I was nearly ten years older than him, but I didn't let on. I didn't want to tell a lie so I changed the subject and he didn't press the point.

While we're eating, he tells me that he lives with his brother and his sister-in-law and that he works at one of the Ministries as a chauffeur.

Straight away, we make love – in his car, parked in the gardens in front of the church of San Giovanni. He's a gentle creature, with soft lips, soft hands. I still remember that, while I was kissing him, I looked up at the white statues on the roof of the church and thought: How sweet this boy is!

I fell in love with him. He liked me, but he wasn't really in love with me. I loved him more than he loved me. It was the first time I had really been in love because what I had felt for my husband wasn't deep love.

I lost my head over this Tonino Santità. I would have done the craziest things for him, and in fact, I did them. We saw each other every evening. We always met at the Bar Genio. Then we went to the cinema, then to dinner, then to a hotel. I always paid because he didn't have enough money.

He had to give everything he earned to his sister and his mother, who had no other means of support. He even had to pay rent for the room at his sister-in-law's house where he slept. He was always skint and he was happy to go out with me because I paid for everything.

Seeing all this money that I had, he asked, 'Excuse me, but how do you manage? Who gives you all this money? Don't be angry, but I can't help wondering . . . I'm not sure, I may be wrong, but . . .'

I said to him, 'You think I go with men for money, don't you? Well, you're wrong. I've earned this money, saved it up. Anyway, you don't have to worry. If you haven't got any it doesn't matter, I'll pay.'

He saw that I was a generous spender, lobbing out 5000-lire notes, and it made him a bit cocky. We'd go out to eat, to a hotel for the night, and I was always the one who shelled out. And I bought him presents.

I bought him a solid gold watch with a gold bracelet-strap – it cost 60,000 lire. I bought him shirts, shoes, cuff-links – a really smashing pair of cuff-links. I spent a whole afternoon shopping for them; they were silver, with a little branch of coral set in four gold links, and on the other part was a gold button with the dome of St Peter's engraved on it.

The moment I had a little bread I bought him presents. And more presents. In his entire life, the only present he ever gave me was a bottle of French liqueur, which he brought back from France when he went there with the Ministers for the Atlantic Treaty.

He was there for a week and he came back with this little bottle of liqueur. Tonino said, 'This is a very fine French liqueur, really high-class stuff.' But I never drank it, I carried it around with me for years and years, as a memento, until I eventually lost it.

For his sake I did a lot of jobs, I really stuck my neck out. Simply to have money in my pocket, to impress him, I risked getting into all kinds of trouble. I did wallets with Dina, shop-lifting with a girl known as Gianna the Bigmouth and her friend, a fellow called the Whisperer. With other girls I went dipping, I did handbags.

They taught me how to do it. 'Stand close to us on the bus,' they said. 'You must look fixedly into people's faces, while you cut the straps of their shoulder-bags or dip into their pockets. If you stare at your chosen victim, he won't notice your hands running over him.' They gave me a regular schooling. And I learned quickly; I became a real ace.

But there was never enough money, I had to have more than one job. Never before had I wheeled and dealed as I did then. I flogged oil, smuggled cigarettes; whatever anybody proposed to me, I did it, even if it meant running the most awful risks. I was always the eager muggins. Simply to have spending money.

In the evenings I went to the Bar Genio to meet Tonino. He

was punctual on the button. He came wearing a blue suit; he was very handsome and everybody looked at him. His eyebrows were dark, clearly-marked, his cheeks were pale and smooth, his lips full and pouting, his teeth small and white.

We went dancing at the April 21 Club. I had even bought myself an evening dress, it was orange velvet. As often as I could, I went to the hairdresser to have my hair done. The one I went to was a queer called Ilario who had a salon near Cinecittà. He was crafty. He'd comb and arrange my hair and say, 'Look how becoming this style is! You'll see, Tonino will be thrilled!' He knew I wanted to look beautiful for Tonino. He had met him – I'd introduced them myself. He gave me the final touches with those dainty hands of his, looked at me, kissed me on the forehead. And I was so grateful that I left him a handsome tip.

Tonino was very keen on good clothes: he liked me to be very elegant, to make a good impression. He took me to places I had never been before and it seemed to me I was discovering a whole new world! We went to a medieval tournament, to target-firing, to the cinema. I was absolutely crazy about him.

But sometimes he would fly into a rage. He'd say, 'Come on, come on, let's get out of here!' and drag me away from some place in a rush. The fact was, he didn't like to be seen with me by certain colleagues of his from the Ministry, because he'd realised that I was a thief and he was afraid.

In August his family went away and the house was empty. He lived in via de Polis. 'Shall we go to your place?' I said. I was going through an unlucky period, I couldn't rustle up a single lira, but I never let him see that. I kept up a pretence. I borrowed money, at 50 per cent interest.

'No,' he said, 'we can't go to my house, people will see us.'

'Who?' I asked.

'The neighbours,' he said. He was afraid of the neighbours, he was afraid of everybody; he set great store by his respectability. In fact, he *was* respectable, very correct, always clean, polite and attentive and as sweet as honey.

One evening, all the same, he decided to take me to his home. He hustled me in secretly, opened a door, shut me up in one room and jumped up every other minute to see if anybody was coming. We didn't put the light on in case it attracted attention.

Next morning he made me get up at half past five because he wanted me out of the house before the porter was awake. He

111

went back to sleep. And I found myself out in the street, without money, and I had to walk all the way home.

I had been stony broke for several days. I hadn't even paid my rent at the pensione where I was living. No jobs came my way. My girl-friends, scenting danger, had made themselves scarce. There are certain periods when everything stagnates and the thieves go to ground because they sense that the police watchdogs are on the alert.

So at night I had to sleep in doorways, or on the landing of some house. I would choose a building where there was no porter, wait till late at night and then ring all the bells. Somebody always pressed the button that opened the outer door. I pushed it open and put my foot in the door to hold it open. I stayed outside, out of sight, till they came to see who had rung. Usually they just leaned over the banisters at the opposite side of the courtyard, peered down and, seeing no one there, went back inside. Then I would go in and walk up to the first floor. I installed myself in front of the door that leads out on to the terrace, where nobody ever goes at that time of night, wrapped myself up in my coat and slept.

In the mornings I went to the public baths to wash. Sometimes I went to Dina's place. She was living in a tiny room with this Domenico of hers, the fellow they called Mimí. It was chaotic: rumpled beds, dirty dishes, blankets and dirty clothes strewn everywhere.

She'd make coffee for me, with milk. She told me I was a fool, that I had gone bonkers over a man who was only after my money. I didn't want to hear these lectures, so I avoided going there as much as possible.

When I had nowhere to go, I slipped into a church, just as I had done when I ran away from home at eighteen. They thought I was a pillar of the church, a pious woman. But I went there only to get warm, to sit down and rest after all that aimless wandering about.

I was really desperate and in a wretched state. I didn't go to meet Tonino because I couldn't pay for dinner and a hotel bed. I knew he would pull a long face; I knew that look of his only too well. He never said anything, but his face spoke volumes. He was too much of a gentleman to reproach me for not having money, but he'd let me see that he was disgruntled, all right.

He'd stand there, at the Bar Genio, with a cup of coffee in

front of him, and say, 'Well, what shall we do?' I'd say, 'We can make love in the car, like we did the first time.' Then he would pull that long face that gave me a stomach-ache just to see it. I already knew what his answer would be: 'We can't it'll mess up the new seat-covers!'

If I had met someone and they'd said, 'Come on, let's pull a job, we'll have to kill someone to do it,' I would have agreed at once. But, as it was, I trailed around the streets, looking and looking for an opportunity that did not come along. All my friends were in prison, or in hiding, or they'd left town.

It was a bad time for everybody, a dangerous time. Police headquarters (for some political reason, I suppose) was displaying great zeal, arresting people right, left and centre, whether they were guilty or not.

I didn't even have money to buy food. I had given up my pensione because I couldn't pay, and I was sleeping in doorways, at the station, wherever I could.

One evening I was with a girl-friend called Giulia. She said to me, 'Listen, I'm broke.'

'Me too,' I said.

Then she says, 'Let's take a little stroll and see. . . .'

'Where to?'

'Oh, around. Come on.'

So we start walking together, not far from Piazza Vittorio. About half an hour later we meet a drunk. Giulia nudges me. 'This fellow's dead drunk,' she says, 'let's take him under our wing, as if we're going to help him, and see if we can lighten his pockets a little.'

We each took hold of him by one arm and towed him along. 'How are you, love?' I said, 'shall we take you somewhere for a coffee?'

This fellow laughed and chattered, but he was absolutely sozzled, out of his head, he didn't know what was going on. Meanwhile, I was looking to see if he had a bracelet, a gold neck-chain or a watch to nick. Giulia ran her hand over his behind to see if she could find his wallet.

She signalled to me that she had found the wallet in the pocket of his trousers. Then I pretended to stumble and crashed into him, while Giulia slipped out his wallet under cover of holding him up.

'Split!' I say, and we start running away. But that drunk,

drowning in wine though he is, grabs me by the arm and holds on, nailing me to the spot. Guilia vanishes with the wallet. And I'm caught.

I'm kicking him and punching him, but he won't let go, it seems as if I'm glued on to him. And he starts yelling, 'Stop, thief! Stop, thief!'

Two fuzz arrived, nicked me and took me to the station. They searched me, but didn't find anything. All the same, they jailed me for 'intent'.

'What does "intent" mean?' I asked.

They said, 'It means you had the intention of carrying out this action, even if you didn't do it.'

I thought: This is a bad look-out, it means they're beginning to know me down here!

And that was how I wound up once more in the Mantellate prison. Tonino dropped me like a hot potato. He was transferred, or asked for a transfer, I don't know which. He disappeared, anyway.

I sent Dina and Giulia to look for him and told them to tell him to write to me. Nothing, not a sign of him. Just the rumour that he had been transferred, but nobody knew where to, except that it was a long way away and it was impossible to get hold of his address.

Like a ninny I waited and waited for a letter from Tonino. I spent my days waiting, waiting for a word from him. I was infatuated, fatally infatuated. He was a good-looking hunk of man, tall, with chestnut hair and sparkling eyes.

All day long I thought about him, his name was always on my lips. I counted the minutes till I would be released and could go and look for him. Tonino was a Venetian. As soon as I'm out, I'll go to Venice, I thought, maybe he's gone up there. I moved heaven and earth to find him. I waited for that letter, day after day I waited.

When the nun brought the post round, I'd say, 'Anything for me?' She didn't even bother to answer me. Well, be patient, I'd say to myself, it'll come tomorrow. And next day it was the same performance. I kept my hopes alive like that.

I got out about a month later, since they had no proof against me and couldn't get a conviction.

I went straight to Tonino's house in via de Polis. There was no one there, not even his sister-in-law. I telephoned the Ministry, searched high and low for him. Nothing. Vanished without trace. He had taken fright and fled.

I went to Dina. I said to her, 'Tonino has disappeared, what can I do?'

'Better lost than found, a man like that,' she said.

'But I'll never find such a sweet, gentle fellow again.'

'Stop being a sentimental idiot,' she said, 'the only thing he fancied was your money. Now, instead of day-dreaming about him, how about doing some wallets with me, starting tomorrow?'

'All right,' I said, 'let's do that. I haven't got a lira.'

Next day, at four o'clock, we go into a shop on via Due Macelli. It's crowded. Dina points out to me a purse that someone's carelessly put down on a glass shelf. I pick it up and start to slither out discreetly.

As I'm crossing the street I hear a shrill voice screeching, 'My purse! Grab her!' and a pack of furious women swarms out of the shop and comes after me.

I don't even have time to turn the corner before five of them seize hold of me. There were too many people around, not a chance of running for it, and if I had tried, those Furies would have torn me to bits. Dina had got out of the shop and, so as not to incriminate her, I pretended not to know her.

Once again, I finished up in the boot – for the theft of the purse. As soon as they nicked me, they took away the purse, with 50,000 lire in it. And they sentenced me to eight months.

# 18

In prison, nobody came to visit me, nobody sent me letters or parcels. Dina had forgotten all about me because she had other fish to fry. She was doing wallets with other girl-friends. She didn't give a bugger about me. As long as I was there by her side, OK, fine, but the moment I was out of sight, she palled up with other girls and forgot me.

Then Dina met a man who fell for her, a very rich gentleman from Catania. I don't know whether she fell in love with him or was simply after the money, but she went off to Catania with him and now she owns a hotel. She left Domenico, or Mimí as they called him, who was madly in love with her.

That girl never got caught, though she had done so many wallets in her time that she'd lost count of them. She stole incessantly, but she never went to prison, not once. I, on the other hand, am unlucky. I always get nicked, they 'feel my collar' and put me inside.

At the Mantellate, I was with the women from Trastevere, where the city's toughs and small-time crooks hang out; they were all dippers and bag-snatchers. They were a gay lot, afraid of nothing. When they received a parcel, they always gave me a bit of fresh bread or a fag; they could see that I was hungry. When they didn't give me anything, I had to make do with slops, the mess-tin full of dirty water and the two rolls the nuns dished out.

There were some who did all right, they had milk, coffee, sugar, meat. But they had to pay for it, everything had to be paid for. I had no money, so I had to eat what I was given. Sometimes, for a cigarette, I would render little services: clean out a cell, darn a stocking, mend a shoe.

I used not to smoke, but Dina showed me how to do it and gave me a taste for it. Inside, it was the one thing I missed most. I did the best I could. I took a little potato peel, dried it and mixed it with some horse-hair pulled out of a mattress. Then I rolled up bits of newspaper, filled them with this stuff, which I'd cut up fine, and smoked it. It left my mouth tasting bitter and foul, but at least I had the illusion of smoking.

The most eagerly-awaited event was the release of a con. Whoever was leaving left behind fags, sweaters, a bit of bread, anything they had left over, in fact. It was a moment of euphoria and the lucky woman played the Lady Bountiful.

Generally, this stuff was shared out amongst the poorest, those who never got parcels and had no money to buy provisions. But if the woman being released had a special friend, a wife so to speak – because there are marriages in there, just as in the outside world – then she left everything to her and that was that.

The married couples were jealous and touchy. They lived quietly as long as nobody disturbed them. But if someone fell in love with one of the partners, it was the end of the world. Out came the knives and they were at each other's throats.

I was always alone. Even in the abstinence imposed by prison, I never went with a woman, because I like men too much. I can be inside for a whole year without a man. All I need is the thought of a man, and I dwell on that. I imagine his body; his beauty, his gentleness, and I appease my own needs.

That year I was in a bad way over Tonino, because he had gone away. I would even have waited two years for him. I thought of him, I sang his favourite songs. For eight months I was constantly with him, he buzzed round my head like a bee in a bonnet.

One day the governor sent for me. I expected to be hauled over the coals because I was rebellious and I was always cheeking the nuns. Now, I thought, he's going to take away what little hope I have, he's going to add two months to my sentence.

While I'm thinking this, he says to me, ever so kindly, 'Teresa, how are you?'

'Very well, sir.' First comes the honey, I think, now he'll put the poison in.

117

Then he says, 'You know all the prisoners pretty well, don't you?'

'Yes, sir, they're all my friends.'

'You never receive any parcels, isn't that so?'

'Unfortunately, yes.'

'How would you like a little extra something to eat?'

'And who's going to give it to me?' I ask.

'Don't you worry about that,' he says, 'you just come and see me from time to time and let me know what your fellow-prisoners are up to.'

Stinking bastard, I think to myself, does he think he can buy me for a scrap of food? 'But, sir,' I say, 'I've nothing to tell you. What can anybody get up to, inside a prison?'

'Plenty,' he says. 'For example, a gypsy woman escaped about a month ago and I am certain you know something about it. Do you know whose fault it is when someone escapes? The governor's. Even if he is blameless and his warders are corrupt and fail to do their duty, it is the governor who carries the can.'

'I don't know anything. You know as well as I do that the gypsies never open their mouths, not even to yawn.'

'But the others do,' he persists, 'they talk, they tell each other everything, and the governor ought to know about it, he cannot be kept in ignorance.'

'You've come to the wrong shop, sir,' I say. 'I don't know what goes on. Nobody ever tells me anything. I'm matey with them all, everybody likes me, but they don't let me in on their secrets. It's every man for himself.'

'You are a liar and a trouble-maker, you will come to a sticky end,' he says.

'What, worse than I am now, sir?' I say.

The truth was, they told me everything, and the governor knew it. That's why he chose me, but it was also because he knew I was always ravenous, that I suffered from a freak appetite, outsize, special. I never received a parcel, and he thought he could turn me into a grass for the price of a few extra goodies.

I'm no grass. Even if I tried to do it, I'd make a balls of it. I'd give myself away in no time. I'd be sure to finish up in a fight and get into worse trouble. I'm too emotional to be a good spy.

I knew all about the gypsy who had escaped. Not that she had told me anything herself, but I'd heard it all from her friend. In the nick, you know everything that's going on. This gypsy was a smashing-looking girl, with long, long legs and a bright red mouth.

There was a certain Rosa who made sheep's eyes at her. This Rosa was old, but powerful, she ruled the roost in the laundry and in the kitchens. She gave the gypsy double portions of everything; pasta, meat, potatoes. The gypsy ate it all and didn't say a word. She never said thank you, nothing. And Rosa always protected her, without asking for a reward. But they both knew that, sooner or later, the thing would come to a head: the gypsy would have to pay for the favours she had received by letting Rosa make love to her. But the gypsy kept putting it off and the other woman bided her time.

Then, one evening, accounts were settled. I don't know how she did it, but Rosa let her know the time had come, and, if she didn't go with her, she was quite capable of killing the gypsy.

Cool as a cucumber, even that evening, the gypsy ate everything, mopped up her plate with a piece of bread and never spoke a word. Then she went to bed.

The girl who shared her cell, Vincenzina, another gypsy, didn't show up that night. Instead, along came Rosa, all bathed and perfumed, with her hair washed and dyed, wearing a new dress, a necklace, lipstick and mascara. But instead of opening the door, the gypsy shut it and pushed the bunk bed across it so that Rosa couldn't get in. Old Rosa was strong, she pushed and shoved. The other girl held the door from the inside. All the cons knew what was afoot, so they had made themselves scarce, leaving these two alone.

At this point, a nun arrived and Rosa had to go back to her cell and wait for a more opportune moment to return to the attack. The gypsy asked if she could go down to the laundry, as she had left her wedding ring on the basin by mistake. The nun believed her tale and let her go. But she never came back.

It happened that evening because things had been pushed to a crisis, but it would have happened, anyway, sooner or later. The gypsy knew the day of reckoning must come and she had prepared her flight.

Rosa was the only one in the prison who didn't know about it. The others knew the gypsy had a plan, but they didn't all know the details. She had knocked nails into the outer wall, this gypsy, without telling anyone, and she just climbed up the wall with the aid of these nails and dropped down on the other side. She jumped down more than thirty feet. I don't know how she didn't break any bones. She must have been as agile as a cat.

Next day, everybody watched Rosa, ready for a good laugh at her expense. But she showed not the slightest sign of grief on her face. She ate cheerfully, was her usual energetic self; if anything, she was happier than ever and we almost began to suspect she had organised the escape herself. She chatted, laughed, haggled over the food. Everybody had been expecting a scene – rage, screams, hysterics. Instead she was calm and friendly. In fact, the brazen old hussy started paying court to a 'star', a new inmate, a twenty-two-year-old girl in on a drugs charge.

Things went on like this for three days. Then suddenly Rosa broke down, she couldn't keep up the pretence. One morning we heard her shrieking in her cell as if she was giving birth. Everybody ran to her. She was crying, vomiting, bashing her head against the wall. The nun comes along: 'What's the matter, Rosa?'

'I'm dying, I've eaten something and it's poisoned me, I'm dying, sister, I'm done for.' And the tears poured down her cheeks like rain.

She was such a good actress that we were all taken in by this story of the poisoned food. But it was the poison of frustrated love, I understood that at once. Because it was delayed, held back, it came out like a torrent and that torrent kept her in bed in the infirmary for a week. She seemed as good as dead. The doctor said he could find nothing wrong with her, but she was dying; she was as white as a ghost and couldn't breathe.

In prison, jealousy and envy are stronger than outside, and every molehill is made into a mountain. On one occasion I had a hair's-breadth escape from being knifed. Two women were both in for murder. One had killed her father for making love to her and the other had killed her brother-in-law for money. The two of them were as good as gold, you never heard a peep out of them. Maria and Venerina, those were their names. They were both about the same age, twenty-eight.

These two, Maria and Venerina, ate together, slept together, exercised together, worked together. They were like twins. They spoke little and never quarrelled. They were meek and mild.

One day, for no apparent reason, Venerina comes over to me and offers me a fag. 'Smoke?' she says to me.

'Thanks,' I say, 'has somebody sent you a parcel?'

'Maria got one from her mother,' she says.

'What! You mean she killed her father and her mother sends her parcels?'

'The mother is delighted that she did her father in, they were in cahoots, she and her mother.'

I smoke my fag and never give a thought to Maria. I presume she hasn't come down to the exercise yard because she's not well. It never occurred to me they might have split up, it was inconceivable. Venerina, who had eyes as green as a snake's, glues her eyes to my face and talks and talks. She seems a bit excited, but I don't take much notice of that.

She says, 'Do you know how I killed my brother-in-law?' and I say, 'No.' I'm a bit taken aback, because inside prison you don't usually talk about what you've been nicked for.

She says, 'I took hold of a "bad-worse" and while he was bending over the well to draw water I let him have it.'

'And what's this "bad-worse"?' I ask.

'It's an iron pick that's bad at one end and worse at the other. Bricklayers use them for smashing down walls – in fact, my brother-in-law was a brickie.'

'So why did you kill this brother-in-law of yours with the "bad-worse"?' I ask.

'Because he'd taken two million lire off me to marry my sister.'

'And where the hell did you get hold of two million?'

'I worked,' she says. 'I took in washing, I washed more clothes than an electric washing-machine. Fourteen hours a day I worked, and every lira I earned I gave to this brother-in-law, because she was pregnant by him and they couldn't get married without money.'

'How long did it take you to get them married off?' I say.

'Two years. My sister had a son; by the time they got married this boy was already weaned, off the breast. But the agreement with my brother-in-law was that he'd pay me back, after they were spliced, little by little out of his wages. But he didn't give me any money. On the contrary, he demanded that I should go on paying rent for him, for my sister and the child. He said that, if I really loved my sister, I should help her because he couldn't support her. Meantime, I found out he was only going to work every other day, and he was bragging to everybody about how he lived off his sister-in-law, and how he'd found another woman, the wife of a bricklayer friend of his, and he was spending *my* money with her. I didn't breathe a word, I wanted to find out if it was true first. So I followed him. And I saw him, him and this woman; they went into the builder's yard at night to make love.

'Still I didn't say a word, not even to my sister, because I didn't want to upset her. Besides, my sister is a baby, she plays with her son as if he were a doll, she understands nothing about men, about the world. All she likes is going to the cheap department stores, like Upim, looking at everything, touching everything, picking up toy cars, pistols, teddy bears, dolls, fake rings, fake necklaces, fake bracelets. In the end, she buys a bar of chocolate and goes home, contented. Once she tied the baby to his cot so she could go to the shops and he nearly got suffocated.

'Well, anyway, I checked up and found out my brother-in-law really was being unfaithful to her, and then, one morning, as he was bringing up water from the well, I bashed him on the head with the "bad-worse". I split his skull open for him and all the brains came out. Then I locked up the house so that my sister, who was out shopping, wouldn't see him when she got back. I bolted all the doors and went and gave myself up.'

'How does your sister manage now?' I ask.

'On my money,' she says, 'don't I work in here, too? Whatever I earn I send to her.'

Then I say, 'But couldn't your sister go out to work?'

'No,' she says, 'she's got the mind of a five-year-old child. How can a five-year-old go out to work?'

It seems that, all this time, Maria has been watching us from the window. They told me afterwards but I didn't know it at the time. All of a sudden, this Maria comes downstairs, creeps up behind me and raises her arm to stick her dagger into my back.

Venerina has seen her coming but doesn't say anything. She has provoked her on purpose, to make her jealous, and now she's waiting for that dagger thrust to prove Maria's love for her. I, the innocent booby, am sitting there listening to this long rigmarole about the brother-in-law!

Luckily, two friends of mine, two old crones with whiskers, had been following the whole drama. So when Maria came at me with the knife, they grabbed her and held on tight. Then a tremendous struggle broke out, punching, kicking, hitting out. Maria was beside herself and determined to murder someone.

122

Venerina started bashing one of the women because this woman was bashing Maria.

So we went at it, hammer and tongs, tooth and nail, in a general scrimmage. I was lashing out, too, because when I realised the danger she'd put me in, I was ready to beat the hell out of Venerina, but there were three people holding me back.

The screws arrived, the nuns arrived. They got hold of us, separated us all. Two were sent off to the punishment block, two who had nothing at all to do with it. They let Maria and Venerina go free. As soon as they'd gone, the brawl broke out again. Then the screws came back and finally realised that it was the fault of those two angelic twins who never said a word, and they separated them.

Venerina was sent to Perugia and Maria to Pozzuoli, to the criminal lunatic asylum. Later, I heard that Venerina had committed suicide, but I don't know how.

# 19

I came out of prison to find myself poorer than ever. I didn't even have a pair of shoes fit to walk in. I went to Dina's place and they told me she'd left.

I went to the Bar Bengasi and met a few of my thief friends. 'How's things, Teresa?' they said.

'Lousy, I've just come out of jail and I haven't got a place to lay my head.'

'Have a coffee, Teresa, and cheer up, the main thing is, you're free! You'll manage somehow,' they said.

Then I went to see Giacoma, a woman I had known inside and who had been released a little while before I was. As soon as she saw me she brought out the cakes, the brandy, the champagne; she treated me like a queen. I tried to find out if I could spend the night there. It seemed there was another bed besides the one she and her husband slept in. Then the mother arrived and I realised there was no room for me. 'Come back, come back tomorrow!' said Giacoma. She was very kind.

That night I slept in a doorway. And for three nights I slept like a stray dog, at the station, in an abandoned car, anywhere.

Then back to visit Giacoma of the cakes and brandy. She hugs me, kisses me, offers me a glass of Strega. She tells me her old man's about to pull off a job – it's stolen cars.

'Why don't you ask your husband if I could help him somehow?' I ask her.

'We'll see,' she says.

A lucky coincidence: that very morning they had arrested Giacoma's mother as an accessory, so for a few nights I was able to sleep in the mother's bed. The husband never showed his face. I began to wonder whether this husband of hers was just a fantasy.

One morning, as I'm going to the Bar Bengasi, I'm seized with violent pains. That's what you get when you're not used to drinking, I say to myself. That Giacoma has been giving me brandy, Strega and malmsey, and I'm not used to alcohol. The pain in my lower abdomen became so strong that, at a certain point, I couldn't bear it any more and I stretched my length on the ground, flat out.

Somebody scooped me up and took me to hospital. They said I had an inflamed peritoneum, pelviperitonitis, something like that. Anyway, they took me to San Giovanni Hospital and put me into a bed. And who should be in the next bed to me but La Spagnola.

'What are you doing here?' she says.

'I don't know, they picked me up in the street, I was taken ill.'

'I've had an operation on my ovaries,' she tells me.

It was lucky for me she was there to keep me company. We spent the next few days telling one another of all our doings. We were very merry and bright. Meanwhile, my health had improved, I was better.

One morning La Spagnola says, 'Shall we discharge ourselves?'

'And where the hell can we go?'

She says, 'To my husband's house. While you were doing time, I got married to this American.'

And she makes me believe she's got a husband. But he wasn't her husband, he was just some fellow she had picked up in the street. 'Are you really married?' I ask her. 'When did it happen?'

'A month ago. He's very nice, this American of mine.'

'Right, then!' I say, 'let's go and sign ourselves out!'

We discharged ourselves and left. This husband, however, was non-existent and so was the house. 'What did you want to get me out of there for? At least we had a roof over our heads. Now where can we go?' I grumbled at her.

'To my sister's,' she says, so off we go to see this sister, Nerina.

She lived at the Batteria Nomentana. She was tall, like La Spagnola, and dark-haired like her, but she was ugly. She had a snout like a dog's and a big mouth with all the teeth sticking out. Nerina let us sleep at her house for one night, but next day she chucked us out because her husband was due home from a business trip and she didn't have room any more.

I said to La Spagnola, 'You're always yakking on about your husband and your sister, but a fat lot of good they do you: you've been booted out on to the street, same as me.'

'Now I wonder where that husband of mine can be hiding himself?' she says. 'I swear to you he exists. He must be tucked away somewhere, but I'll find him sooner or later. My sister's changed, she used to be a good girl, but since she married that commercial traveller she's a different person.'

'That's as may be,' I say, 'but what do we do now?'

'Let's go to Anzio,' she says, 'you've got lots of brothers there, surely one of them will help us.'

So we wound up in Anzio. The moment he clapped eyes on me, my father chased me out. Lanky Dora had her knife into everybody at that time, she was like a bear with a sore head.

I went to Nello, but he couldn't put us up as he was decorating the house. 'We're out of luck,' I said. 'Now what?'

'Back to Rome,' she says.

We start walking. When we're tired, we sit down at the roadside to rest a bit. We try hitch-hiking, but nobody stops. When they saw how bedraggled and poorly-dressed we were, they looked the other way.

Finally, a Fiat 600 stopped. The driver was a student, handsome, very fair-haired, eating sweets out of a paper bag. 'Get in!' he said, nice as pie. When we were in, he started cross-examining us. 'How much do you earn in a day? How many customers do you have in a day? Do you ever have trouble with perverts?'

This boy had taken us for a couple of whores and nothing we said would make him change his ideas. He thought we were ashamed to admit it, and he kept offering us candy, pink candy from a christening, to soften us up.

Stuffing ourselves with candy, we reached Rome. He put us down near Santa Maria Maggiore and we went to look up a friend, Gianna the Bigmouth.

She lived in a pensione in via Panisperna. She had a tiny room overlooking a garage. We had to shout to hear ourselves above the deafening din. All three of us slept in that room, two in the bed and one on the floor, on a blanket.

Next morning, we went out to try and do some wallets. But La Spagnola was no Dina, she didn't have the knack. Me neither. I was clumsy, out of practice. We did a couple of wallets but they were empty. And we nearly got our collars felt twice.

La Spagnola says, 'You know, this job is too dangerous, doing wallets is a risky business. You know what? I'm going to pick up a man, it's the only way to manage without getting nicked.'

That very day, in fact, she dresses up to the nines and goes to the station. She catches herself a nice little fish and carries him off to bed. And that evening the three of us at last ate a meal. We spread a newspaper out on the rickety old bed and sat around it as if we were having a picnic in the open air. We ate bread, *mortadella,* fried fish and oranges.

During the day I went around on my own, dipping or doing wallets, and La Spagnola went on the game. In the evenings we all met up again in Gianna the Bigmouth's room and ate our supper. We didn't always eat, though, because we didn't always have money. La Spagnola had a talent for picking up dead-beats who took her off into the bushes and then didn't pay her. For me, too, it was a black period; I couldn't lay my hand on a well-filled wallet for the life of me.

One evening La Spagnola comes and tells me she's found her husband again, the American.

'Let's have a look at him,' I say.

'Come round this evening,' she says, 'I'll introduce you to him and we'll all go out to dinner together.'

That evening he did actually appear. He was an old man, an engineer. But he was no more American than I am. He had spent two years in the Argentine, he'd made money, but he was not American – he was as Italian as me and La Spagnola.

This Argentinian takes us out to dinner in a posh trattoria: *ossobuco,* pork chops, *tortellini,* chestnut pudding and coffee. While we're wolfing it down, La Spagnola makes a fuss of him, holding his hand, stroking his shoulder.

The old boy was tall, with dyed black hair, distinguished-looking. He had gleaming white dentures but they fitted badly and every time he spoke or laughed they wobbled up and down and I thought at any minute they would land in his plate.

This old fellow gave La Spagnola money, but only a little at a time, a few thousand lire. If she wanted something, she had to go to the shop with him to buy it. He bought her a solid-gold bracelet, two inches wide, with Chinese writing on it. But as for spending money, nothing doing. He held the purse-strings.

La Spagnola asked him for money to rent an apartment, but he was deaf in that ear. 'If you want a home,' he said, 'come and live with me.' She often went to his house, in fact. His ninety-year-old mother lived there with the youngest son. But when they were there she had to look after this brother, who was a mongol, and she soon got fed up with that. She had had hopes of marrying him, but every time she mentioned it he said, 'Do you think I'm going to marry a whore? Bring a whore into my home?' And she had to button her lip.

I said to her, 'Why the hell do you bother with that old geezer with the wobbly teeth? You're wasting your time in that mouldy old house with that idiot brother of his. And don't you see what a mean sod he is?'

'Yes,' she said, 'but I prefer an old man, he's not so demanding, and besides, he pays for everything I want.'

'But he never gives you any money in your hand,' I said.

'No,' she said, 'but he's a good sort, he loves his brother, he tends him with his own hands, and he is also very fond of his mother, and of me.'

'Yes,' I said, 'so fond of you that he won't hear of marrying you, and, if he did, it would only be to make you play nursemaid to that cretinous brother! Listen, let's pinch all his money and split!'

'No, I'm scared,' she said.

'Don't worry, Gianna the Bigmouth and I will help you.'

'What about the mother?' she said.

'The mother's old,' I said, 'what can she do?'

So Gianna the Bigmouth, La Spagnola and I planned the perfect robbery, and, in fact, it went off perfectly.

One evening, La Spagnola goes to spend the night with her 'American' and she leaves the front door unlocked. Then she retires to bed with him, having locked the old woman into her room and put the mongoloid brother to bed.

About three in the morning, Bigmouth and I go into the house. We open the bedroom door. La Spagnola, barefooted and in a nightdress, stares at us, terrorised. 'Ssh, ssh!' she says. She was terrified, quaking. She kept one eye on him, one eye on us. I hope to God she's given him a sleeper, I'm thinking, but I don't speak in case I make a noise.

Bigmouth goes to the wardrobe and takes out the mother's fur coat. I open the drawer in the chest-of-drawers where I know he

128

keeps his bread. I take two bundles of 10,000-lire banknotes which I find there. Then I slip his wallet out of his jacket pocket and Bob's your uncle. We're all ready.

Then we tiptoed out. In her fright, La Spagnola left her bag behind with all her documents in it, but they were false anyway. We got away with it, we never got nicked for that job.

We managed to live for nearly three weeks on that stash. We ate splendid banquets in Bigmouth's room, with wine, Russian salad, mushrooms, roast meat and fried fish. Then it was hungry times again. La Spagnola went back on the game, and she tried to persuade me to do it, too. She said, 'I know a man who'd love to meet you, he's loaded with money.'

'Listen,' I said, 'if you want something nicked, I'm with you, but the thought of making love to some filthy, lecherous bastard makes me vomit. Don't keep on at me, or I'll punch you on the nose.'

'Look,' she says, 'I've got an idea: I'll introduce you to a man with money, you pretend to fancy him, butter him up a little bit, then, at the last moment, I'll go to bed with him instead and we'll share out the proceeds.'

'Hm,' I said, 'that's more like it, we might pull that one off.' And it worked, two or three times. When there was a fellow who fancied me, I played up to him as if I was willing and then at the last minute I popped my friend into bed with him and she had to do the dirty work.

Once, it really worked a treat. We got more than 100,000 lire. This fellow was from the Vatican Embassy, all dressed in black, black socks, black tie, even his underpants were black.

'Whose funeral is it?' I asked.

'What?' he said. He had a big, fat, placid face and lots of grey curls hanging on his neck. It made me sick to look at him, but, to please La Spagnola, I sucked up to him the whole evening. Then, when it was time to go to bed, I said, 'Let's go to a hotel I know, in via Capo le Case.' They didn't ask for any documents there.

At the hotel, when we were right on the point of getting into bed, I said to him, 'Listen, I'm not well, I'll send you a friend of mine instead, a beautiful girl.'

He says, 'But I'm all ready for you now, I might not fancy this other girl.'

'Just think how we feel sometimes,' I say, 'we're always having to go with men whether we fancy them or not.'

129

'But you do it for money,' he says, 'you don't care.'

'Oh, so you think it's all the same to us, that the man doesn't matter?' I say.

'For you, yes, otherwise you wouldn't be much good as a whore, would you?'

'Look, don't make such a song and dance about it,' I say, you'll like my friend, she's much prettier than me and anyway, I'm sick. You wouldn't want to make love to a sick woman, would you?'

'As long as it's not a venereal disease, I don't care,' he says.

'Ah, but I do!' I tell him.

I go out and call La Spagnola, who's waiting round the corner. I go back in with her. The man was standing there, stark naked except for his black socks, admiring himself in the mirror. He had folded his clothes and laid them neatly on the chair. He had a gold crucifix weighing a couple of pounds round his neck and his skin was dead white and hairless. 'Here she is,' I said, 'may I introduce my friend, Ofelia?'

'How do you do?' he said.

La Spagnola quickly undressed and put out the light. He said, 'You stay here, too, I want both of you to stay, I'll pay double.'

'No,' I said, 'I told you, I'm ill.'

'What does it matter?' he said.

'Make love to Ofelia,' I said, 'and afterwards I'll come and cheer you up.'

'When will you come back?' he said.

'Soon,' I said. While we were talking, in the dark, I pulled his wallet out of his trouser pocket. Then I left.

La Spagnola made love to him, she gave him a good work-out, and left him there fast asleep. She met me outside. We ran so fast that our heels touched our heads. In that wallet we found 115,000 lire.

Another time La Spagnola almost got me run in because of her nervousness, her petrified expression. We'd played the same trick on a fellow and he caught us at it and wanted to call the fuzz. We scraped out of that one by the skin of our teeth.

So then I said, 'Listen, Spagnó, if you go on like this I'll wind up inside again, because you're no bloody good at anything, and you drop me in the shit, too.' In fact, she was a hopeless thief, she had no idea how to do it.

La Spagnola was only good in bed. That was her trade: she

went with a man and he paid her. She named her price, the fellow paid out in 100-lire notes and that was that. She didn't know how to do anything else.

In the end she found herself a husband. She got married and now she lives in Trieste. She's well off, she's got a beautiful house, she loves her husband and she makes an excellent wife.

They're always sending me postcards. 'We're longing to see you,' they say, 'come and visit us.' She's got a refrigerator, constant hot water, a washing machine and a bed with a canopy. Her husband goes out to work and she stays at home.

# 20

One day, as I was following a man who had his wallet in full view, sticking out of his trouser pocket, I was seized with another attack of peritonitis.

I was after this little spiv. He stopped at the newspaper stand in Piazza Vittorio. This big fat wallet was poking out of his pocket. I thought I'd follow him and see what he did. But then this attack came on and I fell helplessly to the ground.

I lay there writhing, I couldn't get up. The fellow with the wallet turned round, ran to me and helped me to my feet. 'What's the matter?' he says.

'I'm ill! Oh, oh, God, the pain's terrible!'

I was thinking: If he comes a bit nearer, I'll whip it off him. That wallet was dancing in front of my eyes. At one moment it was within reach of my hand, because he bent down to pick up my handbag. I said to myself: Now! Now take it! But my arm simply wouldn't obey me. I tried to raise my arm but instead I fell down again. I fainted.

When I wake up, I'm in a hospital bed. I recognise San Giovanni, but there are more beds this time than last. They've stuck me right by the door and every time someone goes in or out they bang into my bed. The pain was so fierce that I could scarcely breathe.

That evening they shaved my sex, put me on a trolley and wheeled me along to the operating theatre. While they're preparing me for the operation, a specialist arrives, Professor Matteacci, Matteotti, some name like that.

I still remember, it was raining outside and he arrived with an umbrella. He comes in, takes one look at me and says: 'Leave her alone. If you open her up, she'll only die on you. Leave her as she is.' And so, with my beard shaved off, my belly smeared with iodine, half-frozen, they take me back to the ward.

This doctor, still holding his umbrella, says: 'Try to keep her cold; if we operate, she'll die on the operating table, so keep her cold, chill her, at least she'll die wholesome!'

So that's what they did, they froze my peritonitis. Injections all night long. A little nurse came along with a big fat needle; I remember her clearly, she really gave me a mauling. She was a pretty little thing but she had muscles like iron. She grabbed my bottom with her freezing cold hands and shoved the needle in. She was like a sergeant-major. Then the ice-bag, and as soon as it melted they put another one on.

The peritonitis went away, it was frozen. I could hear them saying: 'Poor woman, what a way to die!' But fortunately the freezing calmed my peritoneum and made it better. When they froze it, however, they froze the ovaries as well, or something, so now I can't have children. From that time on, I was sterile.

Slowly, little by little, I got better, I came back to life. And still that pretty little nurse with arms like Popeye kept giving me injections. I got fat. The pains went away and a fortnight later I was discharged.

I came out and went to the Bar Bengasi. All my thief friends were there. They made a fuss of me, treated me to coffee. But when it came to work, it was every man for himself. No one could help me, there was no work to be had. I started talking to a girl called Lucia who came from Velletri. 'I'll help you!' she said.

This Lucia was on the game. She was small, raven-haired and with a good bosom. She was mad about hats – every time you saw her she had a different hat on: satin, velvet, felt, huge hats that made her head look twice its natural size.

She invited me to her place. She was kind. She lived alone in one room with no running water. But she had a lovely big, soft bed. She invited me to sleep there and she even fed me. I said, 'As soon as I've made a bit of bread, I'll pay you back.'

'Don't worry,' she said. She was good-hearted, generous.

During the day we slept. At night, she went out on the man-hunt and I tried to pull off some kind of job. But it nearly always turned out badly. I was going through an unlucky spell.

I was supposed to pick up a consignment of cigarettes with a

133

black marketeer, but at the last minute he chose a different partner. I was to do an apartment, but then they cut me out because they said I was still weak and couldn't run fast enough.

One morning Lucia says to me, 'Tonight, I'm going to introduce you to a fellow who wants to meet you. He's seen you already, in fact.'

'What's he like?' I ask.

'He's got pots of money, he's a tailor, he's got a shop, he'll make you clothes free of charge. He owns some land, property and houses; he's very well off.'

That evening the tailor turns up. The moment I see him I start to laugh. He's very short, with a big round head, he looks just like a cottage loaf. Besides, he's got one eye that goes off sideways, all by itself, and in fact his nickname is Boss-Eye, they call him that. I didn't fancy this tailor, it made me sick to look at him.

We sit down to table to eat, and we're all very jolly and bright. The tailor keeps looking and looking at me with that wonky eye of his. He was very sociable, eating and laughing and playing footsie-footsie with me under the table.

Lucia flattered him, paid him compliments, treated him like a fine gentleman: Would you like some more wine? Mineral water? A little liqueur? He never said no. That eye of his became madder and madder, squinting all over the place.

Well, after that Boss-Eye started showering me with presents. He came round at all hours of the day, loaded with gifts: handbags, gloves, scarves. He was generous. Lucia said to me, 'Give him a bit for once, he'll treat you like a lady!'

'He's so ugly, I can't bear to look at him!' I said.

'What do you care? Go on, let him have a bit, just once if you like, but get some money out of him, go on!'

No good, I couldn't bring myself to do it. I took his presents and kept putting off the day of reckoning.

One evening he made a date to meet me at a hotel. I had been shilly-shallying long enough and recently he'd bought me a pair of crocodile-skin shoes. I couldn't refuse any longer.

He'd booked a room at the hotel. 'This evening,' he says, 'no excuses, Teresa, either you come with me or I won't give you another thing.'

'All right,' I say, 'don't worry, I'll definitely come with you tonight.'

I turned up for a date. He comes trotting along, all dressed up in a dark suit, carrying a bundle under his arm. 'What've you got there?' I say.

'My pyjamas,' he says, and I think to myself: I'll give you pyjamas!

So we go into this hotel on via Merulana, at the end near San Giovanni. I'm dragging my feet, hanging back, because the thought of it turns my stomach and I'm trying to think up some excuse. But it was difficult. Boss-Eye had given me so many presents, he had bought me a whole new wardrobe, and besides, he was in love with me.

While we're in this hotel, walking down a long, long corridor all painted yellow, I see in the distance a man who looks like Tonino. 'Excuse me a moment,' I say, 'I've just seen a relative of mine, I'll be back in a minute.'

I run after this fellow, catch him at the top of the stairs, take a good look and see that it isn't Tonino after all. But the thought of him comes back so strongly that I feel quite ill.

Boss-Eye was still waiting for me in front of the bedroom door. I said to myself: Wait there, wait as long as you like, you'll never see me again! And I took off, ran away. I left him standing there, all alone with his pyjamas.

That night, I didn't go back to Lucia's in case I ran into him. In fact, I learned later that he had gone straight there from the hotel. He told Lucia, 'Your friend's played a dirty trick on me, did you know? She let me book a hotel room, I even went there the day before and paid for it in advance, then she ran off, left me there with my pyjamas rolled up in a newspaper!'

Lucia said, 'Aha, so that's what she did, is it? I'll give her what-for when I see her! That's no way to treat people. I'll slap her face for her, I'll kick her on the shins.'

'Yes, yes, that's it, we'll kick her.'

But he wouldn't give in, old Boss-Eye. He went to Lucia and told her he must make love to me at all costs, and she must arrange another appointment or it would be the worse for her.

I stayed away from Lucia's for several nights. Then hunger and cold drove me back. I went in and found him sitting there. I immediately stammered some excuse. 'Forgive me,' I said, 'but I bumped into my brother and I had to go with him.'

'What brother?' he says, 'where was he? I saw you going out alone.'

'You're mistaken, I was with my brother,' I say. 'I had to go out with him so that he wouldn't get suspicious.' So I spun him this yarn about running into my brother in the hotel, and he swallowed it.

Once again he started buying me presents: dresses, necklaces, shoes, handbags. Then one evening he made an arrangement with Lucia. He told her, 'I'll make a date with Teresa, but this time you must be there too. I want a guarantee that she won't run off.'

So they agreed it all between them. Lucia was to sleep in a single bed in front of the door, and the two of us, Boss-Eye and me, would sleep in the double bed. They'd got me bound hand and foot! He said, 'She won't do the dirty on me another time, that Teresa!' And to me he said, 'Why did you mess me about like that? You know I don't deserve it. I am not a bad man; whatever you want, you have only to ask for it and I buy it for you. Look at all the presents I've given you! You can't go on taking and taking and giving nothing in return. You owe me something.'

The fateful evening arrived. First, the three of us had a sumptuous meal. Then we went up to this room. Boss-Eye locked the door and gave the key to Lucia for safekeeping.

He started undressing. 'Take your clothes off!' he says to me. Moving at snail's pace, I take off my dress, my petticoat. Then, when I get down to my knickers, I say, 'Oh, mamma mia! My period's started! I'm sorry, but I can't make love. When I get the curse, it's very painful and I get awful flooding. We'll have to put it off.'

'And how long does this curse of yours last?' he says.

'Tomorrow, or the day after, I'll be OK,' I say.

'Very well,' he says, 'we'll delay it till the day after tomorrow. But are you sure? Let me see the blood.'

'Oh, no!' I say, 'I'm embarrassed, those aren't things for men's eyes, it's bad enough having to tell you about it. But wait, in a couple of days' time we'll make love, I promise you.'

'Couldn't we do something now?' he says.

'If you like we can be close, we can sleep together, but don't touch me, because when I'm like this I get nervous, I feel rotten,' I say, and he says, 'Of course, I understand. Excuse me.'

But he wouldn't let me go. I had to sleep in that bed, beside him, under the same sheet. Lucia snored in the little bed by the door and all night long Boss-Eye gazed at me.

Next day I got him to buy me a coat and two pairs of silk stockings. Then, when we were in a bar, I took off the gold chain with the medal of the Madonna that he wore around his neck and said, 'Can I try it on a minute?'

'Go ahead,' he said.

The moment I had it in my hand, I ran away, did a bunk. I left him there with a cup of coffee in his hand and his shirt-collar all undone.

When Lucia saw me, she burst out laughing. 'Christ!' she said, 'you've really fucked up old Boss-Eye, he's looking everywhere for you!'

'What's he after, the fool? If I see him, I'll give him two boss-eyes instead of one!'

She laughed. 'I should stay out of sight for a while. If he claps eyes on you, you'll get a knife in your ribs.'

I went to the Bar Bengasi and there I met a man I really fancied, a certain Alfio. A bunch of us went dancing till three in the morning. We played cards, danced, sang; there was a fellow who played the accordion and another one who played the guitar. We were amongst friends, all of us thieves, and it was really gay and lively.

Then this Alfio says to me, 'Shall we go to bed together?'

'Yes,' I say. I like him, he was my type, tall, handsome, thin. But he had to start work at five, he worked for the transport company, ATAC.

'Never mind,' he says, 'it just means I won't get any sleep tonight.'

'No, let's leave it. Nobody's pushing us. We can make love on Sunday, when you're free,' I say.

During the week I discovered that Alfio was having it off with a girl-friend of mine. It put me off, I didn't trust him any more. He attracted me, he was a good-looking, dark-haired fellow with a beautiful fleshy mouth. But I found out he was going to bed with Teresa, a girl who sold shoes from a little stall in Piazza Vittorio.

She's a friend of mine. I think to myself: Perhaps she'll find out about me and Alfio and we'll fall out. We might even come to blows. Besides, I don't want to take her left-overs. I don't want anybody's left-overs, thank you. I want a man all to myself, otherwise I'll do without.

I was very smart, with all the clothes Boss-Eye had bought me.

I had a new dress, a new coat. If I met Tonino now, I'd really bowl him over! And I roamed about the streets, always thinking of him, always hoping to meet him somewhere.

Things went on like this for a month, and I just couldn't get on my feet again. I had to sell the coat and my crocodile shoes. I went back to Lucia's so that I could sleep in a bed. For some time I'd been dossing down at the station.

When I went in she said, 'Boss-Eye is looking for you. If he sets eyes on you, he'll stab you.'

'Let him,' I said, 'let him just try, if he's got the guts! He'll get more that he bargains for, doesn't he know I eat knives for breakfast?'

I put a brave face on it but I was scared. I knew that Boss-Eye had turned vicious. And one morning I met him outside the house. I was with a friend of mine called Olga. 'Look out!' she said, 'he's got a knife in his pocket!'

As soon as I saw him I turned and ran. I met a friend of mine with a car. I said to him, 'Quick, get me out of here for Christ's sake!'

'What's up?' he said.

'There's a nut chasing me with a knife.'

I decided I'd better not go back to Lucia's ever again.

# 21

Olga and I made a bit of money selling contraband cigarettes. In those days you could get hold of three or four hundred packets and sell them off in small quantities. They let you pay for your stock later, after you'd sold them.

Now it can't be done any more. If you don't pay in advance, nothing doing. This means you have to be rich to start with, if you want to deal in contraband cigarettes. You can't make money unless you've got money already.

At last I had a little cash in my pocket. I decided to set up a home. I saw Olga's smashing new apartment and thought: I'll have one like that, too!

'Listen,' she says, 'I can give you the address of a place that's up for rent. Go to via Enea, you'll find a good room with a kitchen for 12,000 lire. If you're going, go at once!'

So off I went to via Enea, near the Tuscolana station, and I agreed to take this place. But they wanted 20,000 lire deposit. I started selling fags at night, in spite of the risks, and I collected the 20,000.

Now, I thought, what the hell am I going to use for furniture? Olga said. 'I've got an old wardrobe my sister gave me, and a bed-spring. It's rusty, but it's OK. You can buy other things bit by bit.'

So that's what I did. I rented this room, with kitchen. I bought a second-hand mattress. Olga gave me some sheets, patched but still serviceable. Then I bought a few things on the never-never. I signed the H.P. agreement, a thing I had never done before. And I paid. I had become a person who paid bills. And I paid on the dot out of terror of going inside again for non-payment! Nowadays, I never pay for anything. I sign H.P. agreements by the dozen, but I never pay after the first down-payment.

For the first time in my life I had a home of my very own. Just imagine, I was thirty-five years old! I felt like a queen. I thought: At last I have a bed of my own, a room all to myself, I can do what I like. I can sleep to my heart's content, get up when I feel like it.

In fact, I slept all day long. I was greedy for sleep. I got up only to go to the Bar Bengasi or to sell a shipment of cigarettes with my friend Olga.

No sooner had I got a home, a bed, and plenty of sleep, than the kidney pains came back. I got up in pain, I walked about bent double. It was crippling me. Olga said she knew a doctor who didn't charge very much and she urged me to go and see him. This doctor kept me waiting two hours, then he finally examined me and said I had annexitis. Annexitis of the kidneys. 'You must have a course of injections,' he says.

'And who's going to give me the injections?'

'I'll introduce you to a nurse who won't overcharge you,' he says.

He was as good as his word. He introduced me to a male nurse, a fly sort of character with the gift of the gab. The doctor said, 'He works at the San Giovanni Hospital, but he'll visit you at home and charge only 200 lire a time.'

Meanwhile I had furnished my room nicely. There were comfortable chairs, a table, and pretty pink curtains at the window. The nurse was the first stranger I entertained there. I sat him in a brand-new chair and offered him a glass of Kümmel and a biscuit as soon as he arrived. I noticed that he was looking round admiringly. 'It's a small room, but very cosy; you've done it up so nicely, with the curtains and everything, it's as pretty as a chocolate box! And clean,' he says, 'spotless. I'll be glad to drink a glass with you in such a nice clean place.' And he drank the Kümmel down in one gulp.

Each time he came, I gave him a glass of Kümmel. We became friendly and one day he told me he had been in prison, and in and out of all kinds of trouble.

Then he says to me, 'I've got a brother-in-law who's been in prison for robbery with violence. I would like you to meet him.'

140

And he never stops talking about this brother-in-law of his. I didn't even listen, I wasn't interested.

'Why are you always on about your brother-in-law?' I asked him. 'I haven't met him.'

But still he went on about him. Built him up to be something terrific. 'He's handsome,' he says, 'strong and healthy, he's a good man, very intelligent. When he comes out, I'll introduce you.' I took no notice at all. My head was still full of Tonino. I said 'yes, yes,' out of politeness but I didn't give a tinker's cuss for this brother-in-law, in fact I was so sick of hearing about him that I began to dislike the man.

The course of injections lasted a month, and after that I saw no more of the nurse. Till one morning, before I'm even up, I hear a loud knock at the door. It's the nurse shouting, 'Teresa, Teresa! May I come in? Guess who I've brought to see you!'

I open the door and find myself facing three people: the nurse, a woman and another man. 'This is my wife, Alba, and this is my brother-in-law, Ercoletto, the one I told you about.'

'Ah,' I say, 'delighted. Do come in!' I was still in my dressing-gown. I went into the kitchen to do my hair. Then I offered them a glass of Kümmel.

'Or would you prefer a Mandarino, or an Anisetta?' I said.

'Yes,' said this brother-in-law. 'Anisetta, please.' He sipped his drink and looked round the room. I didn't like him. He looked like a clodhopper. He wasn't bad-looking but he seemed uncouth, a real yokel. I was getting on for thirty-six and he was thirty. But he looked younger, more like twenty-six.

We started chatting. I told them about my brother Orlando who had been transferred from Procida prison to Soriano del Cimino because he broke a chair over a warder's head. 'Why did he do that?' they said.

'Because he found out that a certain Pesciolini, with the connivance of the nuns, was stealing the decent provisions and leaving all the rubbish to the prisoners.'

'Yes, it's terrible what goes on in prisons,' said the brother-in-law.

'Exactly,' I said, 'and that's why Orlando denounced this Pesciolini for stealing and selling off all this crap, but they told him that *he* was full of crap, and that made him mad, so he snatched off the nun's coiffe, shouting, "We'll see who's full of crap!" and for this they took him away and tied him to the

141

restraining bed for a month. He got a friend of his to write and tell me.'

This brother-in-law said, 'Listen, I know Carla Capponi, the deputy; if you need any help for your brother, I'll see what I can do. Better still, I'll come and pick you up tomorrow and we'll go and see Carla Capponi together.'

Because he showed an interest in my brother, I warmed to him a little, but I still didn't care for him, he was too much of a country cousin. Besides, I couldn't help wondering if he really did know this politician, Capponi.

He turned up next day. 'Here I am,' he says, 'let's go and see Carla Capponi!' We made our way to via Marconi where this lady deputy lived. He didn't say much on the way, but he was polite and attentive.

We reach the house, walk up the stairs and knock. The maid tells us the deputy is out of town.

'When will she be back?' he asks.

'In a couple of days,' the maid replies.

So we went away. 'Never mind,' he says, 'we'll go another day, we'll go on Saturday.' And we made an appointment for Saturday.

Afterwards, I found out that this business of Carla Capponi was just a pretext. He had discovered beforehand that the deputy was not in Rome. He'd got his eye on me and wanted to make a big impression, that was all.

But I didn't fancy him. He wasn't unattractive, he had a moustache and a lovely smile. He was sentimental, which pleased me, he was very sweet, he said romantic things. But I found him a bit crude. I didn't like the way he dressed, with those awful country bumpkin boots of his and that fustian jacket.

But he was certainly keen on me. Morning, noon and night, even the middle of the night when I was sleeping, he would come round to visit me. A knock at the door: 'Who's there?'

'It's me, Ercoletto. I want to tell you something.'

'What?'

'I want you to be godmother at a christening.'

'And you come here at this time of night to tell me about it?'

'Open the door, I must speak to you.'

I open the door. In he comes, and drinks a glass of Kümmel. He says, 'I must tell you something – I got a servant-girl

142

pregnant and she's had a baby by me. I was quite willing to marry her, but while I was inside she went with friends of mine, so it's all over as far as I'm concerned.'

'I'm not interested in what you do or what you've done,' I say.

He says, 'Well, I'm just telling you, to keep the record straight.' Then he goes on: 'Tomorrow, I have to go to my niece's christening. I'm to be godfather; will you be godmother? You must, I've already accepted on your behalf.'

So I went to the christening of this god-daughter of his. She was a lovely chubby little thing. On the day of the christening, the male nurse from San Giovanni Hospital gave a party in his house.

Ercoletto's father was there, an old man with a yellow moustache, and there were loads of friends. Everyone was busy getting drunk. It was very gay, people were singing and dancing. They were handing round cream cakes and sweets.

That same evening Ercoletto proposed to me. He said straight out that he liked me, that I was the woman for him, his type, and that I should come and live with him. He said, 'You know, I can give you a good life, you can stay at home, like a lady, while I go out to work. We'll set up a nice home together,' etc. etc. I wasn't even listening. I didn't fancy him.

He insisted. I made date after date with him, but at the last moment I always stood him up. He didn't appeal to me. But he wouldn't give in. He came knocking at my door, took me out to dinner, to the cinema. He tried to talk me into loving him. But I am stubborn, I wouldn't let myself be persuaded.

One day, the nurse told me I was invited, together with him and his brother-in-law, to a dinner party in the country. 'Did you know,' he says, 'Ercoletto's found a job?'

'Oh, where?' I say.

'He's working for Count Tolentino,' he says, 'at the Pantano Borghese, he's got a job as bailiff. He's got hold of a lovely chicken and a bit of venison; he's been poaching in the game reserve, we'll have a grand roast. You *must* come, Ercoletto's set his heart on it!' Well, that's what this dirty pimp told me, and I let myself be persuaded.

They came and fetched me and took me there, to this Pantano Borghese. Ercoletto had a very cosy set-up, he was living in the bailiff's house, there was a bedroom and a kitchen, and there was a large wood nearby.

We ate vast quantities of meat and drank wine by the gallon and I got a bit sloshed. When I was really tired out and muzzy with booze, they put me into bed with Ercoletto.

At the time I made a fuss, I wanted to leave. But, partly because I was so tired, partly because my curiosity had been aroused about this man, I stayed with him. And I did the right thing, because he made me happy, and he still does, to this day.

In the morning I woke up quite late. I looked out of the window and saw him riding up and down, exercising the horses in the yard. He was as straight as a ramrod and I began to think: Hmm, he carries himself well. He's not so bad-looking! And I started to fall in love.

The work at the Pantano Borghese was heavy and tiring. It was farm work. Ercoletto had to get up at five every morning to see to the cows, the hens, the horses. He was always humping sacks, loading up the hay, the cattle fodder, the bran. Wearing patched old trousers and a fur cap on his head, he did the work of a farm bailiff. We were never short of food, but there was so much work and the animals needed constant attention, they were for ever eating, breeding, sleeping, shitting, all at the same time.

It was while Ercoletto was working there that this woman turned up and started going for him. She threatened him, struck him in the face. It was Cesira, the woman who had had a child by him. She came there often and made scenes. He couldn't get her off his back.

'You've got no idea how to go about things,' I said to him, 'you'll never get rid of her. Let me have a word with this Cesira.'

'No,' he said, 'I must deal with her myself, discourage her. She's a good woman, you know, we must do things calmly.'

In fact, she wasn't a bad sort, but she was vindictive. She'd turn up, weeping and wailing, with the kid in her arms, and she'd start a row: 'This child is yours! You've got to marry me!' She plagued him so much that even the other farm-people started telling him he ought to get shot of her.

One day Ercoletto says to me, 'You know what I think? If I'm ever going to get rid of Cesira, I'll have to give up my job, disappear. Then she won't see me any more and she'll get over it and settle down quietly.'

So he gave up his work at the Pantano Borghese. He'd been there five months. The pay was good and they gave us vegetables, chickens, wine. But that was the end of it. One of his fellow-workers even came to my house looking for Ercoletto. 'Why don't you come back to work, Ercoletto?' he says. Princess Tolentino says she must talk to you at all costs,' But he wouldn't go. He didn't talk to the Princess. So he lost his position, and all on account of this wretched Cesira who had had his baby.

We had to scratch a living as best we could. We started gathering mushrooms in the Fragonella woods. We picked basketfuls of mushrooms and took them to the greengrocer's. They paid us well. This was the first crop, the early ones.

You have to be careful with mushrooms because there are good edible ones and bad ones that look like them. If there is a good one which is fleshy, brownish, smooth and shiny, right beside it you'll find its double: fleshy, brownish, smooth and shiny – and poisonous. If you eat it, you swell up and up, you vomit your entrails out of your mouth, and then you die. You had to be craftier than the crafty imitative mushrooms and look for certain pinkish veins under the head, like tiny delicate muscles, which are a danger signal. Death is lurking in those little muscles.

Ercoletto had a sharp eye for mushrooms. We went up into the Fragonella woods. We went in a second-hand car we'd bought cheap; as a matter of fact it was third-hand, a white estate car, and it was falling to bits. Every now and then it stopped and Ercoletto had to get underneath, tie the bits together with wire, or stick it together, and get it going somehow.

That car drank oil as if it was dying of thirst. We always had to carry cans of oil on board. It was cheap oil that had already been used and it stank like rotten meat. Once, by mistake, we put in olive oil and the car started to fry!

In the evening we went home and ate mushrooms and potatoes, mushrooms and broccoli or mushrooms and pasta. We drank plenty of wine. Then we went to bed satisfied.

It was the happiest time of my life. In the morning we got up early, drank our coffee and hurried off to the woods to gather mushrooms. We spent all day there under the trees. At midday we sat down on the grass and took out a bit of bread and salami. When it was dark, we loaded the mushrooms into the car and went back home.

Then the mushrooms came to an end. The woods were nothing but mud; we slithered about and sank in; it had become a quagmire. There was nothing left to pick. Then Ercoletto looked around and found a job as a bricklayer while I stayed at home. Working with lime and cement, he always had his hands in water and the skin became all chapped and split. I made him an ointment of olive oil, flour and almond oil, but he didn't like putting it on.

Then one evening he went out drinking with some friends of his and he fell off a wall and broke his leg. When he didn't come home, I went out looking for him and found him dragging himself along the ground saying, 'Oh, God! Help me, help me, I can't move another inch!'

I took him to the hospital. They put him into bed and set his leg in plaster. He had a high temperature. I went to see him every day. I took him *pasta al forno,* fillet steak and almond cake, because the food in the hospital was worse than in prison. On the pretext that you were ill and needed a light diet, they dished out wishy-washy soup and a bit of chicken's wing that wouldn't have satisfied the appetite of a child.

At last, after more than a month, the leg was cured. I had no money left to live on. I had had to sell a cupboard I'd bought in palmier days, as well as the radio, a big mahogany radio with all the stations in the world. I had sold a leather case, which I'd nicked, and even the watch Ercoletto had given me for my birthday.

They mended his leg. But they told him he should wear a support in his shoe for walking, as the broken leg had grown shorter by a few centimetres.

'But how can it grow shorter?' I said.

'I don't know,' he said. 'When it was knitting itself together the bone must have shrunk.'

But I thought they had bungled the job. 'Anyway,' I said, let's be thankful that you can walk.' And I took him home.

For some time we lived on bread and pàsta. We didn't even have the money to buy a little coffee. The landlady was pestering us for the rent which we hadn't paid for five months. Then one day we sold everything and went to Alba, Ercoletto's sister, the one who was married to the male nurse. We didn't say a word to our landlady, so when she came she found the place empty and

146

the tenants flown. She didn't know how to trace us and that was that.

Alba had a lovely big house, near Cinecittà, with two bedrooms, a sitting-room, bathroom and kitchen. Ercoletto and I slept in one room, Alba and her husband in the other.

It's my destiny – always these confounded sisters! I am condemned to have sisters round my neck. First, my husband, who had no mother but those two vipers of sisters, now this one, also motherless, but with a sister.

In the mornings, Ercoletto and I went out to try and earn a little money somehow. The nurse went to the hospital, Alba stayed at home. She was a woman who loved to eat and drink, especially drink. She liked to stay at home. She was always laughing; she was a great nit. She laughed even when there was nothing to laugh at. If she heard about a disaster, instead of crying, she burst out laughing. If she saw someone hurt themselves, she laughed like a lunatic.

One day Ercoletto, Alba and I went to see a dead man. This poor soul had a belly as big as a house. He had swelled up after his death. He was full of wind. Well, we go in. I look at her, she looks at the dead man and bursts out laughing. I take her by the arm and lead her out. People are turning round. They're saying, 'They come to pay their respects to the dead and they laugh!' Meanwhile, her laughter's infected me too and the two of us are laughing like a pair of idiots. We are overcome with giggles at the sight of this huge pot-belly like a drum and we can't contain ourselves, even out in the street.

Now this sister is dead. She died a few months ago. Ercoletto was very fond of her. They squabbled but there was plenty of affection between them, so much so that some people said they had it off together. They said, 'Haven't you noticed that Ercoletto is attached to his sister, as if she was his wife?' But it was all jealousy and lies. Just because they helped one another. They were close, rather like my brother Orlando and me.

At first, in the sister's house, we went hungry. We couldn't find any way of making money. Then Ercoletto managed to do a few deals and we started trading in oil and household linens. We got the oil from a bloke called Bolloni who was an oil merchant. It was labelled 'olive oil' but in fact it was seed-oil flavoured with a little olive. We bought it at 300 lire a kilo and resold it at 500.

The best customers were trattorias out in the country. They would buy 50 or 100 kilos at a time, so we made quite a bit.

Then there was a man called Peppino, who brought us household linen. He worked in a wholesale warehouse; he nicked stuff from there, gave it to us and we sold it. Then we divided the proceeds in half.

But he couldn't pinch too much at a time or he would be found out. Sometimes a week or two went by and we didn't see him. Then he'd turn up again. 'Peppino, what have you brought us this time?' I'd say, and he'd say, 'A load of sheets.'

'How much?'

'Each package is worth 150,000 lire.'

'Right, we'll see what we can get for them.'

We took the packages, brand-new, unopened, to certain dealers we knew. They paid us half, a third, sometimes only a quarter or even a fifth of the value when we had to hurry and we knew the police were on the watch.

We also had private clients. There was a lady in Parioli who'd take any stolen goods, pay us a pittance, and sell the stuff again from house to house at very high prices. I didn't like this Parioli woman and we only went there when there was absolutely nowhere else to go. She treated us like stray dogs and even had the nerve to lecture us: 'Here you are, you thieves, you're the scum of the earth! Why don't you go out and get a decent job? You're too lazy, that's why!'

During these trips, if we had the chance, we pinched a few things here and there. Ercoletto wasn't up to it, but I was. So I'd say to him, 'Stop the car, I'm going to snitch something.' I'd see a house left unattended, a window open . . . I'd climb in, lay my hands on something and carry it off.

Once I stole a glittering, brand-new racing cycle, a Legnano. We tied it on to the roof and everybody looked at it admiringly. It was beautiful. We were sorry to have to sell it. We took it to a fence, a fellow by the name of Massimo who lived in Quadraro. He offered us 15,000 lire. 'No,' I said, 'it's worth more than that. We'll go somewhere else.'

So we go to a certain Giorgio, known as the Worm, because his guts are full of worms and he's always taking medicines. They don't cure him, though. Worms come out of his bottom; every time he pulls one out he puts it in a little jar full of oil.

I don't know whether it's the worms or what, but this Worm is a healthy, strong, robust type, with a puffy face, fat hands, fat legs, fat neck. It looks as if the worms are doing him good, because he's now nearly eighty years old and he's healthier than I am. He offered us 20,000 lire, so we left the bike with him.

We got on reasonably well with Alba. As long as we bought her a few flasks of wine and a pound or two of meat, she was happy. She liked offal best: liver, kidneys, tripe, heart, brains, trotters. She loved meat, she was a real carnivore. But she loved wine above all things. When we brought her a flask, she was as happy as a sandboy. Sometimes we paid her rent, sometimes we didn't. But she never complained.

Her husband worked at the hospital, sometimes as a nurse, sometimes as a porter. But he made quite a bit on the side. He wheeled and dealed, pimped and ponced, he was a Jack-of-all-trades. He found women for everybody at the hospital, the doctors, the porters, the male nurses.

He went to the homes of all these girls on the game, to give them injections, so he knew them all, good and bad alike. He also knew married ladies, young girls of good family, lonely widows, the lot. He'd give them their injections, then sit and talk. He makes himself agreeable, he's a great talker, he worms his way into everybody's confidence, finds out all their business, then he makes a suggestion: 'I know a man who is always thinking of you, he's dying of love for you.' He arranges an appointment and get paid for it.

The little male nurse, Ercoletto's brother-in-law, is as ugly as sin. Once he even had the nerve to make a pass at me. He comes up and starts pawing me, touching me up. 'Look out!' I say, 'keep your mitts to yourself or I'll tell Ercoletto!' But he didn't give a bugger. He kept trying it on, secretly, so that his wife wouldn't see. He squeezed my tits, stroked my legs.

One day, I round on him and say, 'Listen, you ugly bastard, you make me sick, I wouldn't touch you with a barge-pole. If you were good-looking, maybe it would be different, but you're ugly and stupid and I'm fed up with you!'

Then he grabs me, shoves me against the sideboard and presses his mouth to mine. 'Give us a kiss!' he says.

'Piss off!' I say, 'your breath stinks, your teeth are rotten, you pong like a sewer!'

His teeth are all encrusted with black, with yellow half-moons under his gums. For me, teeth are all-important. You could almost say I fell for Ercoletto because of his teeth, they're clean, white, sound. So when I see this black mouth, I say, 'I wouldn't give you a kiss for all the tea in China! You disgust me – if I kissed you, I'd throw up!' And he was so angry he slapped my face.

That evening I told Ercoletto about it. 'A fine thing,' I said, 'your brother-in-law trying to maul me about all the time.'

Ercoletto lost his temper and he had a fight with the nurse. The brother-in-law said, 'But I was only joking! I wanted to see if she was willing, I wanted to test the fidelity of this woman of yours!'

Ercoletto said, 'Never you mind about her fidelity, I'm quite capable of keeping her in order myself!'

Alba was there, too, and she burst out laughing. She pretended she didn't believe me. Later on, however, I heard them having a row in bed.

Next day, this sister's giving me old-fashioned looks, so I say to her, 'If you're jealous on my account, don't bother, I can't stand the sight of your husband. Your old man goes with every whore in town, he goes to give them injections and he undresses them and feels them all over and often they go to bed together – and you're jealous of me! Furthermore, your husband insulted me not once but many times, and if I was a different type, I might have gone with him. But I never did and I never wanted to. First of all, because I respect you and Ercoletto, second, because he revolts me. Excuse me for saying so, but your husband makes me feel like vomiting. I think you're a bloody heroine for taking him on!'

But she wouldn't listen. She was jealous of everybody. As long as she didn't see what was going on, she didn't care, but if she saw something, it upset her. She had no imagination. Only when something happened right under her nose did she notice it. Otherwise, even if that man of hers came home dog tired, with lipstick and mascara all over his collar, she didn't say a dickie-bird.

They were always quarrelling over this business with me. It got so that I'd go out of the house as much as possible. One day he had the cheek to say to me, 'Who are you to make such a fuss, you're nothing but a jailbird!'

'Filthy swine!' I said, 'and what have you been up to all these years at the hospital?'

'I'm an honest man!' he said.

'What?' I said, 'you've been lifting stuff, you've had your fingers into every kind of dirty deal. What do you mean, honest? Just because you've always got away with it, whereas I get nabbed the minute I move a finger! But you're a bigger thief than I am, and a pimp to boot!'

And those hands of his were like a conjurer's! I saw him at his tricks once at a house La Spagnola had rented in the country, at Mentana. She invited us all down to this little house, it was in the middle of a vineyard and my friend paid 15,000 lire a month for it. It was a beautiful new house with a bath, a flush toilet, all conveniences. And all around it was this lovely countryside, with a kitchen-garden, a lawn and fruit-trees. La Spagnola kept hens on the lawn.

She was living in the house with a fellow called Nardo. She asked us there to lunch one Saturday, Ercoletto, Alba and her husband and me. She said, 'I'll kill three chickens if you come, we'll have a banquet.' That's the way she is, she loves parties, eating, drinking, singing.

So we arrive at this place, Mentana. It's all green and lush. La Spagnola welcomes us, all smiles. She was wearing trousers, she looked like a handsome cavalier. She's a tall, voluptuous-looking woman.

She shows us the kitchen-garden with cabbages, beans, onions, and the chickens shut in a wire enclosure. Then she says, 'These hens are so lovely, I'd hate to kill them. I've got some veal, do you mind if we eat veal escalopes instead?'

Now, while she's busy picking the salad greens in the kitchen-garden, I see Alba's husband sneaking up to the chicken coop, but I don't pay much attention. I was carrying the plates out to the table. All of a sudden, bam! I feel something hit my back. 'Shit!' I say, 'whatever's that?'

I turn round and see the ground all smeared with blood. He's thrown a hen at me with one wing torn off. Even my dress is stained. I'm about to say something when he pipes up: 'Ssh! Give me that bag.'

'What bag?' I say. 'La Spagnola's no fool, you know, she'll notice, then she'll fly at me and it'll be all your fault!'

He doesn't even bother to answer. Quick as lightning, he takes that wounded hen, wrings its neck like a murderer and shoves it into his bag.

But I told La Spagnola. I said, 'You know, that son-of-a-bitch pinched one of your hens.' But I didn't tell her till some time later, when she came to visit us.

'Aha!' she said, 'so that's what became of the missing hen!'

Another thing, Alba and the nurse aren't married. They've lived together for twenty years. But he had another wife and kids somewhere or other. He's had five children with Alba, one of them is already married.

He says he left his first wife because he came back from the war to find her in hospital, suffering from venereal disease she'd caught from going with men. He met Alba there, in the hospital; she was visiting her sick mother. They set up together, had five kids, and stayed together till she died.

As for the daughters, one got married this year. She's a bit odd, full of wild ideas. She married a boy who's out of work. She's capricious and pig-headed, and goes and marries this boy who has no job. 'What does it matter?' she says. 'Daddy will look after us! We can always find the money for the rent, a bit here, a bit there, it's not hard to rustle us 20,000 lire for the rent.'

They didn't have a thing when they got married. Then the boy's father bought them some bedroom furniture, a wardrobe and a couple of mattresses. All the rest was provided for by the nurse.

This husband of hers is a vagabond; he's a nit. He has long hair and a moustache; he carries on as if he was Jesus Christ. But he's a dope, he doesn't understand anything. When other people talk, he keeps making faces as if it hurt him. Everything he says delights him, everything other people say gives him a pain in the arse.

Another of the nurse's daughters is working as a shop-assistant at Standa. The rest are still small, one's twelve, another ten; they're good girls, they study hard at school. Only the older one is a bit crazy. She takes after her father, both in looks and character. She's arrogant and as hard as nails. When she walks, she stoops forward. She's not exactly ugly, but she's unappetising. She has this haughty manner. She doesn't know anything and she's never been anywhere, but she dolls herself up, cakes her eyelids with two inches of that green powder, paints herself red, yellow, all colours; she looks like a parrot.

# 22

One day, Ercoletto and I were unloading cans of oil when we bumped into Boss-Eye. He confronted me immediately: 'You've taken up with that stupid peasant there, that bum, yet you wouldn't have anything to do with me!'

'Peasant or not,' I said, 'I like him, and you make me sick. I'm in love with him, and you're nothing but a clown. What do you want with me, anyway?'

'You prefer that yokel to a man like me, who works and makes good money. I would have made a lady of you!'

'Yes,' I said, 'he may dress like a yokel, but Ercoletto is a man and you're not; you're young but you're like a senile old man. And you should just see Ercoletto without his clothes on, he's the seven wonders of the world!'

Then he said, 'You two make a fine pair, you're both jailbirds, stinking lousy peasants! One's as bad as the other, a couple of shit-stirrers and thieving cut-throats!'

At this point, Ercoletto couldn't take any more. He jumped at him and started hitting him. But the swine was ready, he'd got three men hidden in a car. The moment Ercoletto set on him, he called these three friends and they all started laying into us.

We were in front of the Trattoria Annibale, near the Opera House. Ercoletto was alone against these three. They were beating hell out of him. When he saw the things were going against him, he pulled out his knife and stabbed one of them, a friend of Boss-Eye's known as Thirsty. The tailor was hurt too. He got a dagger wound on his arm and they ran away. But later they got their revenge, because they went to the police and laid charges.

Ercoletto and I had to go into hiding. We were on the run for a year. We couldn't go home in case they arrested us. We lived near Frascati, in the caves. There are large holes in the rocks there, in the area where the pine-woods are. We chose a large wide cave and settled in.

Ercoletto gathered firewood and we made a fire on the ground in a circle of stones. I cooked pasta or soup and we ate straight out of the saucepan. We had nothing, no plates, no knives or forks. One saucepan had to serve for everything, and when we needed water we had to go to the public pump to get it, some three miles away.

In the mornings we went down into Frascati to shop. We went in the car, an old, sky-blue rattletrap with the doors held together with string, the brakes gone and the gears broken. I don't know how it went at all, but it did. We'd go into the village and buy a few things in the market. Then we went round selling oil.

We had started up again in the oil business. We sold it in cans, but in the smaller sizes so as not to attract attention, Ercoletto's sister helped us a little, too. She would make an appointment by telephone, meet us in some out-of-the-way place and hand us a bit of money. Then we got things on hire purchase and flogged them. We made a living any way we could.

At night we slept in the car, because the cave was sopping wet and full of snakes. We had two blankets and a tattered old eiderdown I had stolen from a house, and that was how we slept.

Sometimes there were storms: bursts of thunder and lightning. The ground under the car became a sea of mud and rats crept out, black ones as big as dogs. But we never got down-hearted. In fact, it made a better home than some of those hovels you see in villages.

We lived like that for a whole year. Then one day they spotted the car and stopped us. Ercoletto was a wanted man; they recognised him and we wound up in jail. They kept him inside but they let me go, as the charges had been laid against him, not me, and he had struck the blow with the dagger. So he ended up in Regina Coeli.

I started to look for a lawyer, to do what I could. The car had been confiscated so I had to go everywhere on foot. Anyway, I don't know how to drive. I walked. Sometimes I took a bus or a tram but most of the time I walked. Luckily I've got strong legs.

I took parcels to Ercoletto in prison. At first they wouldn't let me in.

'Who are you?' they said.

'His wife.'

'You'll have to prove it.'

'How?'

'You have to produce a certificate stating you're his common-law wife, otherwise no visits, no parcels.'

I went to the judge and asked for this certificate, proving cohabitation. I waited days, weeks. At last they gave it to me. Then I was able to see him and talk to him. I took him cigarettes, *mortadella,* coffee.

At the trial he got eight months. I had to sell a good mattress, worth 50,000 lire, to pay the lawyer. But it was not enough. So I sold all the bedroom furniture and an armchair upholstered in mock leather. When the money was gone, I started dipping again. Doing handbags. I went back to the Bar Bengasi and looked up my bag-snatcher friends again. 'Come with us,' they said, 'these days, we're dipping on the trams.'

The first time, it went off smoothly. And the second. But we didn't make much, 10,000 or 15,000 lire. And we had to divide it into three. I bought things for Ercoletto and visited him.

The third time, I got done. A girl by the name of Peppina got on to a No. 12 tram with me. We mingled with the crowd, pretending we didn't know each other from Adam.

I see that my friend is standing facing a well-dressed man in a hat; he's got such short little arms that he's having a hard time reaching the straps. She looks him in the eye and at the same time stretches out a hand towards the trouser pocket where he keeps his wallet. I'm watching and sweating. I have a horrible presentiment. I don't like this fellow's face, he's got eyes like a sick wolf and I'm sure he's going to notice what's going on at any moment.

In fact, as soon as Peppina's taken the wallet and passed it to me, at the very moment when I take it into my hand, this mangy wolf wakes up. He starts yelling. Orders the tram to stop.

'What's up?' they ask.

'My wallet's been stolen,' he says, and rolls those horrible sick animal's eyes.

'Who took it?' they ask.

The wolf lowers one of his fat little arms and points at me. 'It

155

was her,' he says. By this time I had dropped the wallet, but it had got caught up in my coat. So they nicked me and took me in.

I saw my friend getting off the train; she was in a right old panic. She was afraid I'd put the blame on her and have her arrested. But I didn't. I took all the blame and that was the end of it. I said to myself: What's the point of getting us both into trouble?

The moment they'd clapped me into jail they said, 'You will be brought up for summary trial at once.' I thought: If it's a summary trial, I'm sure to be convicted. What can I do, without a lawyer or anything?

Then one of the cons, by the name of Pina, says to me, 'You know what you should do? Drink some lemon tea, keep the rind of the lemon in your mouth, chew it all up and then, when the nun comes along, pretend to vomit.'

So that's what I do. I take the lemon tea, then I start yelling: 'Ow, ow, the pain, it's terrible!'

Pina calls the nun and says, 'She's feeling ill, sister.'

Lella of the Angels, the nun from the infirmary, comes along. 'What's the complaint?' she says.

'Ow,' I say, 'I can feel a stabbing pain here, it's nearly killing me!' I've got the lemon rind all mushed up in my mouth, so I pretend to vomit, spitting it all out. And the nun sends me straight off to the hospital.

As usual, I wind up in San Giovanni and they operate on me for appendicitis. The other times, when I had been really ill, they didn't operate, but this time, when there was nothing wrong with me, they cut me up!

They made an incision a foot long. I thought: My God! What'll happen when they find out I haven't got this here appendix? I didn't know what an appendix was, I thought it was a kind of little tree that grew inside your belly when you were ill. If I'm well, I thought, the little tree can't be in there. However, it seems there was one, and they took it out.

There was supposed to be a general amnesty about that time – everybody was waiting for it like manna from heaven. But no. I got done for two years, in spite of the operation. There was an amnesty all right, but it didn't apply to me.

So once again I found myself back in Rebibbia with my old friends: Tina, Giulia, Marisa, the gypsies. A few had left. Others, like me, had been released and nicked again. There were some new ones, mostly very young girls in on drugs charges, or women in for soliciting. But the drugs lot kept to themselves, they didn't mix with us old cons, the recidivists.

One of these drugs girls was an extremely beautiful blonde. She must have been nineteen or twenty. She was always closeted in her cell because she was afraid of being assaulted. And, as a matter of fact, five of them had set upon her the night she arrived. One of the nuns rescued her and locked her in an empty cell. The older cons propositioned her, offered her food. But she was rich, she didn't need anything. Every day she received parcels, food, letters. And the nuns treated her like a lady, they were deferential to her. They brought her mineral water, cough syrup and pepper-mint drops because she said she had a sore throat. They tele-phoned her mother for her and later this mother arrived, carry-ing a box of cream cakes for the nuns.

Sister Isabel, known as Big Isabel, is mad about cakes. She's got a sweet tooth but the rest of her is bitter, especially her hands – they're vicious, always hitting out. One word out of place and she wallops you. She's always walloping somebody. She must have hit me a thousand times.

Ercoletto was in prison, and so was my brother Orlando. Nobody sent me anything. I didn't even have the cash to buy a fag. Luckily I was great friends with all the old cons in there, and they knew all the dodges, they had plenty of food. I made them laugh, told them stories, and in exchange they gave me a mouthful of meat, a little cake or half a cigarette.

Whenever he was out, Orlando helped me. But it seemed to work out that each time I got nicked, he was in the boot too. We were both inside and couldn't help one another. We two always got caught. Even as small children, we were always the ones who got the strap from father, our big brothers or our grandmother.

I had never given a shit about sleeping on the floor, or in a cave, or out in the rain. It didn't bother me, I just said, 'Well, I'm tough!' But strength can drain away and now, because of all the damp I'd taken, I got arthritis in my kidneys.

My liver, too, is a bit dicey. My ovaries have been frozen. One tooth is missing. In short, I am not what I was any more. Orlando is ill, too. His heart doesn't work any more, not properly. He said he wouldn't go back to prison for anything in the world. He set up with this woman, she's a dwarf and half-blind. Then he got done for fraud and they chucked him inside again.

# 23

A second amnesty came round and I was released after serving five months. Ercoletto was still inside. I didn't have a home any more. For a while, I went to live with Vanda, a friend from the Bar Bengasi.

For the first few days I couldn't do a thing. I stayed in bed, slept, ate, drank, smoked and that was all. Vanda was kind, she didn't say a word. But I knew it couldn't last. She had her work, her men, and sooner or later I would either have to leave or pay my share of expenses.

I put on a little weight, had my fill of sleeping and smoking. One morning I got up and went back to the Bar Bengasi. I met a few friends. 'Where's Gianni?' I asked them.

'Inside.'

'And Gino?'

'Inside too.'

Quite a lot were in the nick. But not the women, they were working. So I team up with these women, especially two that I got on well with, Ines and Violetta, who was known as Angel-Fingers, because her hands were so slick, so skilful at stealing.

We went dipping. Doing handbags. Ines and I kept watch and helped, while Angel-Fingers slipped in and did her sleight-of-hand. She could take the socks off a man's feet while he was still wearing his shoes, and he wouldn't even notice. She was almost as smart as Dina.

Well, the three of us go dipping, on trams, buses, or in the big stores. When there's a crowd, it's easy. Ines, who has an eye as sharp as a needle, tips me the wink. That means she's seen someone with a bag just asking to be done. Then I get close to her, size up the situation, follow her step by step, try her out with a little shove. That way, I can see whether she's suspicious, or up in the clouds, or in a hurry.

When it looks like a piece of cake, I give Angel-Fingers the go-ahead sign. She comes up to us, and I go away to keep an eye on the victim and on the shop assistant. Ines, meanwhile, is standing on the stairs, surveying the whole interior of the shop.

Angel-Fingers, as dignified as a duchess, opens the woman's bag, slips out the wallet with two fingers and even closes the bag up again. Then, slowly and serenely, she moves away and I move in behind her. Outside, we split up and make our way to the appointed meeting place separately. There, we open the wallet and share out.

For a month, we had terrific luck. Every day we got a good stash. Not huge sums, about 10,000 or 15,000 lire a time. But it was very gratifying. I left Vanda's and took a room on my own, furnished it and settled in.

The following month, we got the Evil Eye on us. Angel-Fingers nicked three or four wallets a day and they were all empty. One thousand lire, two at the most, sometimes not even that. What was there to share out, between three of us? We began to feel the pinch of hunger.

Then Angel-Fingers says: 'I tell you what we'll do today, we'll nick a nice big *mortadella*. I've got a craving for *mortadella*. We'll have a right old blow-out, I haven't had anything but bread and water for four days.'

We go into a big delicatessen near the Casilina. Angel-Fingers says: 'Teresa, you'd better do the job here, it's not a matter of slipping wallets out but of grabbing that *mortadella* and running like hell.'

'All right,' I say, 'I'll do it.' And all three of us go into this shop.

Angel-Fingers takes the shop-assistant to one side and asks, 'How much is this *mortadella*?'

'Four thousand lire,' he says.

'Very well,' she says, 'but you'll let me have discount, won't you? If I'm satisfied with the service I get here I'll send my mother to you, too, she lives near here, and so you will acquire two new customers.'

She keeps talking to him, wasting his time, confusing him.

'How much is this ham?' she says. 'Is it really mountain ham? And is it very salty?'

'No, no,' says the boy, 'it's lovely and sweet, I can guarantee it.' He was a dope, he didn't know his job.

While Angel-Fingers is yakking to him, I choose a moment when the shop is empty, grab a *mortadella* and run. The boy sees me and starts after me at once. Meanwhile, Ines and Angel-Fingers saunter out casually, and head for home as if they haven't a care in the world.

When I run, I go like the wind, and I soon shook off the shop-assistant. Half an hour later we all met up again on via Prenestina. Angel-Fingers came with a boy-friend, Pasquale. He had a Fiat 600. We all got in and drove out to the country.

We stop in a dry, scrubby field, covered with garbage. 'It stinks!' I say, 'why do we have to stop here, of all places? Let's drive on a bit.'

'No,' she says, 'this is fine. I know the place. People come here to rummage through the garbage, so, if they see someone eating, they won't be suspicious.'

We sat down in a semi-circle on the ground, all amongst that half-burned rubbish and the greasy smoke that poured out of the piles of old tin cans, broken china and so on. Pasquale took out his knife and started slicing the *mortadella*. It was a big one, nearly two feet long, and it weighed about four pounds.

Pasquale handed round the slices. Angel-Fingers crammed her mouth full. When it comes to eating, she's worse than I am, she was so greedy she couldn't stuff it down her throat fast enough. We ate one slice each, two, three . . . four . . . another and another. I couldn't eat another mouthful. It was hard work swallowing that *mortadella* without bread or wine, though it was of prime quality.

Angel-Fingers ate more than anyone, she ate almost half of it all by herself. 'What a scrumptious bellyful of *mortadella*!' she said. 'Do you know how long I've been dreaming of it? Every night in prison this *mortadella* would come into my head, and I kept saying: "The moment I'm out, I'm going to eat *mortadella* till I burst." Well, here we are, and I've had my wish at last!'

But even she was bloated. We were all bursting, overstuffed. 'What shall we do with the rest of the *mortadella*?' she said.

'Let's keep it for later,' I said. But Pasquale, who, like me, was forty years old, though he was as playful as a boy, took a piece of *mortadella* and threw it at my head. So I took another bit and slapped him round the face with it. Then Angel-Fingers joined in. It became the Battle of the Mortadella. The fat smeared our hands, our faces, our hair, we were worse than a gang of kids playing truant. We enjoyed ourselves. Bits of *mortadella* were whizzing through the air like shuttlecocks and we laughed till we were helpless.

That same day, when we went back to Pizza Vittorio, I ran into a girl-friend of mine, Nicolina. 'Listen, Teresa,' she says, 'you've got to do me a favour.'

'What sort of favour?' I ask.

'Well, I had this boy-friend and he sucked me dry, took my last lira off me. I'll confess the whole story to you. I even lived in whorehouses for this fellow, brothels in Milan and Turin. I did the rounds. I managed to earn as much as 100,000 lire a day, but I had to give him 90,000 out of that. He left me just enough to scrape along on, barely that. So I had it out with him. I said: "Natalino dear, we can't go on like this. I do all the work and you gobble up all the money." So, to console me, he took me out in his red Jaguar, we had lunch in a posh restaurant with his friends. He introduced me as his fiancée. And I was happy. But then things went on as before. He treated me like dirt and took ninety per cent of what I earned.'

'But he was protecting you, Nicolina!' I say.

'He protected me,' she replies, 'but at a price! Sometimes I didn't even have the money to buy stockings, I went around with ladders in them.'

'Well, now, what's this favour you want me to do?' I say.

'Wait,' she says, 'I'm telling you. I loved this fellow, I put up with all his beastliness. Then one day I saw him with another woman, a new girl, and out of jealousy I denounced him, charged him with pimping.'

'What! You might as well have put a noose round his neck! What will the people of silence* say? Don't you know it's taboo to betray someone? It's an infamous thing to do, you'll be an outcast!'

'Yes,' she says, 'and afterwards I was sorry for what I'd done, especially because of Natalino's father. He's an old man and he keeps coming to me and weeping over his son. He says Christmas is coming, the mother is longing to see her son, and the boy is

* The Mafia (translator's note)

miserable in prison, he cries all the time; he says prison is intolerable for someone who's never been there before. He's begging me to withdraw the charges.'

'Do it, then!' I say. 'If you don't, you know how our people will condemn you, they'll spit in your face, they'll shun you. Besides, we live in a world of vendetta, it won't be safe for you to walk about.'

She says, 'I'll withdraw it, I've made up my mind, but I want them to give me the money I paid out for the case, for the lawyer, Ammazzavacca.'

'And where do I come in?' I ask.

'Let me explain,' she says. 'You must go and see the old man – he's in the market, stall number twelve. And you say to him: "Nicolina wants to speak to you." '

'Well, if that's all there is to it, I'll do it for you. But afterwards I'll clear off and leave you alone with him, I don't want to get involved,' I say.

So I act as mediator. I go to this old man and tell him about Nicolina. I say to him, 'See if you can mend matters, she seems willing enough to withdraw the charge, but she wants you to reimburse her for the money she's shelled out for the lawyer. If you give her half-a-million, she'll do what you want.'

The old man says, 'As long as she withdraws the charge of pimping, she'll get her half-million all right. You will be witness and sign the papers, together with her, then everything will be in order.'

We made an appointment to meet in a bar on the following day. I went to pick up Nicolina and the two of us went to the rendezvous to collect the money and sign the statement withdrawing all charges.

This old man, Balocca, comes into the bar. He was a handsome, solemn looking old man. 'Would you like a coffee?' he says.

'No, no,' I say, 'let's get the business over and done with quickly.'

'I've got the half-million ready,' he says, 'but first Nicolina must sign this paper for me.'

He pulls out a stamped document with these words written on it: 'I, the undersigned, Nicolina Gasperoni, declare that I laid charges against Natalino Balocca only as an act of jealousy, and I further declare that it is not true that he acted as a procurer and lived off my immoral earnings. Personal jealousy was the sole motive for my previous denunciation.'

Then he says, 'Here, Teresa, you sign below as a witness that I have given her the 500,000 lire.'

'But where is it, this 500,000 lire?' says Nicolina, 'we haven't seen it yet.'

The old man pulls out a bundle of notes. 'Here's your half-a-million,' he says, 'but first sign the paper, then I'll give it to you.' So she signs and I sign below her signature.

No sooner have we signed than wham, bam! the door flies open and in come the fuzz. Balocca scarpers with the signed document and the money. And we're marched off to the police station.

'I haven't done a thing,' I say, 'I'm just a witness.' And I told them the whole story, just as it happened. But the filth wouldn't listen to me. They paid no attention whatsoever. Nevertheless, I didn't get excited, I kept quite calm because I thought they were bound to release me, it was nothing to do with me. Witnessing is not an offence.

But they put us both inside for extortion. And extortion is no joke, they'll give you five or six years for it, easy as kiss my arse. Yet I hadn't done any extorting. I just couldn't swallow the idea that they'd put me way for six years, just for signing as an innocent witness!

Ercoletto was almost due to come out. I thought: Now, if he hears that I'm inside again, he'll abandon me. He'll find himself another woman. And, in any case, my home will be broken up. The moment I go inside, my place will be looted and I'll have to start from scratch again. It seems that, for me, having a home brings bad luck. Every time I get a home together, my friends come along, green-eyed, jealous. 'Oh, how lovely! Where did you buy this? Where did you buy that? What a lovely bedroom suite!' And they put the Evil Eye on me, with their envy they destroy me. Then, the minute I'm in jail, they rush into my house and get their claws on everything, clean it out, so that when I come out there's not so much as a pin left.

# 24

In prison, I felt like a damned soul. For six months I'd been shut up in there and still they hadn't brought me to trial.

For the first time I found it impossible to settle down in peace. I couldn't stomach being shut up. I fought all the time, lashing out at everybody in sight.

As for that wretched Nicolina, I really had it in for her. 'Look what a mess that bloody fool's got me into!' I said, and to her: 'Listen, you half-wit, can't you at least call up the judge and tell him I had nothing to do with it?'

'It's not my fault,' she said, 'I'm not to blame.'

'I did you a favour,' I said, 'and I asked nothing in return, isn't that the truth?'

'Right,' she said.

'You see? I didn't ask for anything and you didn't give me anything, I just wanted to help you. Now I'm locked up in here for your sake.'

Sister Carmina of the hard hands came along. 'Shut up, Teresa,' she said in that gravelly voice of hers.

I said, 'You should just try being in my shoes! When I've done something wrong, I resign myself to my fate, but when I haven't, no!'

'Shut up, you old con!' She wouldn't believe I was innocent.

Those were six painful months. I couldn't eat, I hardly spoke. I lay on my bunk brooding. The more I thought about it, the angrier I became. I thought of Ercoletto, who was out by this time – God knows what he was up to.

He didn't send me parcels, he didn't write. He had deserted

me. Orlando was still in prison but I didn't know where. I felt very bitter. The nuns would come in and fling open the windows. 'Get up, Teresa, don't pretend you're sick because no one will believe you!' But I wasn't ill, I was sick at heart. Fed up with life.

My friends understood. They came to my cell now and then to bring me a fag. Even Nicolina came, but I chased her out. I didn't want to see her, even though I knew she had been tricked, same as I had.

I lay there with my eyes closed, but I didn't sleep. Not even at night; I couldn't. I was depressed, half out of my mind and I didn't feel like doing anything. I got up to eat, swallowed half a spoonful of soup and went back to bed. The nun said to me, 'You'll get six years, and serve you right! You're a thoroughly bad lot and God knows what wickedness you and that prostitute Nicolina have been up to!'

I said, 'I'm not doing six years in here when I'm not guilty of any crime. I'd rather kill myself.' And in fact one morning I took a sheet, twisted it into a rope, made a noose, knotted it, tied it to the window-bars and hanged myself.

At that moment Anna Bordoni, who was one of the nun's little pets, happened to pass by. I had calculated that nobody would be about just then, they'd all be in the exercise yard. But this Anna goes by on her way to the toilet – she's got a sudden, urgent desire to go; she glances into my cell and her eyes come out on stalks when she sees me hanging there with my tongue sticking out. She starts screaming, calling people. The nuns come running, get me down, untie the knot, give me injections.

I was out. Dead. But they brought me back to life. They wanted to save me. My neck was all black and blue. My throat hurt, I couldn't even swallow my own saliva. My face was covered in blotches. I don't know how they managed to pull me round. It seems I'm hard to kill.

After that, they were always on my back. They never left me alone for a minute. They shut me up in the infirmary with Lella of the Angels. She never took her eyes off me.

One morning, after I've been in there eight months, Sister Innocenza comes to me and says, 'Teresa, you're free! They've admitted that you're innocent.' After eight months!

'You can go now, you're released,' she says.

'Is it true? It's not just an excuse to send me somewhere else?'

165

'If I say so, you can believe it!' she says.

I said, 'How come they've released me?'

She said, 'You've been acquitted because there is no case against you. Judge Dell'Alba committed a judicial error.'

'There you are!' I said, 'I told you it was an error! Extortion is something that's done secretly, at gun-point, not in a bar with officially-stamped documents, witnesses and all.'

So I came out. Everybody admitted it was a judicial error, on the part of the police as much as the judge. It was a certain Judge Giustiniani who recognised the mistake. He re-examined the case and acknowledged that there had been an error. That's why they let me go. Nicolina was freed too.

I come out and go looking for Ercoletto straight away. I'm thinking: Who knows how many times that wretch has put the horns on my head? He didn't know I was coming out so soon, any more than I did. Meantime, he'd gone to live at his sister's house.

Hearing this news from friends, I immediately went to Alba's place, but the porter told me she didn't live there any more. 'Where have they gone?' I asked.

'I don't know,' he said, 'I think they've moved to the country, but I couldn't tell you where.'

So I took a taxi and went to Quarto Miglio where Ercoletto's brother lived. 'Biagio,' I said, 'do you know where Ercoletto is? Where is he living?'

'He just left here a minute ago,' he said, 'on his Lambretta.'

'Where's he gone?'

'To Alba's.'

'And where's that?'

'Down at the Batteria Nomentana.' And he told me how to get there.

I go down the stairs and run into Annuccia, Ercoletto's niece, in the hallway. 'Come on, I'll buy you an ice cream,' I say. This Annuccia is thirteen.

'How thin you are, Auntie!' she says, 'where shall we go for the ice cream?'

I take her to a nice confectioner's and buy her a big ice cream for 100 lire. Then I ask her, 'Has your uncle Ercoletto seen anything of that Cesira lately, the one with the baby?'

She says, 'The other evening he took her to the cinema, but I don't know where they went afterwards.'

When she said that, I did my nut. I was furious, fit to be tied. I said, 'OK, goodbye!'

Then she said, 'Will you buy me another ice cream, Auntie? I told you what you wanted to know, didn't I?'

'Annuccia, you're a hustler,' I said, 'you're following in your father's footsteps.'

I took a bus to the Batteria Nomentana. It was already dark when I got there. It was winter, just after Christmas. I walked around till I found the street. I found the house, went in, climbed the stairs, stopped on the landing in front of the door. I was just going to knock when I heard voices – Alba's and Ercoletto's: they were talking about me and Orlando.

'That Orlando claims his sister's belongings are his by right,' said Alba, 'the car is his, the furniture is his, everything's his. But you must do something quick,' she said to her brother, 'or he'll have the lot off you. The stuff is yours, you and Teresa bought it together.' She was provoking him.

'Ach,' said Ercoletto, 'if Orlando doesn't lay off I'll punch him on the nose one of these days.'

Alba said, 'That Teresa's just as bad, she's a troublemaker, too. She always makes a mess of things and gets herself arrested. Who told her to go and witness that document? She's got no brains, Teresa, no brains at all.'

I listened for a while then I got fed up with it and started knocking: bang, bang, bang! There was no bell.

'Who is it?'

'It's me, Teresa!' My nerves were all on edge after listening to them speak ill of me.

They open the door. I go in. 'Well, well!' they say, 'look who's here!'

'Right!' I say, 'have you finished tearing me to pieces? I've been listening to you for an hour. I heard every word.'

'But why are you mad at me?' says Ercoletto, and he embraces me.

I say, 'You've got a nerve to embrace me after all you've been saying about me? Do you think I'm deaf? I heard it all, and now I'm off, this is no place for me.'

I open the door and pretend I'm leaving. Ercoletto grabs hold of me. 'Where are you off to?' he says, 'you're crazy! Come on now, where do you think you're going on a freezing cold night

167

like this?' And he locks the door. 'Come on,' he says, 'let's go to bed.'

We fought all night long. I didn't want to make love. I said, 'I'm not staying with you any longer, I'm not sharing my man with anyone.' And I pretended I meant it.

'Where are you going, then? Out on the roof?' he said.

For several days, I refused to let him make love to me, because I was certain he'd been with Cesira again. He said, 'But you know you're the only woman I love!'

'Drop dead!' I said. 'Go back to her, because I'm sick of you, sick of her, sick of everything! I've had a husband of my own, I don't need your name, thanks very much!'

Ercoletto said, 'I would have married you, you know that, if you hadn't been married already. In fact, I'm still willing, right now, if you like!'

And it's true that, now my husband, Sisto, is dead, he would be happy to marry me. But I didn't want to. 'Marry you!' I said, 'what would that make me – a queen? I don't give a shit for you and your name!'

The fact is, I don't want to remarry because I'm still hoping they will give me my husband's pension, the railwayman's pension. 'Anyway,' I said, 'I'm old now, what do I care about getting married?'

Well, after Ercoletto had gone on begging and imploring me for some time, we finally made love again, and I was glad because he is my man and he makes me very happy. He said, 'As for Cesira, I don't give a damn for her, I swear to you. If I'd wanted to, I could have married her by now, couldn't I?'

He was so persuasive, with those gentle manners of his, that fond smile, that in the end he convinced me, we made our peace and started living together again in love and harmony.

Later on I found out he was still seeing Cesira, because of the baby. He even brought the kid to our house. Now he's grown-up, and last year he went off to be a soldier. I've got a photo of him. He's a good-looking boy. A rascal, always demanding money and more money. He eats a lot, laughs a lot, often gets drunk. With him, it's all wine, women and song. That's the way he is, the sensual devil.

He worked as a painter, then as a waiter. He got a job in a restaurant but he played the fool and they gave him the sack.

Then he went to work in a studio where they made statuettes from coral and jade. He got the bullet from that place, too.

Wherever he goes, he gets into fights. They even found him a hospital job, serving out meals, taking round food and coffee to the patients. But he got into a scrap there, as well. It's all laughter and good times till he suddenly flies into a rage. He's always pulling people's legs; sometimes they get huffy, then he takes offence and it turns into a punch-up.

The mother, Cesira, is a bit lame. She works as a maid. She's a scatterbrained creature and when it comes to eating she's even worse than me, she's greedy. She's two or three years younger than me, but she's let herself go, she's tatty, a pathetic-looking object. Ugly, too. The first time I saw her, I said to Ercoletto: 'Crikey! I don't admire your taste!'

'Well,' he said, 'what of it? I was stuck way out in the country and this girl came along and slept with me. We were at it day and night, so what can you expect? Naturally, this kid was born. If she'd behaved herself, I would have married her, not for her sake, because she turns my stomach, but for the child's.'

'Aha, now you despise her,' I said, 'but you didn't despise her at first, did you? Men are all the same, they treat everybody like dirt. First you fancied her and now you cast her off, but, you know, you haven't grown any prettier over the years, either.'

Cesira, when you come down to it, isn't all that plain. She's in a bad state, that's all. But he fancied her, I know he did, and I'm certain they made love while I was in clink.

But she certainly put the horns on him later. She even had an abortion. Then she swore she'd been faithful to him, she wept and carried on. She's a bloody liar. But Ercoletto heard that she'd had the abortion at the Policlinico, so he went there and checked up. Yes, they told him, she had indeed had a miscarriage. And after that he left her, he despised her, he wouldn't believe a word she said.

They had taken her to the Policlinico because she had started haemorrhaging. They scraped her womb and took out her ovaries. That's why she couldn't have any more children. Otherwise, who knows, I might have found Ercoletto with another son when I came out of prison.

She wanted to have another kid. She would have given her right arm to have one by Ercoletto, and he wanted it too. Ercoletto loves babies and he'd have had dozens if he could.

He would have loved to have a child by me. I would have loved it too, but because of that inflammation, that peritonitis, when they froze my ovaries, I can't have any more babies. He would give his life to have a child by me.

# 25

We started trading in oil and household linens again. We bought and sold, never earning very much, but at least it was regular. We managed to rent a house on the via Tuscolana. It was a pretty little house with a verandah. We paid 15,000 a month for it.

There were four of us going around together, Ercoletto and me, Giulietto and Lalla, two friends from the Bar Bengasi. We had a car, a second-hand 1100 that had done more than 190,000 miles, though it still went like a bomb. It was bright blue. The only trouble was, it had a perpetual thirst, it drank petrol like nobody's business.

One day, we were travelling in the direction of Littoria with our two friends. We stopped in Nettuno to pick up a parcel of linen and some money, but we couldn't find our contact man. The porter said, 'Come back later, he's not here at the moment.'

The fellow we were looking for was a Neapolitan who bought wholesale and dealt in smuggled goods. 'Shall we have a look round Nettuno while we're waiting?' I said. The others agreed.

It was cold, the place was deserted, even the dogs had gone to earth. We had some coffee and went back to the warehouse. A clerk told us our man was not back yet.

We go for another tour round, but this time we take the road down to the beach. We stop the car. I go down to the sea. It was green, foaming, the whole surface ruffled into little waves. It was that sea that was so familiar to me, the sea I had known at Anzio when I was little. I was like a child again, gazing at this dark and restless sea. As I'm walking along, lost in thought, I catch a glimpse of something white, a kind of bundle it looks like, sticking out from behind a rock. I take a closer look. I realise it's two naked human legs. Oh, God, it's a dead body! I say to myself. Going still closer, I see an old man and an old woman, they must be eighty years old apiece, stark naked, white as snow, clasped together, locked one inside the other. In the extremity of their passion, they don't even notice me. I think to myself: Good God, look how ugly they are! And I start climbing up the dunes at a run.

I get back into the car and tell them what I've seen. 'Really?' they say, 'then let's all go back and play a joke on the old folks, we'll embarrass them!'

Ercoletto says, 'Oh, let them be! If they're making love in this freezing cold, they must be madly in love.'

Giulietto insists. 'Let's go down and pinch their clothes!' he says.

Lalla starts laughing. 'Yes, come on!' she says, but I say, 'It's late, let's go home!'

In the end, the cold won. We stayed in the car, chatting and joking, smoking cigarettes for a while, then we went back to Nettuno to look for the Neapolitan.

But he wasn't there, and the clerk couldn't tell us when he'd be back. Later on we heard that he had absconded with all the money in the till, 2,600,000 lire. He stole it from his partners.

'It's late,' said Giulietto, 'what shall we do? We haven't even got enough money to buy a sandwich. How much have you got?' I had 300 lire, Ercoletto 500, Lalla 600. We bought a few litres of petrol and set out again.

We had 50 lire left. We were approaching Littoria. 'I'm starving,' I said, 'let's stop at a café and buy a bit of bread with this 50 lire.' We drove slowly, looking for a refreshment place.

We found a little tumbledown trattoria with rickety tables, a pergola and chairs blackened with rain. The door was open. I went in. 'Signora!' I call out, 'is there anybody here?' It's about half past three by now. They'll have gone for their siesta, I think. I call again. 'Signora! Signora!' but nobody appears.

Standing in the middle of this trattoria there's a huge refrigerator with a big door all stained with rust. I go up to it, open it, stick my head inside. There's a lobster lying on a plate and, beside it, a boiled fowl and some chicory. I grab the lobster and the chicken and run like lightning.

I get back into the car and say, 'Quick, let's get going! Step on it!'

'What's up?' They thought I had nicked some money. When they saw the chicken instead, they were disappointed. 'What are we going to do with that hen?' they said.

'What do you mean?' I said, 'we're going to eat it, of course!'

And while the car was speeding along towards Rome, we broke the chicken into portions and shared it out. We wolfed it down greedily. We hadn't eaten since one o'clock the previous day. That chicken brought us back to life.

Then we split the lobster. The boiled flesh was white, plump, succulent. We divided it into four equal portions. Giuletto said, 'Give me a claw to suck!'

'Me, too!' said Lalla, and we started tearing off the claws, which snapped off with a sharp clack! And we burst out laughing.

We laughed and we guzzled. Ercoletto said, 'I'd love to be there and see the owner's face when she opens the door and finds the fridge empty. She'll say, "What on earth's happened to my chicken? Has it flown away? And the lobster! It must have swum away"!' And we all laughed like mad, we laughed so much that we couldn't eat.

Back in Rome a few days later Ercoletto said to me, 'I'm going home to Sant'Agata to take a headstone for my father's grave. I made a promise at the time of his death, and I must keep it.'

'All right,' I said, 'when will you be back?'

'Couple of days, three at the most.'

'Are you taking the train?'

'No, the car. I'm going with two friends, Nino and Ciapparelli.'

'All right, then,' I said, 'goodbye!'

And so they set off, him and his two friends, carrying the marble headstone with them. They went to the cemetery, set up the stone, and started on the return journey.

On the road, soon after they'd left Sant'Agata, they stopped for a bite to eat. And there, in a little village, they spot a shop that sells fabrics, and there's no one keeping an eye on the goods except the manageress. It's that dead hour of the day, about two o'clock.

So they get the idea of pulling a job. Nino goes in and starts spinning some yarn to the manageress, he flirts, butters her up,

173

pretends to fall in love with her. In the end, he persuades her to come round to the back of the shop and smoke a fag with him.

While she's outside with Nino, Ercoletto and Ciaparelli load three or four rolls of cloth into the car, in frantic haste, ready to make their get-away the minute she returns.

But the woman noticed; she took a scrap of paper and wrote down the registration number of the car. When they saw what she was doing, Ciapparelli got out and snatched the paper out of her hand.

That's the story they told me, anyway. Ercoletto said, 'We're not worried. That fool couldn't have written down the number, we snatched it out of her hand at once.'

But, in fact, the woman had written the number on the palm of her hand. I learned all this later. I don't even know whether it was true that Ercoletto went to put up the headstone on his father's grave in the cemetery of Sant-Agata, in the Abruzzi, though he says he did.

If only they had told me sooner, I would have gone to the police station and reported that the car had been stolen; in that way, I would have been clear of all involvement. But the car was registered in my name. And out of sheer funk, Ercoletto kept his mouth shut.

So they dropped me in it, too.

Then I found out that these idiots had even gone back to the shop. The truth only came out bit by bit. They turned back because they were afraid the woman might have memorised the number of the car.

They gave all the stuff back to her, they even apologised. They tried to ingratiate themselves with her by saying, 'Please excuse our friend, my dear lady, he's a lunatic, he's been in the asylum. He has a mania for putting everything he sees into the car. He's a kleptomaniac.' They made out Ercoletto was a nut-case to excuse themselves. And they gave back every last bit of cloth.

The manageress was furious. She wanted not only the cloth but compensation money as well, the greedy bitch! They told her they hadn't taken any money. And she said, 'But I'm 8000 lire short in the till.' In the end, just to keep her quiet, they gave her the 8000 lire. They went there to con her, and she conned them instead!

As soon as they'd gone, she reported them to the police. And the fuzz came looking for me. They didn't find me, though,

174

because I hadn't reported my last change of address. Otherwise I'd have been nicked at once, because the car was in my name.

They caught Ercoletto a few weeks later. They traced him through me, and he was arrested at his sister's house. That Abruzzese bitch recognised him and he got done for six months.

# 26

I was trying to find out where my brother Orlando had been sent. The last letter had come from Soriano del Cimino. So I took the train and went to this place, Soriano, but they told me there was no Orlando Numa there.

'Where's he been transferred to?' I asked.

'We don't know. Apply to the Ministry.'

I went to the Ministry but they didn't know anything either. 'Ask at Police Headquarters,' they said. At Police Headquarters they sent me from one office to another and finally threw me out.

That very day I received a letter from him. My heart melted when I saw the envelope with his writing scrawled all over it. But when I read the letter it upset me no end:

'Dearly beloved sister, They transferred me from Soriano to the prison at Palliano, but even there I didn't last long because I complained to the *maresciallo,* La Cosa, about the uneatable food, and this man had me tied to the restraining bed. They left me there for a week, tightly bound, half off my head with rage. You can imagine how I suffered. When they untied me, my arms were paralysed, my bottom was covered in weals, my wrists and ankles lacerated by the cords. And I was so weak I could not stand up. So they put me out in the yard to get some sun and somebody, out of pity, gave me some tinned meat. In that yard I found a cat that had just had kittens. I took a black kitten and looked after it. By good luck. I have managed to keep it with me until now. But, as this La Cosa wouldn't leave me in peace, and I kept needling him, too, on account of this lousy food that was worse than the muck they give to pigs, he had me tied to the restraining bed again. After two days, however, I succeeded in freeing myself; I pinched a knife from the kitchen and took refuge on the roof. A prison officer and a lifer came up to get me, there was a ferocious struggle. I stabbed the con in the chest and wounded the *brigadiere* in the left arm. About an hour later, they caught me and put me in a padded cell. I stayed in there for seven days, then they sent me back to Porto Azzurro, And that's where I am now.

'I've made friends with a fellow called Ezio Nardini. Three weeks went by, and then I got into a fight with a con by the name of Rebecchini, another one called Ciccotti and two lifers because they kicked my little cat: punishment cell and bread and water for fifteen days. During this time a friend of Ezio's came to my cell and gave me a couple of tomatoes. The guard noticed and came in to take them away from me, but I gobbled them down quick. It was very cold, I was lying on the plank-bed: the guard, whose name was Panetti, was enraged by my swallowing the tomatoes, so he threw a jug of cold water over me. I bided my time, and one afternoon, pretending to feel ill, I got them to call Panetti to my cell. I threw a pot full of urine and shit right in his face; ten minutes later, his colleagues came in and beat me up. Four days after that, the governor summoned me to a disciplinary council. In the waiting-room I met La Parca, the bandit, who's serving two life sentences and three thirty-year stretches. I had a home-made fag and, when I asked him for a light, he didn't say a word, he just slapped my face with all his strength. I had my interview with the governor, then they took me back to a cell, which was already occupied by a couple of Neapolitans. My cheek was still red and inflamed. I asked one of these fellows to lend me a knife, so that I could hide a bit of tobacco and some fag papers in the heel of my shoe. A few minutes later La Parca came along and saw me with the knife in my hand. Thinking it's for him, he calls me a coward and comes at me with a piece of broken glass; we stalked round and round each other till I stabbed him three times in the chest and he fell to the floor. They called the guards and rushed him off to hospital. He's still lying there, wounded, and I hope he stays there a long time.

'How is Ercoletto, and how are you, my dearest sister? I'll find some means of sending the cat to you, because if it stays here somebody is sure to cook it, if only out of spite, as I am not very popular. I hope to see you soon. Come and visit me, and bring something for me as I am short of everything here, and I am wasting away. With much love, your brother Orlando.'

That was how the letter ended. Immediately, I stirred my stumps, trying to rustle up a little money. Then I bought a big cardboard suitcase and filled it with rice, biscuits, salami, dried fish, sugar, oil, wine, grapes and oranges. And I went to Porto Azzurro.

I found him on special punishment in the Polveriera, a dungeon below sea-level that was always damp and salty. There were two of them shut up in there, him and a friend. They told me at the entrance that he was in the punishment cell and couldn't come out. I said, 'But I'm his sister, I've come all the way from Rome, let me see him just for a minute!'

'Can't be done today,' they said, 'come back tomorrow morning at eight and ask the governor.'

'And where am I supposed to go now, carrying this case that weighs a ton?' They didn't even answer, they simply shut the door in my face.

I didn't have enough money to go to a hotel. Luckily I found some country people who let me have a bed very cheap, a huge bed with a mattress that must have been impregnated with the piss of four generations, because it gave off a violent stench.

Early next morning I presented myself at the fortress of Porto Azzurro, which used to be called Portolongone, and is known as the 'Living Tomb'.

I waited and waited and at last, towards midday, the governor received me. 'What do you want?' he says.

'I've come to see my brother, Orlando Numa.'

'That thug! Don't you mention his name to me, get out of here, go away!'

Then I think to myself: I'll have to put on a big act here, or they'll send me back to Rome, suitcase and all. So I throw myself down on my knees, weeping, imploring, tearing my hair.

In the end, either to get rid of me or because the scene distressed him, the governor says, 'Very well, I'll have the prisoner called, but make it short and don't let me hear one more word about it.'

'Thank you, sir!' I say, 'you are very kind!' But he could tell I was saying it with my tongue in my cheek, and he sent me out with a kick from behind.

178

Anyway, at least I was allowed to see my poor unfortunate brother. He was nothing but skin and bone. Bits of skin flaked off his body the minute you touched him, his hair was all shorn off and his scalp covered with sores.

'How are you?' I said.

'In a bad way,' he replied.

'Don't they feed you?'

'Yes, potatoes.'

'Never any meat?'

'Twice a week.'

'Well, then,' I said, 'they treat you better than at the Mantellate.'

'Yes,' he said, 'but you can't imagine what the meat's like, it comes from the Argentine, it's frozen, dehydrated, God knows what. It stinks of medicine and it's tough and colourless.'

'How is it down in that powder-magazine?' I said.

'They keep us down there, half-naked, in that damp, salty atmosphere, and when we protest they throw cold water over us. But nobody rebels, they're all half-dead, they're afraid of the governor, De Martis – remember the name, he's the biggest tyrant in history!'

I said, 'I've noticed that. He wouldn't let me see you, I had to make a scene. I went down on my knees and at last he took pity on me.'

'That bastard doesn't pity anyone,' he said. 'He did it to get you off his back, or because you made him feel important. He might show you mercy, condescend like a king, but he'll make you humble yourself, make you grovel at his feet first. If you dare to raise your head, you're done for. That's why everybody here creeps about with their heads bowed, they're shit-scared.'

We were talking like this when the guard came up, seized Orlando by one shoulder and led him away without a word. He didn't protest, though, because he was delighted to have seen me, and even though he was going back to that dungeon in the powder-magazine of the fortress, at least he had some good nourishing food to take with him.

I had to walk the nine miles back to Portoferraio. From there, I took the train-ferry back to Rome. When I got home, I found a telegram saying my father was dying. I left for Anzio at once.

He was dead when I arrived. I found Lanky Dora playing the widow: stern-faced, all polished up.

179

'How did he die?' I said.

'Arthritis,' she said, 'your family disease. He was bed-ridden for a while, then he got thrombosis.'

In short, these two creatures from Friuli, Dora and her sister, had destroyed him. And he, too proud to ask advice, had let himself be conned by those two vipers. He had sold everything. He died as poor as a hermit.

When I came in, the house had already been cleared out, there was nothing left, not so much as a chair to sit on. In the middle of the room, which was suffocatingly hot, was the bed, and, on top of the bed, my father, and, on top of my father, the flies.

They had washed him, dressed him, combed his hair. He had shrunk away to nothing. They had put gleaming new shoes on his feet. I thought to myself: Well! As if they didn't make him march far enough on this earth, now they're going to make him march in the next world, too!

I looked at that hard, savage father of mine, proud as the devil himself. I tried to remember all the times he had taken the strap to me, beaten me with a stick, kicked and punched me, but I couldn't do it.

There was this pale, timid, clean-looking man, with a gentle face, his work-worn hands clutching a rosary of blue beads. His body was light, dried out, and his feet in those great big hikers' boots!

I said to him: 'Papà, they fucked you up, too! For all your strength, your roaring, your lashing out, you didn't manage to die like a lion. You look more like a plucked cockerel, and it was those two murdering females who wrung your neck. Rest in Peace. Amen.'

Lanky Dora looked at me. With her sleeves rolled up, she was washing the floor. 'Now,' she said, 'now you respect him, now that he's dead, you and your brothers and sisters! When he was alive, not one of you gave a bugger for your father, you left him stranded. Now that he's dead, you cry, you make your solemn faces!'

'Respect!' I said, 'what respect, you fool? And what did I ever get from my father except kicks and beatings? It's true my brothers have made money, they've become rich, they're gentlemen now, but I'm as poor as I ever was, so I couldn't have helped him even if I'd wanted to. And perhaps I wouldn't have wanted to, even if I was rich. He turned me out of the house, that father of mine, he left me to wander the streets like a stray dog. Or perhaps I would have helped him, as a grand gesture, who knows? Anyway, I don't owe you anything, you're nothing to me, neither mother nor sister.'

We started fighting, and it almost came to blows right there in front of the corpse. Luckily some people arrived and the old nag shut her mouth. All my brothers came, wearing dark suits and suitably mournful faces; their wives had all grown fat, dull, pompous.

They treated me like a leper, hardly deigning to glance my way. They shunned me. I said to myself: A fine lot you are! You're so busy hanging on to your money, you have no eyes for your brothers and sisters any more! You left me and Orlando to rot in prison, you washed your hands of us, and now you're afraid of getting contaminated. You really are fine ladies and gentlemen!

They said to me. 'You, our sister, have put yourself completely outside the law, that is why we do not acknowledge you as a member of the family.'

I said, 'Better an outlaw than a miserable, law-abiding, castrated bastard like you lot!'

During the funeral service, inside the church, they tried to make me sit to one side away from them all. After a while I'd had enough. I packed up my things and went back to Rome.

# 27

At the Bar Bengasi I made friends with a girl called Zina Teta, who was said to deal in travellers' cheques. One day when I was desperate, without a job, I went to her and said, 'Listen, I hear you deal in American cheques, is there any chance for me to get in on it?'

'Yes,' she said, 'as a matter of fact, I was looking for someone to help me.'

This Zina bought travellers' cheques off the dippers, at 20 per cent, then she used them to buy good stuff in the shops.

'But how do you manage to change them?' I asked, 'you have to have an American signature on here.'

'I'll teach you,' she said. And she showed me how to copy the genuine signature. You put the cheque on a piece of glass, with a strong light underneath, and you trace the name, with the flourishes and all. She was marvellous at it, she'd learned her craft. But I'm quick to learn and I soon got the hang of it, even though my fingers were a bit unsteady. Anyway, this Zina taught me, she gave me lessons and I went to work with her.

We worked hand-in-glove with a fellow called Pippo. This Pippo took us around in his car. He'd stop at the end of the street and say, 'Now, go into that goldsmith's, or into that shoe shop.' And I'd go. Sometimes Zina came with me, sometimes not.

'What about you, Pippo?' I say, 'don't you ever show your face?'

'I'm too well known,' he says. 'I wouldn't stand an ice-cream's chance in hell, but you're new to the job. Just walk in, buy something, and pay with a travellers' cheque.' And that's what I did.

This Zina helped me to dress like a lady. A lovely rose-pink coat, a crocodile handbag, a gold watch, a ruby ring (fakes, of course) – all to throw dust in the shopkeepers' eyes. Perfumed, elegant, I was as smart as a fashion-model.

All tarted up like this, I stroll along, stop in front of a shop window, look in, half-close my eyes as if I'm considering making a purchase. Then I go in. 'Listen,' I say, 'I'd like to buy that bracelet with the paste diamonds in it, but I don't have enough Italian money on me, would you accept foreign money?'

'What money?' they ask.

'American dollars. Do you take them?'

'Ah, yes,' they say, 'if it's dollars, we can accept them.' So I pull out a cheque-book. 'Oh, travellers' cheques?' they say.

'Yes, but they're still dollars.'

I see them hesitating. So, with an ingenuous air and an innocent voice, I say, 'My sister gave them to me, she's just come back from the States. I've changed some already and some I've left in dollars, well, in cheques, that is.'

'Just a moment,' they say, 'I'll ask my wife.'

Back he comes and says, 'All right, we will change them. Are they signed?'

'Yes,' I say, 'look, here's the signature.' And I put the cheque right under his nose with a confident air, casually, like someone who deals in travellers' cheques every day of the week. Then I say, 'Oh, while I'm here, I think I might take that pearl necklace, too. How much is it?'

When I see they're willing to accept them, I try to cash in quick. And, in fact, I get them to parcel up the paste bracelet and the pearl necklace, which is worth 300,000 on its own, and they even hand me the change: 10,000 lire.

'Thank you, *gud-bai*,' I say in English, and, without hurrying, pulling on my glacé kid gloves, I saunter towards the exit, as serene and unruffled as a princess.

Outside, I say to myself: My, my! What a smart girl I've become! I soon learned that trick! It was Dina who taught me to keep my cool, at the time when we were doing wallets together. The cooler you are, the less anyone suspects you. As long as you're smiling and serene, you could take the pants off a man while he's standing there, and he wouldn't even notice.

Zina was pleased. 'Well done, Teresa!' she said. 'I see you know what you're doing!' I was delighted. Then we took the jewellery to a fence. We divided the spoils in three, between Zina, Pippo and me.

It nearly always went off smoothly. The shopkeepers swallowed the bait. Sometimes they weren't keen to accept them, so I walked out, still very calm, but in a slight huff, like a society woman who feels she has been offended. I pulled the corners of my mouth down, very subtly, as much as to say: 'Just look at these stingy country clods who don't trust me!' And they'd get embarrassed. That pout of mine was a work of art, very convincing; I tried to imitate Tonino's grimace when I did it.

Sometimes I took articles worth 300,000 or even half a million lire. But it was easier with less expensive items, things worth 30 to 50,000 lire. At times, I changed as many as four of these small cheques in a day.

Then we hurried off to the fence – the Worm, or that other fellow at Santa Maria Maggiore, the one they called Christopher Columbus because he claimed to have discovered America. I don't know which America he meant, perhaps the America of Money. He certainly made a mint of money out of stolen goods. But he was very cagey and, if he saw us coming too often, he sent us away.

Occasionally the fences wouldn't take our stuff. Then we went to uncle's, pawned everything and sold the tickets. We were up to all sorts of tricks, just to ensure that a little bit of money was coming in regularly every day.

I thought to myself: I've found a good profession! The work is light, I enjoy myself and earn money without effort. It's true you need to have your wits about you, you had to be quick and cunning and know how to talk your way out of sticky situations. You needed the gift of the gab.

Meanwhile, I kept taking parcels to Ercoletto, I never neglected him. I know only too well how awful it is to be left in there, abandoned and forgotten. Even if I was short of money, I'd put a few things in a box – pears, a bit of cheese, some pasta – and take it to him.

One day I went to Regina Coeli and they told me, 'We can't deliver the parcel, the prisoner isn't here.'

'Where is he?'

'God knows.'

It took me days and days to find out that he had been transferred to Isarenas Ardus, in Sardinia. Then I took the train to
Civitavecchia, boarded the boat and sailed for Sardinia. It was
hot, the end of August. And the sea was rough.

I arrive at Cagliari, get off the boat and ask where the penal
colony is. They tell me, 'You have to go to so-and-so and such-
and-such, but the bus drops you two miles from the prison.'

'I'd better take a taxi, then,' I say. 'I haven't got much money,
but I can't walk two miles with a knapsack slung round my
neck and a case in my hand.'

So I take a taxi. The driver goes like a bomb all the way, then
suddenly stops in the middle of nowhere.

'Where the hell are we?' I ask.

'I can't go any further,' he says, 'the road's too bad.'

'But how far is it from here to the prison?'

'Oh,' he says, 'three-quarters of a mile, a mile maybe. . . .'

And I have to pay him and let him go. Humping the knapsack
and the suitcase, I start walking towards the prison, under the
midday sun. After I've been walking for a little while, the heel
comes off one shoe. I try walking with only one, but it's impossible, I have to take the good shoe off as well.

And that's how I turned up at the penal colony of Isarenas
Ardus (also known as 'the valley of the lepers'): barefoot, with
my feet raw and blistered, one shoulder bruised from the knapsack and one arm almost broken from carrying the case. And I
was in a muck sweat.

I was so hot and exhausted I could hardly speak. Ercoletto was
good to me, he got a bucket of water and sluiced me down and
washed my feet. He embraced me, he was happy to see me. He
took all the good things I had brought him and hugged me and
thanked me.

Then the warder comes along. He wants to send me away immediately. But Ercoletto says, 'Please, can't you see she's done
in? She's come all this way for my sake. Leave her alone.' But no,
he insists on turning me out. Then Ercoletto starts insulting him,
and as a punishment for those insults he gets himself sent to
Portolongone, amongst the lifers and the cons doing long
stretches. He didn't even have the consolation of finding Orlando
there, because he, meanwhile, had been transferred to Rebibbia.

As soon as I got back to Rome I started doing travellers'
cheques again with Zina and Pippo. We bought and bought, and

it almost always went off smoothly. It was an easy life.

One day Pippo says to me, 'Today, we're going to a shop where they sell electrical household appliances, I know they take dollars there. You go in and buy a fair amount of stuff, we'll load it into a friend's car and take it away.'

We drive to this shop on the via Nazionale. I go in. I'm all done up like a fine lady, wearing a new coat with gilt buttons, a brooch on my lapel, bracelets, rings – I'm decked with jewels like a Madonna.

I buy a refrigerator, a television set, a transistor radio, a record-player with a built-in table-lamp, a food-mixer and a hair-dryer. Then, with the most assured air in the world, I say, 'By the way, I've only got American money.'

'Dollars?'

'Yes, but in travellers' cheques.'

'Ah, yes,' they say, 'travellers' cheques are as good as dollars.' So I pull out a wad of these cheques and pay. Then, while they're making out the bill and geting the change, I tell the boy to load the things into the car, which is waiting outside.

Just at that moment, I see the manager lifting the telephone and dialling a number. Oh, Dio mio! I think, I hope he's not ringing the bank! And in my haste to get way I leave the change behind, about 40,000 lire.

The Worm took all that stuff off us for 100,000 lire. The total value was about six times that amount. 'Now,' says Pippo, 'we'll go and have a real slap-up meal!' And we go into a grand restaurant, with a fountain in the entrance spouting green and rose-coloured jets of water. It was a place for the rich, the waiters spoke French, there was a carpet on the floor so deep that you sank in up to your knees, there were red cloths on the tables and it was so dark you couldn't see what you were eating. A magnificent place.

We ate an hors d'oeuvre of seafood, then truffled pheasant, salmon in aspic, spinach pancakes, fried potatoes, strawberry ices with whipped cream.

'Ah,' I said, 'what a delicious meal! The money was well spent!'

'Not a bit of it,' says Pippo, 'we'll save our money. They're sure to cough up here, so we'll pay by cheque.' I didn't want to, but Zina sided with him, so it was two against one and I lost.

When the waiter came with the bill, Pippo said, 'You do accept dollars, of course?'

'Certainly, sir.'

Then Pippo, very cocksure, says, 'Wait, we haven't finished yet,' He turns to Zina and says, 'What else would you like, sweetheart?'

Like me, Zina was full up to the eyebrows, in another minute she would vomit. 'Nothing for me,' she said, 'I'm full.'

But he insisted: 'Well, we can have a drink, can't we?' And he said to the waiter, 'Have you got some sweet liqueur? A digestive?' They brought us Sambuca. Pippo looked at it, scowled and said, 'No, this is too ordinary. Bring us something a bit exotic, something strong and expensive.'

They bring a green liqueur that burns our mouths when we drink it. Then something transparent, but it tastes salty so I spit it out. The others pronounce it excellent, but I can still taste salt.

In the end we pay with travellers' cheques and they even give us the change, in cash, 'Now,' I say, 'let's get out of here fast, before they find out.'

But Pippo takes his time. 'Let's buy a bottle of that liqueur to take home,' he saids, 'and one of those ice gâteaux!' And he pulls out more travellers' cheques, mumbling and fumbling, because he's half-sozzled.

I'm thinking: Now they'll nab us, we'll finish up inside. But instead, it all goes off beautifully. They even escort us out to the car with an umbrella.

It was raining cats and dogs, you couldn't see your hand in front of your face. The waiter came right out to the car with us. We left him a handsome tip. 'Thank you, sir,' he said, and, 'goodbye ladies, we hope to see you again soon.' He was all smiles.

Not even the tips of my shoes got wet. I was casually dressed, with a shoulder bag, a blue blouse, a sky-blue suit – I looked just like an air hostess.

We got into the car and burst out laughing. We made fun of the waiter with the umbrella. He had an impediment in his speech, a lisp. I imitated him, putting my tongue between my teeth and we laughed till we almost died. 'Oh, Christ,' said Zina, 'don't make me laugh any more or I'll be sick,' and she belched up a piece of black truffle that stuck to her chin.

When we were well away from the restaurant, Pippo said,

'Now where shall we go?'

'Take me back to the pensione,' I said, 'I want to sleep for a while.'

'No,' he said, 'first we must go back to the electrical shop and pick up the change, the 40,000 lire you left behind.'

'No,' I said, 'better forget it.'

'We must go,' he said.

'Well, then,' I said, 'you go in by yourself.'

'No, you should go. They never suspect a woman so much.'

We reach the corner of the street and Pippo stops the car. I get out, start walking. Then I realise I've left my handbag in the car. I turn back to get it, thinking: You never know, they might pinch my money!

I go into the shop, unwillingly, because my instinct is warning me not to. And in fact they're waiting for me. The moment I arrive, they nick me.

A red-haired *maresciallo* from the Flying Squad is there. 'Would you mind coming down to the station with me?' he says.

Zina and Pippo were in the car at the end of the street and they saw it all happen. They saw me arrested, they saw them put me into the Black Maria. I walked right by them but I made no sign, I didn't even glance at them. So, once again, I wound up in clink.

I spent two days in a cell without light, then they called me for interrogation. 'Where did you get these travellers' cheques?' they said.

I said, 'I'm a prostitute, I go with Americans, they give me these cheques as payment.'

'What a coincidence!' they said, 'every one of these Americans you've been with has laid charges against you. How come?'

'How the hell do I know?'

'And have you been going with women, too?'

'What women?'

'Some of these signatures are women's names. Do you go with American women, too?'

'They must be the sisters of the men I go with,' I said.

'Oh, naturally, the sisters!' they said. 'Stand there against the wall and we'll call in the shopkeepers you've robbed and see if they recognise you.'

They pushed me out into a corridor. At the end of it I could see a line of people sitting on benches. They were the people from all the shops I had robbed, they had come to identify me. I take a look and see them all peering at me, craning their necks. The faces of murderers, a lynching party! 'Aha,' I think to myself, 'I'll fix you lot!'

I call the *maresciallo:* 'May I go to the toilet, please, it's urgent.' I go into the wash-room, take a run at it and bash my face against the edge of the door, splitting my head open. The blood pours down, spurting all over the place, one eye is closed up. My face swells up like a balloon. Then I come out.

'What happened?' they ask.

'I slipped and fell against the door.' They had to take me to the hospital. First, however, they made me pass in front of all those cretins, who goggled at me pop-eyed. But they couldn't tell whether it was me or not.

I would have got away scot-free if they hadn't nicked that idiot Pippo three days later. At the first blow, he grassed. Blurted out the whole story. He was a slob, an ex-policeman. He told them all the details, about me, Zina, the cheques, the shops we had done. The snivelling, pox-ridden grass!

When he was in Regina Coeli prison, his companions said to him, 'How come Teresa, who's a woman, held her tongue, denied everything, and you, who are a man, couldn't stand up to the fuzz?' They told him: 'In the eyes of the people of silence, you're a contemptible rat, your name stinks, they call you the executioner, nobody will have anything more to do with you.' And they warned him: 'Now, when you go in front of the judge again, try to get yourself out of the shit, retract everything you said to the fuzz, tell them it's all lies. Deny it, deny everything.'

So he withdrew his statement. In front of the judge, he said he wanted to deny it all. But the first deposition carries a certain weight, they give it more credit than the one you make before the beak. That's why, to avoid snarling myself up, I always stick to the same story, I never change. I deny the charge to the police and I go on denying it stolidly.

189

# 28

They jail me for the business of the travellers' cheques, and the moment I get inside I come across a serpent, a real snake-in-the-grass. This fellow had had a grudge against my brother Orlando when he was in Soriano del Cimino. Then Orlando was transferred to Palliano, and this serpent, whose name was actually Manlio Serpente, was transferred to Rebibbia. He was a prison officer, a *maresciallo*.

The snake had had fights with my brother because Orlando was a Communist and he was a Fascist. Orlando shouted communist slogans at him – 'We will take power and throw all you fuzz into jail!' and things like that.

Then he put a red scarf round his neck to show his contempt for the serpent. In fact he wrote to me, asking me to send him this red scarf. I sent it and he wore it round his neck. Queuing up in the canteen, he would sing, 'The red flag will triumph!'

The *maresciallo* got his knife into him, he persecuted him, sent him to the punishment cell. One day, in a rage, Orlando set the straw mattress on fire. He nearly died of suffocation. The *maresciallo* dragged him out and beat the living daylights out of him. Then he had him transferred to Palliano prison.

Anyway, I end up in Rebibbia with this *maresciallo* Serpente. The moment he lays eyes on me he says, 'Ah! So you're Orlando Numa's sister, I'll soon get you sorted out!' And he kept his eyes on me constantly. If I stepped out of line, even for an instant, he made me sleep on the plank-bed. No matter what I said or did, even if I was in the right, he found fault with me because he hated my brother like poison.

They put a girl called Rita into my cell. She was an out-and-out lesbian. She was a nasty bit of work, hypocritically playing the puritan while secretly putting her hands up everybody's skirts. She was violent and a bully.

'I don't want to share a cell with that Rita!' I said, and the moment the serpent got to hear of it he put another one in with us, a certain Mungelbino, who was a friend of Rita's.

Mungelbino and Rita were kissing and cuddling all day long. Rita gave the orders and the other girl obeyed; she cleaned her shoes for her, cooked for her, washed for her, massaged her, waited on her hand and foot.

Rita made her go to bed with the *maresciallo,* so as to get certain concessions, and she sent her off to the old women, to let them touch her up for money. She was insatiable, a blood-sucker.

This Mungelbino was nicknamed the Princess, but, if you ask me, she was more like a skivvy. I don't know how she got her nickname, perhaps it was because of her long nose.

One day I said to this Princess, 'What a fool you are! Don't you see she's just making use of you? She packs you off to the old women, she packs you off to the *maresciallo,* as if you were a parcel! You really are a twit!'

Mungelbino didn't say anything at the time, but later, she told Rita what I had said and Rita complained to the *maresciallo.* The serpent went to the governor and said, 'That Teresa Numa is worse than her brother, she's a bully, an anarchist, a vicious criminal, it's in her blood.'

The governor sent for me. 'Is it true you incite the other convicts?' he says to me, 'and that you set them against the authorities?'

'No, sir, it's not true.'

'Nevertheless,' he says, 'there have been complaints. I am warning you for your own good, stop being a trouble-maker or it will end badly for you.'

I thought that was the end of it. But no. As I'm going out the door he says, 'Well then, six days on the plank-bed!' And I think to myself: Fuck that slimy serpent, it's all his doing! He was always saying to me, 'You're just like your brother, a carbon copy, identical twin turds!'

He said it to me once, he said it to me twice, he said it to me a third time and I rounded on him. 'You're getting on my tits about that brother of mine – stop bringing his name into everything! If you're a man, go out, confront him face to face, take off your policeman's uniform and see if you can beat him! You're always insulting me, throwing my brother in my face, but what have I got to do with him? If you don't belt up, I'll bash your head in for you, then you can really say I'm like my brother!'

When he heard this tirade, he sent me to the punishment cell at once. Three days in a room the size of a toilet on a train, a plank to sleep on, without blankets or sheets. It was cold. My kidneys were playing me up, too. All night long I stamped my feet against the wall to try and keep warm, until I finally dropped off, exhausted, in the frosty air of morning.

When I came out of the punishment cell they said to me, 'Get ready to leave.'

'Where am I going?'

'Don't know.'

They never tell you a bloody thing. Everything is shrouded in mystery. They made me get into the Black Maria, closed the doors, and off we went. Two hours later we stopped. They open the doors, I get out. We've landed up at another prison.

'Where's this?' I ask.

'Montepulciano.'

There's not so much as an ant in this prison – just me. It's night time. I walk around. The place is like a ruined castle, rubble and debris strewn all over the grounds, rusty pipes sticking out of walls, the floor-tiles all broken, the walls bulging, peeling, filthy, cracked. It's dreary and dismal as hell, all on my own. 'Where have these pigs brought me to?' I wonder.

They shove me into a tiny little room with a window that is nothing more than a hole in the ceiling. There's a cold, thin light trickling in; it's like being in a tomb.

I start knocking, shouting: 'Let me out of here! Let me out! Let me out!' I was used to being in the midst of uproar, amongst my friends. This solitude was breaking my heart. 'Signora!' I call out, 'Signora, I feel ill! I feel sick, I can't breathe!' And it's true, I'm suffocating, shut up in there with nothing but that little hole for a window. Oh, Dio! Dear Mother of God! Where have they brought me to? 'Listen, I haven't murdered anyone!' I shout, 'I'm not a killer, you don't have to shut me up in solitary! Let me out, let me out!'

From behind the door the wardress keeps saying, 'You'll get

out, all in good time! Pray God to send you someone for company!'

'What!' I say, 'pray to God to send some poor sod to prison to keep me company? I'd rather pray to Him to kill you all off first!' I was raving, furious, off my head. 'Who was it?' I said. 'Whose idea to have me locked up like this?' And I found out it was that accursed serpent who had requested that I be cooped up all alone in this hole, out of spite. I had guessed as much, I knew it, and I cursed his guts.

I spent the whole day shrieking: 'Governor, governor! I want to get out of here! Let me speak to the governor, call the governor!'

The governor was a Sardinian, God rot his soul, and he'd gone off to Sardinia on holiday. He wasn't there. The *maresciallo*, Andirivieni by name, said to me, 'Be good, behave yourself and they're sure to transfer you.'

'But when?' I said.

'As soon as the judge comes back from his holidays. They've all gone home for Christmas,' he said. It was true, there wasn't a soul in that prison, the place was empty.

'But have you all gone mad?' I said. 'I can't wait here till the judge gets back from his holidays. I refuse to stay here!'

'Well,' they said, 'they're away, they won't come back yet.'

'But when *will* they come?' I said.

'Maybe in a week, maybe longer.'

I racked my brains to think of some way of getting out of there. If only they would send me to a prison where there were other people, where I could talk to someone.

Even Andirivieni kept out of sight. 'What's he doing?' I said.

'Wrapping up Christmas presents for his family,' they told me. So he, too, was all hung up on Christmas, doing up his presents, at home with his family.

'Signora,' I said, 'I can't stand it, all alone in here like a rat.'

'Be patient,' she said.

'Patient!' I shouted, 'I'm burning up with rage, I'm dying! I'm not an animal, you know, you can't just shut me up in a cage and forget all about me!'

Trying to calm me down, the wardress said, 'You'll see, they'll arrest somebody soon, then you'll have someone to keep you company. Even here we have our criminals, you know. As soon as we get hold of one, I'll put her in with you, then you'll have someone to chat to.'

'I'll see you all in hell first, you and all the filth!' I said. 'Because you're torturing me without reason! I'm not going to wish for someone to get nicked now, at Christmas time, just to keep me company – I'm not a cynic like you lot! All I want is to get out of here!'

Meanwhile, the days were passing. Nearly a month had gone by since my arrival. I couldn't stand it any more. I was getting claustrophobia. Then I made up my mind. 'Right,' I said to myself, 'I'll scare the shit out of them, I'll pretend to try and commit suicide, then they'll have to send me away.'

Every day, for an hour, I was allowed to go down into a courtyard full of cockroaches, with the cracked and chipped flagstones covered in slime, and there I paced up and down like a caged lion.

I counted the flagstones, one, two, three, four, for something to do. I counted them out loud, just to hear a human voice. The wardress was upstairs, keeping an eye on me from a window.

'Come here, Teresa!' she'd say, 'tell me a story or something.'

'I don't want to talk to you,' I'd say, 'I've got nothing to tell you.'

I didn't feel like talking to her, with her mean, villainous face. She tried to wheedle and cajole me, but I wasn't having any. Talking to myself was preferable to talking to her.

In that courtyard there was a little window, low down, a grotty little hole with a bit of glass sticking out of the frame. I sat down close to it and when the wardress wasn't looking I slipped out the splinter of glass. It was jagged, sharp as a knife. Now I'll fix them, they'll have to take me away whether they like it or not, I thought. I took the glass and cut myself on the arm, in two or three places. I didn't injure myself badly, just enough to make it bleed. I knew the wardress was still watching me up there.

When I'd done it, I hid the bit of glass in my clothing, ostentatiously. The wardress saw me and came down at once, she came swooping down into the yard like an old crow.

'What are you hiding there?' she says. She frisks me, finds the bit of glass. That's just what I'm hoping for. She takes the glass and confiscates it. Then wham, bam! she slaps me twice across the face and leaves me there with my arm bleeding.

Along come Andirivieni, who's in charge. 'Numa,' he says to me, 'why do you want to kill yourself? You mustn't do that, you must be a good girl, we are fond of you, you know.'

'I want to get out of here,' I say, 'take me to a hospital!'

'Tomorrow,' he says, 'on my word of honour, I'll send you away from here.'

'Meanwhile, send me to the infirmary, can't you see I'm bleeding?' But no, nothing doing. The wardress binds my arm up as tight as anything and chucks me back in the cell.

## 29

Handcuffs, guards, the train. 'Where are you taking me?' No answer. They never answer a con because a con must never know. You are never allowed to know your fate until afterwards, and then you're in it up to your neck. A convict is a parcel, a bit of baggage, to be sent hither and thither. Who bothers to tell a parcel where it's going?

We arrive, we get out. I see written up on an iron plaque: Pozzuoli. Pozzuoli! I say to myself, then this is where the criminal lunatic asylum is. And I was right.

They take me to this lunatic asylum, which has been bombed, it's in an awful mess, but the walls are thick and solid and the place is crammed to the roof with women.

'But this is where they put crazy people!' I say, 'I'm not crazy! There are murderers in here, women who chopped up their babies with razor-blades, boiled their husbands and ate them, or strangled their mothers and fathers with a stocking.'

'Those are our orders,' they say, 'and that's that!'

They put me in with a girl called Astor, who had painted her baby gold all over and put him in a box to send him to the Pope. She didn't like the look of me, she scowled, made faces, and pissed on my bed. 'Look,' I said, 'if you don't stop that, I'll thump you. I don't care if you *are* mad.'

She crouched down on the bed, she was scared of me. You could see she was used to being beaten up. When I turned my back, she made the 'sign of the horns' at me, but I thought: What's the use of flying at her, the poor thing's mad, she's worse off that I am.

And so I let her get on with it, even if she made evil signs at me and pulled faces. Only when she wanted to piss on my bed did I threaten her: 'Watch it, Astor, or I'll do you,' and she ran away. She knew only too well what it meant to be knocked about.

The first night I couldn't get to sleep. I watched Astor, who was laughing in her sleep and kicking her legs in the air, and I felt doomed. I thought: Being amongst all these nuts will send me round the bend, too.

In the morning I was famished! They made us dress, but we couldn't wash because there was no water. They'd been without it six days. In fact, the stink of shit was enough to asphyxiate you. These madwomen shit everywhere, then spent the rest of the day with their backsides caked with shit and piss, and if they complained, the nurses popped a pill into their mouths and that kept them dopey again till evening.

They took us into a large room with long narrow tables. We sat down and they gave us coffee made of chicory. Some of the women had to be spoon-fed. I saw that they tied them to their chairs and, if they wriggled about, they threw a bucket of cold water over them.

Near me there was a beautiful girl, about nineteen years old. She had shit even in her hair. With that stench next to me I couldn't even swallow a sip of coffee. I slid along the bench, further away from this girl, hoping she wouldn't take offence. But she didn't even notice.

Now I was sitting next to a short, hunchbacked creature, with her arms tied tightly behind her back. She said, 'Would you help me eat my bread?'

I helped her, and she nearly bit my finger off. 'Look out!' I said.

She said to me, 'I am the colonel's wife, you know. Tomorrow, I shall go to the colonel and tell him everything.'

'What colonel?' I asked.

She said, 'Shut up and feed me, you sow!'

They turned us out into the courtyard, into the cold, and people were scattered about like so many bundles of old rags, some tied to chairs with a hole through the seat, some lying on the ground, some leaning against a wall. Who can I talk to? I wondered, they're all bonkers here, if I start talking to someone, she may spit in my face. I'd better not speak to them till I know them a bit better. Astor was crouched on the ground at the far end of the yard, looking at me cross-eyed. Watching me.

I sat down and started thinking about Ercoletto. I had heard, through Zina, that he'd been released and then gone in again a month later on a charge of swindling. But during that month he had deserted me. This too I had learned from Zina.

His sister, Alba, had put him into bed with another woman, a certain Bruna. This girl was about twenty-five and good-looking. Ercoletto wanted to marry her. Later, years later, he told me that he only wanted to marry her so as to forget me, because they had told him that I had been unfaithful, put the horns on him with a fellow called Rocco. But it was all lies, just an excuse. The truth was, since I was in for two years, he didn't fancy being alone all that time, without a woman. So he got himself another woman, it was as simple as that.

I, on the other hand, had never once betrayed him when he was inside. I had travelled all the way to Sardinia to see him, I had even walked the last part on foot, without shoes, humping a heavy case and a knapsack, sweating, dusty, under the August sun. And this, I thought, this is the thanks I get!

Anyway, I kept thinking about Ercoletto and I couldn't rid myself of these thoughts. I was sitting there lost in meditation and I didn't even notice that, with the cold, my nose had started running. I came to with a snot on my collar. 'Oh, Christ!' I said, 'I've only been here half a day and already I've become as filthy as they are, filthy and off my head!'

At midday, we were herded into that big damp room again where the draughts whistled through sharp enough to cut your legs off. They gave us a mess-tin full of cold, sour-tasting pasta. 'Sit down and eat!' they said.

I look around me and see that they keep the pasta in a saucepan as big as a bath-tub. It takes two of them to lift it. Those sick women, the convicts, put their hands into the tub, and their hands were foul with piss and shit.

'I'm not eating that!' I say, but, just as I'm saying it, I see a woman opposite me being grabbed, tied and force-fed. She too had refused to eat. So then I think: Better keep my mouth shut, or they'll force me to eat this muck.

I pretended to eat, then, as soon as the wardress took her eyes off me, threw the food into the rubbish bin. I got up, made out I was going to fetch a glass of water, emptied my mess-tin into the dustbin, covered it with a scrap of paper and went back to my seat.

About five o'clock I was overcome with a feeling of weakness. Now what do I do? I thought. Hunger was gnawing at my stomach. I stopped one of the wardresses and said, 'I'm hungry, could I have a bit of bread?'

'Have you got the money to pay for it?'

'No.'

'Not a chance, then.'

I had to put up with hunger, stomach cramp, the lot. I went hunting around for something to put in my mouth, anything. I found a few scraps and swallowed them. I found some little clover plants in the yard and I ate those. In the evening they gave me a murky-looking broth with bits of overcooked potato in it. I gulped it down, in spite of the bitter taste and the stink of shit. I was past caring.

Next morning they issued me with regulation clothing: two pairs of government knickers, all stained and with the crutch torn; a woollen vest with two great sweat-stains on it, a woollen overall the colour of lead, a pair of white stockings as stiff as boards and a pair of canvas shoes, shapeless, patched and darned a thousand times.

'I'm not putting on this rubbish,' I said, 'it's disgusting!'

They said, 'Either you put it on or we put it on for you, by force.'

So I had to put it on. The underwear was stiff with years of dirt, there were stains of blood and urine on it. I turned it over and over and I couldn't bring myself to put it on.

I said, 'I've got a pair of knickers of my own, let me put those on.'

'No,' they said, 'you must wear government issue here.'

'Well, then, give me a new pair!'

But the new knickers had been carefully put away, only the nuns knew where they were. The inmates were given nothing but these torn and dirt-encrusted rags. They said, 'The cons here don't know the difference, anyway.'

But I knew. At the time, I put those knickers on, but I took them off later. I preferred to go naked rather than wear that stuff stained with other women's shit. Later, I fished out my own knickers and put them on. But, after two months of constant wear, there was nothing left of them but rags. I didn't wear a bra, one can do without that, but I kept the rough old sweater they gave me because of the bitter cold.

Every evening I found myself closeted once more with that crazy Astor. I looked to see if she had peed on my bed, but she didn't do it any more. Instead, I often found that she had spat on it. There would be a great gob of yellow spit on the sheet.

'Right,' I said, 'this time, I'm going to give you what-for, you filthy bitch!' She panicked and started screaming. The nun came. I told her I couldn't stay with Astor any longer.

'Why not?' she said.

'Because I can't, that's why. She's mad.'

The nun said, 'You're mad, too.'

'I'm not mad,' I said, 'and you know it as well as I do.'

'If you don't treat me with more respect, I'll have you tied to the bed!' she said. So I had to keep my mouth shut. I turned the sheet over and slept with my head under the covers, so as not to see, not to hear.

One morning I got up and asked sister if the water had come back. 'Yes,' she says, 'but get in line and don't talk.' There's a queue ten yards long. I stand there with the others. I wait and wait, and when the line has moved about half-way up, the hot water runs out. I can hear the madwomen shrieking and yelling.

'What's happened?' I ask.

'The hot water's finished and they're chucking them under the icy shower, that's why they're screaming.'

'No wonder,' I say, 'and where am I supposed to wash?'

They say, 'Unless you want a ducking, too, you'd better hide, get lost!'

So that's what I did. But just as I am slipping away, somebody grabs my arm. 'Come and help!' she says. She was a strong, sturdy girl with jet black hair and steely eyes. 'Get hold of her!' she says. There was this fat old woman, yelling her head off, she didn't want to be washed. Her arse and thighs were encrusted with shit. She gave me the horrors. I drew back.

Then this black-haired girl, who is a con too, slaps me on the mouth with the flat of her hand and nearly sends me flying. 'What are you doing, are you crazy?' I say.

She says, 'Grab hold of this old woman, or she'll fall over.'

So I seized hold of the sick woman by the neck and, using my knees and elbows, I managed to keep her under the cold shower while the girl washed her.

Afterwards, this black-haired girl and I became friends. Her name was Sarabella, she was Sicilian. She wasn't insane, but she had pretended to be mad so as to get a lighter sentence. She was young. She was in for dipping and she had a record as long as your arm. On the last occasion, they had admitted diminished responsibility, and for that reason had sent her to Pozzuoli.

She ruled the roost in there. Since the nuns knew she was sane, they entrusted her with all the dirtiest chores, such as washing the filthy women and tying them up. In exchange, she received double rations of food. She had free access to the kitchen. She took bread, potatoes, beans.

Like me, she was poor and abandoned. Nobody ever came to visit her, nobody ever sent her a parcel. But, inside, she was the boss, she ordered everybody about. She understood right away that I was as sane as she was and, from that day on, she always called on me to help her. Then she rewarded me with something extra to eat.

We were together morning, noon and night. I discovered that she was a miser. When she earned a bit of money, she didn't spend it, she saved it up, lira by lira, against the day when she would be released. I'm not capable of saving; when I have money I spend it, down to the last red cent. It's a defect with me, I'm a spender. But Sarabella wasn't tempted to buy olive oil, butter, wine, fags, all the good things you could buy in there. She hoarded her money, keeping it hidden under her skirt.

# 30

One day, at lunch, they set a bowl of cabbage soup in front of me and it was full of earth. I took a spoonful of soup and heard grit scrunching between my teeth, so I spat it all out. Sister Bleeding Heart of Jesus saw me, grabbed the plate and threw the soup in my face.

My first instinct was to murder her, beat her to death. But I stopped myself in time, because I knew that if I played up, she would have me strapped down. And to be tied is the bitter end. They're quite capable of leaving you nailed down there for a fortnight. So I kept mum.

Another time, out in the yard, I was watching some workmen fixing tiles on the roof. As I'm standing there watching, wham! A clout on the head. Sister Bleeding Heart grabs me by one arm and swings me against a wall. She says, 'What are you doing?'

'Watching the men at work.'

'No, you were talking to them, to those men.'

'No,' I say, 'I was just watching.' Bang! Another bash on the face that splits my lip open.

She was very ready with her hands, that Sister Bleeding Heart, and she was strong. When she walloped you, she left the mark of all five fingers on you. She was rough and ferocious. She wouldn't stand for any nonsense. One word out of place and she clobbered you.

My one desire was to strangle her, but I always contained myself. I thought: Be a good girl, Teresa, they've got you by the short and curlies, and once they tie you down, you're done for. You'll never get out. I didn't want to end up like these poor lunatics, strapped to their beds, tossing and turning in their own filth night and day.

It was rumoured, in there, that the governor was a kind, understanding sort of man. So one day I went to Sister Bleeding Heart and said, 'Sister, I would like to speak to the governor.'

'Fill up this application form,' she said, 'then we'll see.'

I needed a pen to fill up the form. Nobody had one and Bleeding Heart wouldn't lend me one. So I couldn't write out my request. I was about to give up the idea when Sarabella managed to find me a stub of pencil.

I handed my request to the nun. I waited two days, three days, then at last I was summoned by the governor. I was in such a state of nerves that my legs were trembling. I knocked and heard the governor's voice say, 'Come in.' I stood hesitatingly on the threshold. He was sitting at his desk; he didn't lift his head, didn't speak, nothing.

I wait patiently while he continues to read his letters, with his head bent over the desk. In the end, thinking perhaps he's forgotten me, I say, 'Excuse me, sir, may I speak?'

'Come in, come in!' he says. He looks up for a moment, with his wrinkled face, then bends over his reading again.

So I begin: 'Sir, listen to me, sir, does it seem fair to you that I should be shut up in here amongst all these madwomen who can't even talk properly? They put me here as a punishment, and it serves me right because I asked for it. I was all alone in a place and I couldn't stand it, I tried to get out, I took a piece of glass and cut myself on purpose, so they'd send me away, because I was desperate. Well, I was punished for it, fair enough. But I thought they'd send me to another prison, not a lunatic asylum. I'm not mad, sir. I'm not saying a word against this prison, sir, it's well-run, it's a very orderly place, but what has it got to do with me? Besides, it was awful at Montepulciano but at least I got something to eat. I can't eat here. Not with all these crazy women round me.'

Without raising his head, the governor, who's busy writing now, says, 'Go away, my child.'

'But did you hear what I said, sir?'

'Out!' he says.

So I have to go. I didn't keep on about it because I was afraid he'd take me for a lunatic. I just said, 'Very well, sir, good day,' and left.

203

I thought my interview with the governor had been a failure. I said, 'A bloody fine governor we've got, he doesn't even listen to you! If you speak to him, it's no more than the buzzing of a fly to him.' But I was wrong, because that interview had its effect: two days later, the order came through that we sane ones were to sleep together in a room far away from the lunatics.

There were twelve of us, and they transferred the lot of us to a room on the floor above. It was a bit crowded, but at least it was clean, it didn't stink of shit, and, better still, we could hold a reasonable conversation amongst ourselves and at night we didn't have to listen to shouts and lamentations.

No sooner had I settled in to my new bed than the kidney pains came back. I woke up at night with these pains and couldn't get back to sleep. The cold had caught me in the kidneys, the cold out in the yard, the cold in the rooms, the cold of the cold shower. Because I always washed myself, I can't bear to be dirty; even if the water is cold I have to wash. But that cold water numbed me.

The doctor gave me injections of vitamin B. I asked for hot compresses but they wouldn't give them to me. I had some twenty injections and felt a little better.

At night, to conquer the cold, I wound my vest round my head, my towel round my middle, put on the two pairs of woollen stockings I possessed, tucked the pillow in against my kidneys and slept like that, more like a bundle than a human being.

In the daytime I helped Sarabella in exchange for a bowl of hot soup without grit in it. Lately, another girl had joined us, her name was Palmira, She'd been in for ages, though she was sane. She was fat and cheerful, with a belly like a pork-butcher's. 'We ought to take a photo of ourselves, the three of us amongst these poor benighted wretches. We'd have a good laugh over it one of these days!' she said.

Me and Sarabella and this Palmira got some consolation from talking to each other. We told each other our life stories. Palmira was a country girl from Tuscany. She had stolen a lorry full of melons and they'd given her three years for it. But she was a hot-head, she played up like the very devil, sauced the nuns, fought with the other cons, tried to escape. The third time she tried to escape, they caught her and put her in the punishment cell. But Palmira is wilder than me, she couldn't stand being shut up, so she smashed the place to pieces. With the strength of a lion, she

204

broke the bed, shattered the window and even knocked down part of the wall. Then they got hold of her and packed her off to Pozzuoli, double-quick. And there she stayed.

We talked and talked. In the end Sarabella said, 'Let's go to the governor. He's not a bad sort, and if we don't even try to get out we'll be here for ever.'

'It's all very well for you to talk,' I said, 'you'll soon be going to Rome for your appeal, but what if the governor gets annoyed with us?'

'That's true, I'll be going anyway, but you two should try to speak to the governor and get out of here. He's a good man.' Sarabella advised me on how to behave when I went to see him, because she had more experience than me.

Once again, then, I went to see the governor. I was all submissive, quiet and docile, out of terror that he'd write me off as a nut. 'Sir,' I said, 'I have no one to help me, my brother is inside again, my husband – that is, my common law husband – is also in prison. Please let me work because the food they give us is full of bromide, it's poisoning me. I really don't need bromide. Give me a job to do, because I can't go on like this, my stomach is crying out for food.'

The governor, bent over his letters, absent-minded as ever, didn't look at me, he didn't smile. He was a puzzle, that governor. Has he heard or hasn't he? I thought. I stood there waiting. He opened some more letters, a mountain of letters in fact, then he made a sign with his hand and said, 'Get out!'

This time, too, I thought I had been writing on water. But three days later he sent me to work in the laundry. They gave me an iron full of hot charcoal and set me to iron the linen. Only the wardresses' stuff gets ironed, the cons' things are chucked into one of those steam machines that grind everything up and spew it out again, stinking and stiff as cardboard.

They gave me 5000 lire a month. I tried to iron as well as I could, but they said I was no good at it. Sister Fiordaliso said I ironed the pleats crooked. After a few days they moved me to the sewing-room.

There, you only worked on the inmates' clothes. I sewed very slowly, so as not to tangle the thread. But when they handed me some of the government knickers stained with blood and filth, I felt like vomiting. When the nun wasn't looking, I got hold of the spittoon and had a good spit. What with the dust and those stinking garments, I had to turn my head and spit every now and then.

One day, Fiordaliso noticed me spitting. She said, 'Listen, if it upsets you to darn these clothes, don't come any more.'

'Oh, no,' I said, 'it's not that. It's just that I've got a stomach-ache, I have to spit occasionally.'

But there was a lousy, boot-licking grass listening to us – a woman who was in for procuring – and that night she went and told Fiordaliso that it wasn't true, that I was always grumbling about the work and saying that those rags made me spit. Next day the nun said to me, 'You've done enough spitting, Teresa! Clear off and don't come back, you won't be allowed to work any more.' And that was that. I went back to being idle and hungry.

One day, when I was really desperate with hunger, I said to myself: If only I had a fag! Smoking deadens hunger pangs. At that moment I saw a bandaged hand holding out half a fag towards me. I turned round. It was a girl who had been in there for ten years, a certain Marina, known as Christ because she had the stigmata. Everybody knew she secretly kept the wounds in the palms of her hands open by using her nails and a bit of metal. But nobody cared. They called her Christ, and that made her happy.

This Christ was twenty-nine years old, short, pretty, with black hair and green eyes. She was inside because she had killed her father and mother. Her hands were bandaged because of the sores, but the more they wrapped her up, the more she picked away at the wounds and made them bleed. She loved them, she was very proud of her stigmata.

I said, 'Thanks!' and took the fag. She held out a lighted match to me. I lit up, inhaled. 'Ah, lovely!' I said. I took a drag, then another. I held that cigarette between my fingers as if it were a diamond. I really enjoyed it.

And while I am happily puffing away, I notice out of the corner of my eye that Christ's bandaged hand is on my leg. 'Christ,' I say, 'what are you up to?'

Christ doesn't say a word. But her hand comes sliding up towards my thigh, greedily, slowly, rumpling my skirt as it moves. Up and up creeps that hand like a rat sneaking into a sack of corn. When her hand is right there, at the crutch of my knickers, I jump up suddenly and throw the cigarette-stub on the floor.

'Do you think you can buy me for half a fag?' I say, and with that I stump off.

Christ, in a rage, loosens her bandages and starts gnawing ferociously at her sores and scratching them with her nails till the blood pours out. Then Sister Bleeding Heart comes along, wallops her and binds her tightly, right up to the elbows.

I told Sarabella the story and she burst out laughing. She said, 'But surely you know that women in here sell their cunts for just one drag on a cigarette?'

'That may be so,' I said, 'but not me. I wouldn't sell myself for a million!'

'No,' she said, 'because you've got a cold fanny.'

'What do you mean, cold?'

'You can go four months, six months, a year without making love. All you need is the thought of Ercoletto. Others, on the other hand, have hot fannies and they haven't got a man to think about, they have to do it, do it any way they can, with their girl friends.'

Then I found out that she too had a hot fanny. That's why she spoke like that. Instead of paying with money, she paid with favours, because she was powerful. Once she set her eye on a pretty girl, she made a pet of her, slipped her extra food, saw that she got hot water in the shower, and this girl, out of gratitude, would let her do whatever she liked with her.

But one day they caught her, shut her into the pantry and beat her up. A con, Carmela, told me about it. She'd been in the pantry with Sarabella to fetch some potatoes. She told me they got hold of her, and held her so tight that you could hear her bones cracking. They bit her, squeezed her, and left her a mass of bruises.

Out of all the convicts, there were only about ten with cold fannies, like me. The rest were all married, or had lovers, or were ready to sell themselves; they thought of nothing else. Even the very sick women had their love affairs and sometimes they bit each other to death over love quarrels.

The nuns pretended not to understand. As long as it didn't disturb them, they didn't care what the lunatics got up to amongst themselves. Only when violent fights broke out did they interfere, separate the participants and punish them. But most of the time, when they heard weeping or squabbling, they just laughed.

Many women sold themselves for food – an apple, a bit of cheese, a fag, some coffee. Those who received parcels from loving relatives and friends were pampered and sought after. Everybody fought for their favours. These lucky ones could buy whoever they fancied, including the nuns and the wardresses. Then there were others who worked and spent all their earnings on their lovers.

The nuns too had their protégées. They didn't often go to bed with them, because nuns are puritans. But they did fall in love, and when someone became a nun's little darling, she could do what she liked. All she had to do was be a hypocrite, pretend to be docile and run to church every minute.

I was always out of favour because I answered back, I didn't say my prayers, I got into fights and I protested at the top of my voice. I was a thorn in the nuns' flesh. And yet, in that place, I was more patient than usual, because I was afraid. But my nature came out all the same.

Luckily there was Sarabella to defend me. And she was crafty, she knew how to twist the nuns round her little finger. And they let her get away with it because she was so capable and helped them with the inmates. And all the time she worked and saved up money. She was a real tower of strength.

One day I got a card from Ercoletto. When I saw it, my blood fired up. I said to myself: Oh, Dio, Ercoletto has remembered me! But when I took a closer look at the card, I was sadly disappointed.

It showed a picture of a couple lying down, kissing one another. He was young and handsome and held a heart in his hand, she was young and beautiful and held an arrow which pierced the young man's heart. On the other side he had written: 'Think of your Rocco, Greeting, Ercoletto.'

'To hell with Rocco!' I said. Even Ercoletto knew this Rocco was a queer. Now I'll write *him* a letter, I said to myself, the same to him, with knobs on! Luckily I still had the stub of pencil Serabella had given me. I wrote to him:

'Dear Ercoletto, Apart from the fact that, if I had wanted to take myself a man, I would have taken a real one and not a fairy like Rocco, you must surely know how I feel about these things? Even if I was madly infatuated over someone, I wouldn't do you wrong, because you're my man. And even if I did, I'd choose a proper man, a type like Tonino, though Tonino didn't behave like a man at the end. Anyway, your accusation is just an excuse to leave me and go with that woman your sister, the procuress, found for you. Listen, I'm in a really bad way here, amongst a lot of heartless lunatics. I haven't even got the money to buy myself a fag. I'm wearing knickers tied up with string, they're in tatters. Try to come and see me if you can, or send me something in memory of all those parcels I sent you when you were inside. Goodbye, your own Teresa.'

Later, I learned that Ercoletto had pulled off a swindle for twelve million lire for this girl. He and a friend of his shared out the stash, six million each. Ercoletto gobbled up his share, together with that Bruna, down to the last cent. And meanwhile, I was begging for one cigarette!

Every now and then Orlando wrote to me from prison. We two unfortunate wretches wrote to one another, but we couldn't help each other, we couldn't send anything. He too was in a bad way because his wife had left him for another man, a road-sweeper, and she had even had a son by him, called Elio.

One day I decided to write to La Spagnola. I thought: Well, she won't reply, but it won't do any harm to write. 'Dear Marisa, I am reduced to skin and bone,' I wrote, 'I haven't even got a bit of soap left to wash myself with, nor the money to buy a fag. I'm not telling you this out of self-pity, I don't want to make a tragedy of it, but unfortunately it's the truth. They've dumped me here amongst a lot of brainless criminals, although I'm not mad. Hunger devours me, and I am losing my pride and my good health. I have come to the point of begging for alms. Be a pal and send me something, even if it's only a pair of knickers. Your friend, Teresa Numa.'

I sent off the letter, but without hope. I had to mend three pairs of shoes to pay for the stamp. 'She will never answer,' I said. But I couldn't help having just a glimmer of hope, and, as the days passed fruitlessly, I grew more and more melancholy.

One morning they sent for me. 'What do those butchers want?' I said. I thought I was in for a reprimand. I dragged my feet, slow and unwilling, as I went to the offices.

But it was her, La Spagnola, with a case full of stuff. I was so moved that I couldn't speak, I just stood there rooted to the ground. Then she saw me, my face pale and sallow, in that grey overall. I looked like a corpse risen from the tomb. She said, 'What the hell are you doing here amongst all these crazy women? How did you get into such a wretched state? It frightens me to see you sunk so low!'

'It's hunger,' I said, 'I haven't got a lira. You know, sometimes I collect the peel of the mandarines that the nuns throw away, and I eat them. I rummage through the dustbin like a dog.'

'But haven't you got anyone to help you?' she said.

'Yes, one. My friend Sarabella, she took pity on me. But it's an on-and-off sort of thing – when she falls in love with somebody new, she forgets all about me and I go hungry.'

I opened that case. There were six packets of Sport cigarettes. A vest, some flannel knickers, two pairs of woollen stockings. It was the kind of stuff you can buy off a stall in the Piazza Vittorio, but at that moment it seemed to me the height of luxury. And there was meat, cheese, coffee, biscuits.

For a few days, I felt elated. I ate, I changed my clothes. I even gave Sarabella food. I smoked to my heart's content. I was a queen. I gave myself the satisfaction of returning the presents from those bitches who had treated me like a beggar.

Then it was hungry days again, just as before. The only good thing was that the winter was drawing to a close and it was no longer so cold. In fact, the sun was beginning to warm up and when I was out in the yard, crouched against a wall, I felt well and happy. The pain in my kidneys had also passed off thanks to those new knickers, they were warm and snug.

But you never got a chance to be quiet, on your own. Some lunatic always came along and made a nuisance of herself. One day, a woman comes up to me in a flaming temper.

'You've pinched my egg!' she says.

'What egg?'

'It was there on the table,' she says, 'and you've pinched it!'

I had stolen eggs by the dozen, but that particular egg I never laid eyes on.

'Look,' I say, 'clear off and leave me in peace, my nerves are all on edge. I've never seen your blasted egg and I don't know anything about it.'

Then this girl starts yelling that I'm a thief, I've stolen her egg and she's going to report me. I make a grab for her, meaning to slap her on the mouth. Luckily, just at that moment along comes Milena, a strong young thief, and she starts slanging her: 'To hell with you and your fucking egg! Piss off, you stupid, crazy half-wit!'

So now, instead of wanting to murder me, she wants to murder Milena. She accuses her of stealing the egg. Then she grabs her by the hair and flings her to the ground.

Milena is so surprised that she doesn't react for a moment, then she gets up, jumps on her, seizes her by the throat and tries to strangle her. The other woman, to get her off, bites her ear so hard that a bit of flesh comes away in her mouth.

I wade in and try to defend Milena. But insanity gives people the strength of the devil. The two of us could do nothing against that fury who was determined, at all costs, to rip the flesh off our bones with her bare teeth.

Sister Bleeding Heart and Fiordaliso put in an appearance. The moment I see them, I extricate myself, out of terror of being tied down. The nuns grab Milena and the other girl by the hair, tie them up and strap them to their beds. Then, as they are still struggling, they give them that injection that makes your tongue swell, so that you can neither speak nor breathe.

Another day, I was sitting in the yard, taking the sun, when I saw someone crawling along on all fours. I pretended not to notice, that's the safest way with lunatics. I supposed she thought she was a dog. And I was right. Only this dog was just looking for somebody to bite. She crouched down level with me, as good as gold. 'What do you want?' I said. Instead of answering, Grrrrr . . . ow! She fastened her fangs into me. To this day, you can still see the marks of her teeth in my shoulder.

But I didn't hit her. I let her get away with it. I kept as quiet as a mouse, because I wanted to get out of that place. I knew a girl called Andreini who, like me, had been brought here as a punishment. She was sane, intelligent even, but spoke up for herself, shouted, swore, called the nuns whores. Well, when it came to the end of her sentence, that girl was given another six months. Then another six, so in the end she had to serve three years.

# 31

After five months and eight days, they sent me away from Pozzuoli, to Rome. And so I found myself back in Rebibbia, and I was happy, because at least I could eat like a Christian there, and I didn't spend the whole day surrounded by shit. I laughed with my friends, I fooled around, I traded. Compared to Pozzuoli, it was the life of a grand lady.

Then they let me go, because I had served my time. I came out and went straight to La Spagnola's place. In fact, she came to pick me up in a car belonging to an old boy who was keeping her, a certain Italo. She took me to her house, fed me, gave me a bed.

It was she who got me fit again. The first evening, she cooked some veal escalopes and when she saw me eating she was so moved that she started to cry. I hadn't tasted meat as tender and good as that for two years.

Then she put the whole dish in front of me and said, 'Eat, Teresa, I don't want any of it.' And I took her helping, and the old man's, and polished off the lot.

I ate and they watched me. I never lifted my eyes from my plate. La Spagnola said, 'You're making up for lost time! Here, have some wine, and more bread.' And I drank, I gulped it all down. Then I vomited, because when the stomach is accustomed to frugal meals it will not tolerate sudden abundance. La Spagnola said, 'Eat, eat, build up your strength. You won't go short of anything in my house.'

But I was intent on finding Ercoletto again. I searched for him and felt terrible because I couldn't find him. La Spagnola couldn't bear to hear his name mentioned. 'Listen,' she said, 'forget all about Ercoletto, I can't bear to think of that swine, he abandoned you for two years in prisons and lunatic asylums.'

'But I'm fond of him,' I said.

'I know you are,' she said, otherwise you wouldn't have gone to Sardinia, traipsing around for miles with your feet bleeding. You took parcels to him, and this man left you alone and helpless in prison.'

'Yes,' I said, 'on the one hand, I hate him. But we've been together so many years I can't forget him, he's become a habit by now. Besides, I want to ask him why he deserted me and have it out with him. By rights, I should shoot him like a dog!'

Then she tried to take my mind off it. She took me to the market, to the cinema, out walking. She wouldn't let me go out alone.

'Listen,' I said to her, 'I can't stay shut up in here, I've only just got out of the boot, I want to walk, to feel my freedom.'

She said, 'Are you comparing my house to a prison? You know you can do what you like here, eat all you want, sleep as much as you like, make yourself comfortable.'

But I went out all the same. I liked to walk. I walked and walked without even looking where I was going. It was enough just to be out in the street, free to go where I liked.

I walked along via Tuscolana, I went as far as Cinecittà, still on foot. I hung around the bars near Cinecittà because I had heard that Ercoletto was somewhere in that neighbourhood. Each bar I came to, I went in, looked around, pretended to use the phone, so as not to have to buy a drink, and went out again.

One day I went to Alba's. 'Yes,' she said, 'Ercoletto pops in from time to time, but I haven't seen him for quite a while now.' But she started giggling as usual, and she put her hand over her mouth to stop herself from laughing. I knew quite well she knew where her brother was hiding himself. But the whore denied it. 'Who knows where that brother of mine has got to?' she said, 'I don't know where he is.'

The truth was that Ercoletto's friends were trying to prevent him from seeing me, because they knew that, once he saw me, he was done for. Apparently, he himself had said: 'As long as I don't see her, it's all right, but the moment I lay eyes on her, I'm lost.'

His friends reported this to me. For this reason they took him to the seaside, to the mountains, anywhere where he wouldn't run into me. As long as the money lasted, they wanted to keep him to themselves.

But then the money ran out, and the gang of useless lay-abouts who called themselves his friends persuaded him to start swindling again. They made him sign dud cheques. Ercoletto is weak, easily led, they twisted him round their little fingers.

Well, there I was, looking everywhere for him, but I couldn't find him. Easter came. La Spagnola gave me a lovely chocolate egg with an enamel wrist-watch inside.

Ercoletto, meanwhile, was whooping it up with that girl. He was having a good time, and he kept telling everyone cheerfully, 'As long as I don't see Teresa, I'll be all right.'

Then one day, I do not know why, he came to see me. He came to La Spagnola's house in his car. I was out, but he told her he'd come back later. I had been out walking for quite a while. In fact, I came home, but when I reached the front door I changed my mind, and I was just setting out for Cinecittà when a car stopped in front of me. It was a bright blue Fiat 600, brand new; I'd never seen it before, that's why I didn't recognise him in it.

It stopped, kapow! with a screech of brakes. 'Shit!' I said, 'this son-of-a-bitch nearly ran me down!'

At that moment, he got out and came towards me. But he was cautious, a bit windy, because he had been told I was ready to shoot him. So he called out from a distance, 'Hello there! I was just coming up to your place.'

'My place?' I said, 'do you mean you've got the nerve to come and see me?'

'How are you?' he said.

He wanted to shake hands with me. 'Go and shake hands with that filthy bitch who's living with you,' I said, 'you're not fit to touch me!'

'Listen,' he said, 'let's talk things over. But no scenes, eh? We'll talk quietly and reasonably, and see who's right, you or me. Come on, get into the car.'

'No,' I said, 'I'm not going to sit in her place. Your woman may be jealous.'

Then he said, 'Don't talk like that, there's a good girl!' And he looked quite desperate.

I said, 'Well, let's talk then. I'd like to see just how many lies you can think up!'

I was acting as hard as nails, but I was really moved. I sat there rigid and surly, I wouldn't give him an inch. 'I'm not interested in you any more,' I said, 'you deserted me, you left me to rot for two years in various prisons, I was even in a lunatic asylum, and never a word from you.'

He said, 'I'm sorry you were in the asylum, I didn't know.'

'What?' I said, 'but you sent me a postcard there!'

'I sent the card to the prison,' he said, 'they must have forwarded it. Anyway, I didn't know you were in the asylum.'

'Prison or asylum, it's all the same, except that the asylum is worse,' I said. 'In any case, you don't care, you never have cared about me. Let's forget the whole thing.'

He tried to reason with me, to explain, to win me round. Then he said, 'Have you had supper?'

'That's my business,' I said.

'Come on now,' he said, 'I haven't eaten, let's go and have dinner somewhere, then we can talk. I'm hungry.'

'All right, then, let's go. Just to please you I'll nibble a little something. Besides, I don't feel guilty letting you spend money on me, God knows you've gobbled up enough of my money, now I can eat at your expense for once.'

I ordered steak and salad. It was a fine restaurant, all polished and gleaming, near Cinecittà. He was very affable and attentive, but he had changed, he'd become colder. I was worse than him. pretending to be indifferent, he kept watching me out of the Ice cold. But I could see that, although he was playing it cool, corner of his eye.

He said, 'You've put on weight, eh?'

'Yes,' I said, 'I've grown fat on all the parcels you sent me!'

'Don't be smart!' he said.

Then I said, 'I've fattened up a bit recently because I've been at La Spagnola's place, I've been eating her out of house and home. She's more than a friend to me, she's a sister. She's the only true friend I've got, and she had advised me to forget all about you because you've behaved like a swine.'

'I'm sorry about it,' he said, 'but I left you because of that Rocco, they said you were cheating on me with him.'

I said, 'That's just a handy excuse. But I was told it was your friends who wouldn't let you see me.'

215

'That's true,' he said.

'Aha,' I said, 'so you're not your own master, you act on orders from others! If I did that, I'd be ashamed of myself. I'm only a woman, but I do what I like, I'm mistress of myself, nobody tells me what I should do.'

Then he said, 'I realise I've been a bloody fool listening to my friends, but I always had that nagging doubt about Rocco.'

'Listen,' I said, 'if it's true that I went to bed with Rocco, may the worst misfortune in the world fall on me. May I go inside for ever and never come out again!'

When he heard that, it convinced him. 'Well, then,' he said, 'I suppose my friends must have deceived me out of envy.'

'No,' I said, 'they lied to you because you possessed millions of lire, they were on your back because of the money. Now the money's all gone, you come crawling back to me. Do you think I want to come with you and struggle for a mere existence? I'm tired and fed up, I want to stay at home, I don't want to go to prison any more, I want to be kept, because I'm worn out, I can't carry on.'

'All right,' he said, 'you stay at home, I'll go out to work and you won't want for anything. It's true I haven't got millions any more, but you won't have to do without necessities.'

'Well, then,' I said, 'let's try, but if you don't keep your promise, I'll be off like a shot.'

And so we made our peace again. He too came to stay at La Spagnola's and we paid her rent for our room. I stayed at home and he went out with his friends, Otello and Birmana. They bought linen on hire purchase and flogged it, they bought up pawn tickets for gold and jewellery. One way and another, they got by.

Sometimes they bought and sold oil. There was an oil-merchant's on via Tuscolana where they mixed peanut oil with olive oil, poured it into carboys and sealed them with wax. Then they stuck a label on: Virgin Olive Oil Extrafine Quality from Sabina.' In fact, it was a mixture that included purified asses' fat and cocoa oil from Tunisia.

I stayed at home, sleeping. It was lovely having someone to work for me while I serenely ate and slept. If Ercoletto started telling me what he had done during the day, I said, 'I don't want to know, from now on I'm a housewife. If the fuzz come, I'm innocent, they can't charge me. Do what you like, steal anything, only don't tell me about it.'

For a few months I really enjoyed playing the part of a lady. I got up at ten, soaked in the bath-tub for an hour or two, singing and playing in the water. Then I lounged about, doing my nails, yawning, listening to the radio. Slowly, slowly, I dressed, tarted myself up and went out shopping.

I couldn't be bothered to cook, so I bought ready-cooked food: frozen stuffed cannelloni, tinned veal stew, peaches in syrup. At one, I sat down to eat, sometimes alone, sometimes with Ercoletto. La Spangola always ate out with her old man. After lunch, I washed the dishes and lay down for a rest.

I slept, read romantic magazines, picked my teeth, smoked the cigars Ercoletto brought home. At five, I put my feet down and sauntered through the house with the intention of doing some ironing, but as the iron was broken and I couldn't be bothered to have it mended, I put it off. Instead, I washed my hair, getting up a lovely lather, put it in curlers and dried it with the hair-dryer.

That year I had my fiftieth birthday, but everybody took me for fifteen years younger. If it hadn't been for the missing tooth in front, which rather spoiled my smile, I would still have been very attractive. It was 1967.

In the evenings we all had dinner together: Birmana, Otello, Ercoletto, La Spagnola, the old man Italo and me. We drank, laughed, larked about: it was really a beautiful life.

At night Ercoletto was tired, he fell asleep at once. But I had been resting all day, I was feeling voluptuous, randy. And I caressed him, did all the things that pleased and aroused him, till in the end we made love. Then at last I fell asleep, happy and satisfied.

After a few months of this life I began to get sick of it. I felt bored when I got up, I was fed up with taking baths, doing my hair bored me to death, drying it was even worse. Pedicuring my feet had become unbearable, reading comics made me want to throw up, listening to the radio exasperated me.

In short, I was drowning in boredom and became a bore myself. I no longer enjoyed being a lady, having nothing to do. Even the sound of water running into the bath got on my nerves, and the silence when everyone else was out of the house brought on a headache.

So one evening I said to Ercoletto. 'You know what, tomorrow I'm coming out with you.'

'What's this?' he said. 'You told me you wanted to stay at home and be a housewife.'

'I've changed my mind,' I said, 'it seems I'm not cut out to be a housewife, I'm bored stiff.'

The very next day I began going with him to get the oil. I loaded the cans into the car, went into the trattorias, haggled over the price, collected the money, went back to the oil-merchant, and all the time I was on the alert so that the police wouldn't catch us. I took up my former life, and at once the boredom evaporated.

# 32

With the money from the oil, we took a room with a kitchen in the Borgata Alessandrina district. There was light, but no running water and no flush lavatory. Just a black hole. We complained, because the hole was already full, but they wouldn't do anything about it.

After a while the privy overflowed and the stench came right into the house, bringing rats and flies. At night these enterprising, half-starved rats came in and devoured everything. They even opened the fridge – God knows how, perhaps they stood on tiptoe and opened it with their teeth, or their tails, I don't know, but they got that heavy door open and ate the lot.

'Listen, Ercoletto,' I said, 'you'll have to empty that black hole or we'll be eaten alive by rats.'

'Yes, yes,' he said, 'tomorrow I'll bring a couple of friends along and we'll empty it.' But the friends never came and the stink got more and more overpowering.

In the afternoons we met Otello and Birmana in a bar at Porta Maggiore. Together we went and loaded up the oil, then we went round selling it till about eight o'clock, when we counted our earnings and shared them out.

I wasn't too keen on those two because, although they were nice enough to my face, I knew they wanted to split us up and get Ercoletto involved in all sorts of swindles without me. They didn't like me because I am independent, whereas Ercoletto is like a child, they could lead him around by the nose. He is not lacking in courage, and he can be crafty enough, but he's soft.

'Aren't you satisfied yet?' I said to Birmana. 'You made him desert me for two years, and I suffered hell all alone in prison! I was always gazing out, waiting for that unfaithful creature!'

It was true. I had spent whole days with my face glued to the grille at Rebibia. I was obsessed, like a madwoman with her hallucinations. On Sundays I looked at every face that passed, and all because, in the early days, he had come to stand on that lawn once or twice and wave to me. Then he gave up coming.

But that Birmana wouldn't take any reproaches from me. She said, 'You talk too much, I'm going to teach you a lesson!' And she comes straight at me with her hands. She's a sturdily-built woman, fatter than me, domineering and aggressive. She's been living hand-to-mouth with that Otello for thirty years. Neither she nor her husband have ever done a day's work, yet they own a car and a house. And they've never done time. That's because they always hide behind someone else, use someone else as a front.

So first she slaps me round the face, then she takes her shoe and bangs me on the head with the heel. That makes me wild, I lose my head, pick up a brick and smash her face with it.

Meanwhile, her husband has gone sneaking off to get help, and he comes back later with some other people. Amongst them is a great, fat gypsy who works as a film extra at Cinecittà. He's a rich money-lender who charges 150 per cent. I know all about him, because I've had dealings with him before.

Once, I borrowed money off him, when I was desperate, but I couldn't rustle up the cash to pay him back. Instead, I gave him a television, a tape-recorder, a radio and a whole lot of stuff I'd got on hire-purchase. Still he wasn't satisfied. He said, 'You've messed me about and made me lose a big deal. I reckon you still owe me 80,000 lire.' It seemed a bit thick to me, but, to avoid arguing, I promised to get him something else. 'Right,' he said, 'I want a washing-machine, a Zoppa.'

I went to various shops in Rome, but I couldn't get hold of a Zoppa anywhere. Then I had an idea. I went to Anzio, to a shop where they knew my family. 'I'm Eligio Numa's sister,' I said.

'Ah, signora, do come in!' they said. And, on the strength of my brother's good reputation, they gave me a Zoppa, on H.P.

Otello came to take it away. I trusted him, I was sure he was taking it straight to the gypsy, but instead the two of them plotted together and later the gypsy swore he'd never received the washing-machine. He came and threatened me, demanding the Zoppa.

One day I sent him a message: 'Tell the gypsy if he doesn't leave off threatening me, I'll be more of a gypsy than he is and stick a dagger in his guts!' When he heard this, he decided to get his revenge, and he started hunting for me.

So, this day, the day of the fight with Birmana, it happens that my brother Nello is with us, and the three of us are just going down the street, about to leave for Anzio in Ercoletto's car, when we run into Otello and Birmana. And that's when the row starts and I end up throwing the brick in her face.

Now, the gypsy is lying in wait round the corner with his wife and some other friends, so Otello goes and calls him and the whole pack appears.

'What do you want?' I say to the gypsy.

'Is it right,' he says, 'that I'm still waiting for my Zoppa and you won't give it to me? Do you think I'm the sort of man you can fool around with?'

Nello says, 'Let's get out of here, they've got knives!'

But I stand my ground, I stand and face this gypsy because I hate him and I'm sick of listening to him. 'Now,' I say, 'listen to me. It's time you gave up, because you know damn well I sent you the Zoppa, via your friend, and the two of you were in cahoots and you sold it. I don't owe you anything. Piss off, or I'll take out my dagger and shove it through your chest.' I say this knowing gypsies always carry knives. I don't really have any kind of knife on me, I'm just trying to frighten them off.

But before I've finished speaking I feel a fist land in my eye. A stream of blood runs down, my eyebrow's split open. At once Ercoletto jumps on the gypsy and Nello joins in, but gently, because he's had heart trouble. In fact, he died the following year. He tries to get between Ercoletto and the gypsy but the fat man gives him a shove and sends him sprawling.

At this point the whole gang of them jump on Ercoletto and wham, bang, crash! he's stretched out on the ground. I go to his aid, with one eye blinded and my mouth full of blood. Then the gypsy woman comes at me with a knife in her hand.

I twist around, leap like a cat and finish up glued to a friend of theirs, a certain Tullio. The gypsy woman strikes, meaning to stab me, but she gets Tullio instead.

As soon as they see they've wounded their friend instead of me, they panic. I take advantage of this moment to escape. I run and run till I get to the station. There I stop and try to staunch the

221

blood that's spouting out of my eyebrow, dabbing it with my skirt.

But I'm worried about Ercoletto and Nello, who are still lying there on the ground, so, as soon as I've regained my breath, I go back. Fortunately the others have gone, taking the wounded man with them.

Ercoletto's on the ground, still unconscious, and Nello's trying to revive him. As soon as he sees me he starts yelling, 'Look what you've done! We've got to get away from here, quick.'

'No,' I say, 'if we go away now it'll be worse, they'll be waiting for us outside the house this evening. This way, in a sense, the problem is resolved.'

Nello says, 'I thought you were a goner, that knife was long and she was pointing it straight at you, my dear sister.'

We took Nello back to Anzio. And there, in his house, I met my other brother, Eligio. The moment he saw me he started accusing me: 'You, my own sister, how could you make so much trouble for me!'

'What trouble?' I said, but I knew he meant the washing-machine I'd got on H.P. for the gypsy.

'The owner of the shop where you got the Zoppa is always coming to me and asking me to pay the second and third instalments, he says it's up to me to put matters right. I'm not paying out, it was your signature on the agreement, but you've ruined my good name!'

I said, 'I don't give a bugger for your good name. When did you ever help me? Did you visit me in prison, did you send me a parcel, or a postcard even? I was all alone, deserted, in a lunatic asylum. What the hell do you expect? If I died, you wouldn't give a hoot, as long as I didn't disgrace your good name!'

Ercoletto's nose and mouth were still streaming with blood. 'Instead of all this yak,' I said, 'go and fetch a doctor!' And Eligio went out to find a doctor.

He came back a little later with a fellow called Branca. This man looked at Ercoletto's wounds but he didn't lay a finger on him. He said, 'Put on some vinegar and hydrogen peroxide, then bandage him up.' With that, he left. So we patched ourselves up as best we could. We were all bruised and swollen, the three of us.

Later, we learned that Tullio had been taken to hospital with that stab wound. They said he almost died, one millimetre more

222

and the blade would have struck his heart. He had pleurisy as a result and was at the point of death.

I thought: So much the worse for you! You came to defend the gypsy, so you asked for it! This Tullio found clients for the gypsy, thieves who needed some money to pull off a fraud job. The gypsy dished out the money, made them repay him twice over, and gave Tullio a percentage.

I said to Ercoletto, 'Now, are you proud of your charming friends? You see what they're capable of? Otello and that Birmana nearly did for you!'

'You're right, Teresa,' he said, 'they're a pair of fiends, capable of anything!'

So I got Birmana and Otello off my back and I lived peacefully with Ercoletto. We dealt in oil on our own account. We didn't need accomplices. We lived well, we were happy.

It was during this period that Orlando went inside again and I took his youngest son, Orlandino, to live with me. I am very fond of this child, I don't want the mother to have him or she'll send him away to boarding-school. This sister-in-law of mine, the dwarf, is as ugly as a toad, but she's always got men around. She doesn't do it for money, but for pleasure. And so do the men. I can't fathom it at all. She's as blind as a bat into the bargain. She wears glasses an inch thick and without them she can't even see the way to her own mouth.

She takes in a man, sleeps with him, eats with him, keeps him in her house for a month or two. Then he goes and she takes another one in. They're all penniless bums, half potty, derelicts like her.

This dwarf has six children and they're all in convent boarding-schools. It makes me mad when I see them because they're skinny, dirty, covered in sores, it wrings your heart. I say to her, 'Can't you keep them at home?' And she says, 'I haven't got the money to support them.' In fact it's true, because Orlando is always in prison. She goes out charring, but at the most she gets 30,000 lire a month and she can't manage.

Orlando has left her so many times, because of her infidelities. But then, every time he comes out of clink, he goes back to her. Two years ago the dwarf made him a present of this son who is his spitting image, red-haired, gay, demanding and a rascal. Then my brother got nicked again and I went and took the child before she could pack him off to boarding-school, like the other six.

He was three months old when I took him and already he was a holy terror. The dwarf couldn't cope with him. She said, 'He's always crying, messing himself, fidgeting, shouting, bawling, kicking up a din, I can't stand it. I get hold of him and bash him against the wall.'

I bought him a feeding-bottle and some new clothes and I kept him at my place. He was naughty, and he's naughty still, but he's become very affectionate with me. We sleep together, I put my arms around him and he nestles against my breast.

In the morning when he wakes up, he kisses my face and says, 'Wake up, it's late! Move your great fat arse! Get up, you lazy slut!' He makes me laugh. He has a terrible habit of doing his business everywhere. When I put him on his potty, he'll sit there for half an hour or more and nothing happens. When I've got him clean and tidy, all dressed up and we're ready to go out, he says, 'Mamma, I've done it in my pants!' And I have to undress him and change him and start all over again.

# 33

Early one morning, while we're still in bed, I hear a shout: 'Teresa Numa, open in the name of the law!' There are twelve fuzz outside, armed with revolvers. They surround the house, bang on the walls, the doors. 'Open up! Open up!' roars the captain.

'Wait a minute, for Christ's sake!' I say, 'give me time to put something on, at least, I'm still in bed!' Meanwhile, I'm kicking Ercoletto out of bed. 'Hurry up,' I say, 'run, these bastards have come for you!'

'Open the door, Teresa Numa!' A voice like a butcher's.

'What's up?' I say, 'I haven't murdered anyone, have I? Keep calm, I'm coming. And don't frighten the baby or I'll wring your neck.'

I am dragging it out to give Ercoletto time to slip on his trousers and get out of the window. When I see that he's crouched safely in a corner of the skylight overlooking the court-yard, I open the door.

They come in and start searching everywhere. I just stand there looking at them. They are furious, raging, they know I've hidden him somewhere but they don't know where. At last it looks as if they're going. The captain bustles about, issuing orders, he would have liked to beat hell out of those good-for-nothing flat feet of his, if he could. I look at them and jeer.

Just as they're going out through the door, there's a crash and a tinkling of glass and down goes Ercoletto, skylight and all. The fuzz hear it and rush out into the courtyard.

Ercoletto, who can be as swift and agile as a cat when he wants to, has clambered over the roofs and slipped away between the other houses. The captain yells, 'There he is! There he is! Shoot him!' Two policemen fire their rifles at him. But instead of hitting him, they hit someone else. They shoot some poor devil who is running because he is late for work. They wound this man in the legs and back.

'We've got him,' they shout, 'quick, after him! Grab him!' They run over and see that it's the wrong man.

The captain turns green. 'Who told you to fire?' he says, but it was him, I heard him give the order. 'Call an ambulance and take this gentleman to hospital, at once!' he says. 'Please forgive us for our mistake, I beg your pardon on behalf of the police,' he says to the clerk who is gasping on the pavement. The poor man didn't even have breath enough to answer.

I thought it was all over. But no, a moment later the whole merry-go-round started up again, because a neighbour saw Ercoletto hidden amongst a lot of crates and started shouting, 'There he is, there he is, catch him!' Ercoletto started running again and this time they didn't open fire, but, with the help of some of the neighbours, they caught him and put the handcuffs on him.

Two days later the fuzz were back. I was calm because I didn't know I had been incriminated. However, they were after me too, and in fact I had a two-year sentence hanging over me.

They came in and made me dress in a mad rush. 'What's it got to do with me?' I said, 'you've got Ercoletto, what do you need me for?'

'Shut up and come along with us,' they said.

I left the baby with a neighbour. 'Take good care of him,' I said, 'I'll send someone to take him as soon as I can.'

'Yes, yes, don't worry, Teresa,' she said, 'I'll look after him.' She was a kind-hearted soul, but dirty.

A week later, my brother went to fetch him and take him to Anzio. I was inside, eating my heart out, but I was consoled by the thought that he was with his father, that Orlando would take care of him. Then, three days later, my brother was arrested again. He wrote to me from prison: 'My dear sister, Orlandino is in the Hospital of the Child Jesus. He's got scabies and some kind of infection. Try to get him out of there or he'll die.'

The baby had caught scabies. God knows how that neighbour

had kept him! Obviously she had never washed him, she was a filthy pig.

In the hospital they cut off his hair; then, as he kept scratching himself, they bound up his hands and his feet. It was torture. He gnawed and gnawed at the bandages but he couldn't scratch himself. And they couldn't cure him.

I kept imploring Persichetti, the social worker, to bring me this poor little mite, he couldn't stay in that place! I went to the Mother Superior and begged her to bring the baby to me. 'There's room for him in the infirmary,' I said, 'I can take proper care of him there.'

'He's all right, he's fine,' said Mother Superior.

'What about the scabies?' I said, 'has he got over it yet?'

'They have discovered,' said the social worker, 'that there's something slightly wrong with his heart.'

'What, his heart!' I said, 'what's wrong with it?'

'Nothing serious, they may have to do a little operation,' she said.

I was off my head with worry. Suppose this little boy goes and dies on me, I thought, what will I do without him? Later, I found out there was nothing wrong with his heart, they had just told me that out of malice.

By the end of the month I had saved up 12,000 lire. I had been working in the paper workshop, making envelopes and labels. At first I was assigned to the cutting machine. Clack, clack, boom, boom! The blade came down and cut thousands of sheets of paper at one go. One day a moron by the name of Mariella playfully gave me a shove and it was only by a hair's breadth that I escaped having both my hands chopped off under that cutter.

Then I played merry hell, I refused to work on that dangerous machine any longer. But they said, 'If you want to earn money, you'll have to stay where you are. Otherwise no work.' So I had to put up with it. But I lived in constant dread of that guillotine, and by the end of the month I was a nervous wreck. I suffered from nausea and dizziness, so at last they transferred me and let me make envelopes.

With my savings I bought two lovely dolls with glass eyes and pigtails. I asked Persichetti to take them to Orlandino as a present for Epiphany. 'All right, Teresa,' she said, 'I won't let you down. I'll come the day after tomorrow and take them to the little one.'

But she didn't turn up, neither on New Year's Eve nor Epiphany. The dolls stayed under my bed, in a biscuit tin.

I went to the nun. 'Tomorrow is Epiphany,' I said. 'I'd like to send these two dolls to my nephew, he's in the Hospital of the Child Jesus.'

'My dear girl,' she said, 'there's no need. The children in there have more toys than they know what to do with. He's so well off in there, he doesn't need anything.'

But, in fact, he was in a dreadful state. A friend of mine went to see him. She found him lying in a little cot, frozen stiff and half-starved to death. I protested, wrote letters. But there was nothing I could do. As long as I was inside, I could not take care of him.

One evening some of the cons got drunk in one of the cells. They ate biscuits, salami, pickled gherkins, and drank cognac. Nora Selecta had bought it with money sent from home. Then they started laughing like lunatics. Everybody heard them; the nuns heard them too but they pretended not to.

Amongst them was a woman called Scisci. In her drunken state she laid a hand on Nora Selecta's woman, and Selecta, out of jealousy, broke a bottle over her head. It ended up in a fight. The nun had to call the governor. He came, looked, nodded his head and went away. I thought they would be transferred or punished, but nothing happened.

The fact was that this Scisci was useful to the governor, she cleaned his office, polished his shoes, darned his socks and even acted as his informer. As a reward, he let her get away with it. He turned a blind eye – two blind eyes in fact. And the nuns just laughed.

If that had been me, I would have been sent to Pozzuoli; I've only got to say one word out of place and I get sent to the lunatic asylum, but some of the cons could get away with murder.

It happened that, when I came in this time, they gave me a mattress that was almost empty of horsehair. I couldn't sleep at night because the cold metal springs made my kidneys ache. Zina Teta, who was in prison with me that time, said, 'Go and see the governor. Ask him to change the mattresses, and tell him that half the showers are broken; we can't go on like this, we're dying of the cold.'

All these women are snivelling cowards – they're scared to go to the governor and make a complaint, so they find some reckless crackpot like me to do their dirty work for them. Then, if the governor gives me a cool reception, they draw back: 'What?' they say, 'we didn't tell you to protest, we've got no complaints, everything's fine.'

Another thing, that Teta is really a dirty bitch. If she goes to the toilet you have to run in behind her and pull the chain. In the cell, I was always cleaning up after her. I went to the Mother Superior and told her I couldn't stand being with that dirty Zina Teta. 'Why don't you move me?' I said, 'have I signed a marriage contract with her, or did the judge condemn me to do my time with her?'

'You must stay with her,' they said, 'you're a good influence on her. You've got a sense of responsibility, of cleanliness, and she hasn't.'

They flattered me because it was convenient for them to put me in with her, they knew I'd clean up her mess.

Then I went to the governor and told him that empty mattress was breaking my bones.

'Well,' he said, 'we can soon fix that, go to the stores and get some horsehair, you can stuff the mattress yourself.'

'Aha!' I say, 'so I have to go and get the horsehair, clean it, stuff the mattress and sew it up. Was I sent here to work as an upholsterer?'

'Look,' he says, 'this is a prison, not the Grand Hotel. If you want to sleep comfortably, do as I say.'

'And who's going to pay me for my work?' I say. 'Well, never mind, I won't split hairs, I'll do it. But, sir, there's a nice, dry, empty cell near mine, at least let me move in there.'

'That cell has to be kept empty,' he says.

'Why, are you renting it out? You said yourself this wasn't a hotel,' I say.

'None of your business,' he says, 'I don't have to account to you for my actions.'

Anyway, I went down and when the nun wasn't looking, I took the two lovely, soft, fluffy mattresses from the empty cell and put them into mine. I gave one to Teta and put the other on my bed. That night I had marvellous dreams. I dreamed someone was chasing me with a knife. I ran and ran. Then just as he was about to stab me, I started to fly. The murderer couldn't fly; he looked up and said: 'Shit! Where are you going?' I looked down on him from above, as if he was a worm, and I laughed at him. I flew, I was so good at it that I skimmed through the air, somer-saulted, stretched out my arms, which I used like a bird uses its wings. Everything looked tiny below me; the colours were bright, as if washed with water. I remember that flight to this day, it was truly wonderful.

The following afternoon Mother Goose, the old Mother Superior, came to my cell. 'Go down to the gate at once, Teresa!' she said, 'there's news for you!'

'What news, Mother?' I said, 'who's it from?' As Orlando had recently had two heart attacks, I was very worried. 'Is it about my brother?' I said. I knew she knew what the news was, that's why I persisted, so as to steel myself to face it. In prison, they like to terrorise you with diabolical mysteries. When they feel like it, they give you just a hint, enough to tantalise you.

'Yes, I think it's about your brother, go down quickly, it may be serious news.'

'Oh, God!' I said, 'he must be dead!' And I ran downstairs. I nearly fell down the stairs in the dark and I was breathless when I reached the gate.

'Are you Teresa Numa?' they said.

'Yes, tell me quickly!'

'You are leaving, you've been transferred.'

That bloody-minded, rotten bitch! Mother Goose knew what the news was all along, and she played this trick on me! I nearly had a fit. I cursed her, and the mother who bore her.

As Perugia, where I was sent, I told the Mother Superior there, Sister Pazienza, about the trick Mother Goose had played on me. And at once she said, 'Oh, yes, I know Mother Supplitiis, she was just an ordinary nun; now they've made her a Mother Superior, but she can't even read or write, she's an ignoramus, a country clod. Can you imagine, I used to ask her to read to me from the newspapers sometimes, and she read like a child, without even pausing for full stops and commas.'

# 34

At Perugia, I was entitled to be in with the remand prisoners, but, on the excuse that there was no room, they slapped me right in with the lifers and the long-term cons. I had to put a brave face on it. 'Good evening, how are you?' they said, 'where have you come from? What did you get done for? Don't worry, you'll be all right here. Got any money? Just hand over what you've got and everything will be fine.'

Luckily I had nothing, because they don't mince matters there, they search you inside out! If you try to hide something, they beat you up and leave you half-dead. Six of them got hold of me immediately; they frisked me, searched me, shoved a finger up my arse to see if I had anything hidden there. Finding nothing, they let me go.

That bitch Mother Supplitiis has certainly fixed me! I thought, not only has she sent me to Perugia, but she's had me shut up with all these murderesses! After tricking me like that, she didn't have the nerve to look me in the eye, so she made me wait in the entrance hall and sent my stuff down to me via another con. This woman kept half my things: a plate, a glass, a cup, two forks, a tin of coffee, a brown woollen sweater, a pair of stockings and two pairs of pants stuck to her fingers. I needed those things – without them I was left practically starkers. But who was I supposed to complain to, the wall?

Anyway, after they've searched me, an old woman with white hair comes up to me and says, 'I advise you not to protest, because those who make trouble here get a bad name and they send them off to Pozzuoli.'

'I know,' I say, 'I've already had that experience.'

'If you make a fuss, they soon lay their beady eyes on you, so keep quiet,' she says. 'If we can, we'll help you.'

'But you manage to adapt yourselves, you pretend to be soft in the head, you lick the nuns' feet, kiss their hands and smile — how do you do it?'

Then this old woman looks me straight in the eye and says, 'We don't give a bugger about you, so be good. Behave yourself or we'll soon knock any idea of protesting out of you!'

I didn't answer, because I realised the old hag was speaking not for herself but for the others; she was a kind of leader. I knew, too, that the long-termers, the old lags, have a completely different attitude, because they have to reckon their accounts over a long period; they have to spend their lives with these nuns, and for that reason they behave themselves, even if it means playing the hypocrite one hundred per cent.

But then, secretly, under the surface, they do what they like. They never protest, they keep up an appearance of order, but it's only an appearance. Moreover, every last one of them has her companion, her lover, and she knows that she must keep her for twenty or thirty years. They're affectionate with each other, they don't run risks.

I, who was not a lifer and knew I would be out within a year, had to act differently. But I felt really uncomfortable amongst all those murderesses, I didn't know how to fend them off. They were tough, violent, and if you upset them you were liable to get lynched.

One day I went to Sister Eburnea, a little nun with a very pretty, swarthy face. 'Sister,' I said, 'try to get me sent away from here, it's awful being among the lifers.'

'But why?' she said, 'they're so good.'

'Yes,' I said, 'good as gold, but they're butchers, they've committed murder, and as they have to stay here all their lives they've become bitter, hard and perverted.'

'Oh, no, Teresa, they're just resigned. They eat, drink, keep quiet.'

I said, 'Yes, quiet!' But, since I am not a grass, I didn't say a word about what went on amongst these women, though of course she knew quite well. I said, 'Yes, quiet they may be, but I get depressed with them. I haven't killed anyone and I don't like being in with killers.'

'We'll see what we can do,' she said. 'For the moment, stay where you are and resign yourself to the Lord's will.'

'It's nothing to do with the Lord,' I said. 'It's your will! Oh Christ bloody Jesus! Fuck the Madonna!' and I started blaspheming at the top of my voice. She got up, slapped my face and went away.

In the mornings we got up at seven. We had to wash, dress, make our beds, do everything at the double and queue up for the toilet. If you didn't hurry up, Sister Caritatis locked you in. At a certain time she bolted all the doors and anyone left inside missed the breakfast of bread and milk.

I often had to forego my breakfast because I wanted to wash. Sometimes I managed without going to the toilet so that I could get the bread and milk. You had to choose: either a wash or breakfast or the toilet. You couldn't do all three. Almost everyone did without a wash.

The milk was watered down, and they put a bit of chicory in it to give it some taste. The bread was yesterday's; we had to save it up from the day before, as it was dished out only at midday. But you had to keep it hidden in a safe place, or on you, under your sweater, or someone would knock it off.

Now that the prison in Perugia has been done up, it's not so bad, but at that time there were no showers, and the only toilets were holes in the ground, like men use. One hole for every fifteen people. As for the wash-basin, it was so small you just had room to wash your face and that was all. If you had money, you could buy a plastic bowl and wash yourself in a little freezing-cold water. We could have baths, down in the basement, once a fortnight, and you had to queue up for them. Once a week you could take your washing down to the laundry in a bundle. You had to wash your things, all standing in line, in a mad rush, everything at the double – it was like the navy. And this is still the same, it hasn't changed.

The food was better in Perugia than in Rome. You got meat every day, a bit of boiled beef, a sausage or a stew. It was so tough you needed teeth of iron, but at least they gave us meat every day. And soup with egg, a little cheese, and lots and lots of potatoes.

As I was only in for a few months, they didn't put me to work. There were few jobs and they were snapped up by those serving long sentences. Besides, I was still fuming over the fact that at

Rebibbia they hadn't paid me for the last three months, I don't know why. I paid for my stamps, too, all the time I was working and they didn't give me my superannuation when I left, I never got a penny of it – perhaps because I was always being transferred. The money kept arriving after I'd left, and, somewhere along the way, it vanished and nobody knew anything about it.

At Perugia I was dying of boredom, sitting all day long at that little table. I wanted a book to read, something to keep me amused. But I can't see well at close quarters, so I asked for a pair of glasses.

Sister said, 'You have to apply to the Ministry if you want glasses.'

I applied, but the glasses never came. Then I said, 'Sister, how can I get hold of some glasses? I'd like to read, educate myself a little.'

'Petition for them.'

So I petitioned, but – no glasses. Then Sister said to me, 'The Contessa Bartolomei comes every Friday with alms for the women convicts. Go up to her, kiss her hand, ask her politely for these glasses and she'll get them for you, you'll see. You'll have to butter her up a bit, tell her a sad tale, she's like St Vincent, she carries her heart in her hand, she's easily moved. Tell her you're half-blind, that you haven't got a cent, and you can't see to read your prayer-book.'

So this Contessa arrives, a big blonde matron with black dress, black stockings, a huge diamond brooch on her bosom and a hat covered in black bows. As soon as she arrives, everybody pounces on her. And she gives out presents: a bra for one, a vest for another, a pair of shoes for a third. All second-hand stuff, of course, but beggars can't be choosers, we're glad of it all the same.

I step forward and say, 'Contessa, I need a pair of glasses, I don't see very well.' I've got a whole string of complaints and lamentations memorised, but when it comes to the point, I forget them all. I can't squeeze out a tear, in fact I feel more like laughing when I look at that stout lady in her hat all decorated with black bows.

Then the Contessa asks me how many years I've got to serve.

'Five months,' I say.

She says, 'I'm sorry, but I give preference to those poor souls who have to spend years and years here. However, since you are

234

so poor, I will make you a gift of this hot-water bottle.'

'But what am I supposed to do with this?' I say. 'I need glasses, so that I can read.'

'And what do you want to read?'

'Educational books, something instructive.'

'Ah,' she says, 'you're not in prison to educate yourself, but to expiate your crimes. Resign yourself and pray, you don't need glasses to say your prayers.'

At about five in the afternoon, Sister Caritatis came and said, 'Who wants to go down for hot water?' Up till then I had never bothered, but from that day on, with my rubber bottle, I rushed down to the laundry with the others. There are geysers down there that pour hot water all day long. We were allowed to fill our bottles with this and then run back upstairs. On that occasion, I tried to take a little extra water, to wash my hair or my bottom, because they never gave you a bidet in that place, but each time Sister Caritatis made me pour it away, saying, 'Just enough for the hot-water bottle, Teresa, and no more!'

Once the stampede for hot water was over there was nothing else to do till television time. Sometimes I lay down and slept on the bench. Then Sister Eburnea would come along and give me a slap. She'd say, 'Wake up! You can sleep later on, in bed.'

I said, 'But I'm bored stiff, I don't know what to do!'

'Reflect on your sins,' she said.

'That's even more boring!'

'Then pray.'

'I've prayed so much my tongue is sore.'

'Yes,' she said, 'that's because you pray with bad words.'

'Yes, that's my way of praying,' I said. I knew that I was putting myself in a bad light by talking like that, but I couldn't help it, I disliked the nuns and I wasn't going to be all mealy-mouthed with them.

When TV time came, it was a mad scramble to get the best seats. The cons were happy and sat there with their mouths open, no matter what programme the authorities had decided to let us see. Every programme was studied by the nuns, the Mother Superior, the governor and the guards. Everybody had their say as to what was 'suitable' or 'not suitable'. 'Suitable' included songs, games where contestants won money, discussion programmes featuring priests, a few documentaries and the odd 'weepie' play. 'Unsuitable' were all news bulletins, even when

235

they talked about the Pope, detective stories, trials, even fictitious ones, all kinds of films, anything about war, debates, enquiries, discussions.

Once, there was a terrible battle over 'Anna Karenina'. The governor had declared it suitable and we had already seen one episode. Then Mother Pazienza came along and said it was unsuitable and switched off the TV set without another word. Uproar ensued. Even those who never made a murmur were up in arms. We screamed, we banged the chairs on the floor, they had to call in the guards to quieten us down. I was the most hotheaded of the lot. I grabbed the nun by the veil and pulled, hoping to leave her with her bald head exposed. But the moment she felt me tugging, she started wriggling like an eel and managed to slip out of my grasp.

When there was television we stayed up till nine or ten, otherwise we went to bed at seven. We slept in a huge room, a sort of stable for horses. In the middle of this stable there was a stove, one stove for all of us. It heated an area of about two yards round the stove, but the rest of the room was freezing cold. There were something like forty beds. Only four or five of these got any warmth from the stove; for the rest it was worse than being in a refrigerator. This stove burned wood, and to make it last a bit longer we would steal odd bits of chairs from the carpenter's shop and smuggle them in.

As soon as Sister Caritatis left the room, we huddled round the stove. We warmed our feet, put our socks to scorch on the metal pipes, we swarmed round like flies. If you didn't hug the stove, the cold killed you stone dead, because the walls of the penal colony stream with water and the damp rots your bones. Very often, when we were huddled round the stove warming ourselves, somebody would say, 'Fucking pigs! Teresa, when you get out of here, you must go to the Ministry, see the Minister himself and tell him to set up an enquiry about this place!'

'Yes,' I said, 'this time I'll do it for sure.'

'Go and tell him we live in a stable with one solitary stove, one toilet, and the pigs here wipe their feet on us as if we were doormats. Nobody can live like this!'

'I'll go to the Minister,' I said, 'I'll tell him everything.'

At eight o'clock, Sister Caritatis locked us into the stable and went to bed. She slept in a room at the end of the corridor, together with four other nuns.

One night I felt ill, I got an attack of renal colic. I got up and knocked on the door. I knocked and hammered till I couldn't knock any more, and I was too weak to call out. The rest of them, the hypocrites, pretended to be asleep, they took not a blind bit of notice. With all the din I was making, they carried on snoring! They were afraid. They were thinking: She's kicking up a hell of a row and she'll get into trouble, we don't want to get drawn into it. Sister will be furious.

After two hours Sister Caritatis finally appeared. 'What do you want?' she says, pale-faced and sleepy.

'I'm dying, I've got colic,' I say.

'Here you are,' she says, 'take this suppository and don't wake me up any more, you miserable wretch!' She locks everything up again and leaves.

For a while the suppository relieves the pain. Then, just as I'm dropping off, I wake up with a start, the pains are nearly killing me. So I shriek, knock, call out, hammer at the door, kick it. But the nun takes no notice.

So there I stay, bent double with the pain and I can't even get back to my bed. Nobody comes to help me. I have to drag myself along on all fours and then haul myself up slowly, hanging on to the blankets.

Next morning they put me in the infirmary. I was rigid and numb with pain.

'Get me the doctor,' I said.

'Yes, yes,' they said, but the doctor didn't come. They gave me suppositories but they no longer had any effect. I was petrified, turned to stone with the pain.

'Do something!' I said, 'do something!'

The nun hurried by, taking thermometers, cough syrup and syringes with her. 'Later,' she said, 'later. Just keep calm now.' And she went away.

At last the doctor came. He gave me an injection. I felt better at once, but I was still numb. And I couldn't stand up. At night the pains came on again. I called the sister and asked her to give me another injection.

'I can't do anything without the doctor's permission,' she said.

'Call the doctor, then.'

'Tomorrow,' she said, 'tomorrow.'

Next day the doctor never showed his face, and I kept begging for this injection. The pains had come on strong again, like the first evening. They told me, 'The doctor only comes when the Mother Superior sends for him.

'And why can't she send for him now?'

'She's gone to Rome on a mission, she'll be back in a few days.'

So I was left without a doctor. I protested, lost my temper. Then the sister said, 'There's a doctor at the prison today, I'll call him if you like.'

'Call him at once,' I said.

After a while, this doctor arrives, tall, beaming, handsome. He says, 'I'm a dental surgeon, do you need a tooth extracted, signora?'

'No,' I say, 'I've got a tooth missing in the front here, though, it was knocked out by the guards. But I haven't got the money to have a new one fitted.'

'Well,' he says, 'you can pay me when you've got the money. I can fix you up for 12,000 lire. Give me 6000 at once and the rest in a month's time.'

'Oh, yes,' I say, 'and who's going to give me the 6000 lire?'

So I didn't get my tooth fixed and I had to endure the kidney pains until they went away of their own accord at the end of a week.

# 35

Two months later I came out, thin and haggard. Ercoletto was still inside, he had got longer than me. As usual, our house had been ransacked. Every time I go in, my friends and relatives come and take everything away. So when I come out I find myself as naked and forlorn as if I'd just emerged from the tomb.

I went to La Spagnola, my only real friend.

'My God!' she said, 'you're wasted away!'

'Yes,' I said, 'in prison one wastes away.'

'Here, eat!' she said, and she gave me a plate of potatoes dressed with oil and parsley. 'I can't give you meat any more,' she said, 'I'm not with the old man now, I'm short of money, and prices have gone up. Veal's gone up from 1500 lire a kilo to 2000 or more, I can't manage.'

'Don't worry,' I said, 'I'll try and work something out. I'll buy meat for you.'

The first thing I did was go and get Orlandino back. I found him covered in sores. He had a rash of yellow pustules all over his bottom and legs; as soon as one burst another started to form and no medicine could cure him.

Meanwhile I tried to find out where my brother had been transferred to. Then a letter came from him, saying: 'My dear sister and my dear little son, Orlandino, my case came up before the Livorno Tribunal. I was tried for my fight with the bandit, La Parca, and for the stab wound given him by Yours Truly. From there, I was transferred to Rome, where I remained about a month and witnessed things more diabolical than hell itself, for I was present at the death of the young man, Cocota – they tied him to the restraining bed and murdered him, they beat him to death. On that occasion I attacked the *brigadiere* and split his left eyebrow open with a chamber pot. For this, I was done for one year's imprisonment and again they transferred me to Porto Azzurro, where I suffered tortures. It was there that I received news of our father's death, and seeing from the date on the telegram that the prison chaplain had kept it back for twenty-four days, I hurled myself at him and split the chaplain's head open with a broom handle. Meantime, we changed governors, and a certain Sozzi came to us from Rome. He knew all about me, knew everything I had been through, and he was kind enough to let me act as rat-catcher and set traps. For every rat I caught, he gave me a packet of cut tobacco, and after three months he sent me to Civitavecchia, where I learned to make shawls and children's garments. After eight months at Civitavecchia I was interviewed by an illustrated magazine; they wrote a lot about me, saying it was enough to speak in the wrong tone of voice for them to drag you off before the beak, that the guards didn't hesitate to knock you about with their fists and with sticks, and that at Civitavecchia I had become a model prisoner.

'And so, my dear sister, I spent six months of consolation and then regained my freedom. You were still inside at that time. I went to my woman, the dwarf, and that same night I tried to throw myself under a train, but a railway worker saw me and, with the help of three other people, escorted me back to my home. The following morning my woman and I were reconciled and for some time everything went well. During the day I worked for the Council and at night I went fishing. One fine morning, returning from a fishing trip, I saw a number of people looking into a shop which had been burgled during the night. I too stopped to have a look. All of a sudden the owner of the shop, a fellow named Rollini, pointed a gun at my chest and shouted, "Here he is, the thief in the night!" Sure of myself, I laughed in his face and said, "You're a fool!" but at that moment I saw the Sergeant of the *carabinieri*, and he arrested me, not hesitating to slap and punch me brutally. I spent two nights and two days in jail. They had to let me out on the testimony of our brother Luciano, at whose house I had called, and of the fishermen I had been out with. Two days later I went to Nettuno, our brother Eligio gave me a room in his house, I paid 10,000 lire a month rent for it. But then Eligio's wife made trouble, she was jealous, so for the sake of family peace I left the house and went to Anzio, where I again started living with the dwarf, Carmela Andando, whom you know. I went to work as a porter down at the port and I earned 5000 lire a day. That Saturday evening some workmates and I unloaded two truck-loads of manure, then we decided to go and eat some mussels and a pizza together. And while we were sitting there drinking and eating, a certain Romoletto, known as Old Scratch, said he had seen the men who robbed Rollini's shop, although he'd never breathed a word about it to anyone or revealed the names, and that, a few minutes before the robbery, he had seen these two thieves talking to the *maresciallo* of *carabinieri*. So I drank a bottle of red wine, made an excuse about taking my woman out to the cinema, said goodbye to my friends and left.

'I went straight to a friend who let me have a pistol, then to the barracks and asked for an urgent interview with the *maresciallo*. In his presence, I said, "Hurry, *maresciallo*, I've found the men who robbed the fabrics shop, they're dividing up the loot and talking about it this very minute." At these words, he ordered the *carabinieri* to arm themselves, we went down the street I indicated, and then I told them to spread out. The *maresciallo* and I, together with a lance-corporal who was armed with a tommy-gun, went down another dark street. At a certain point I pulled out my revolver and pointed it at the lance-corporal. I took the tommy-gun off him, took the *maresciallo*'s revolver and in the end I rounded them all up, disarmed them, and marched them back to the barracks, still covering them with the tommy-gun.

'On the way I met a man I knew and sent him to fetch our brother Luciano, who, in fact, arrived at the barracks at the same moment as we did. Seeing me with the gun pointed, he begged me to behave myself. I told him to telephone the mayor at once because I had caught the thieves and the charge against me must be dropped at once and I must be vindicated.

'The mayor arrived and said he had phoned H.Q. to send a senior officer to the barracks at once, to unravel this affair. Some fifty minutes later a *brigadiere* came in and I immediately levelled the tommy-gun at him. They were trying to persuade me, one way and another, to put that gun down, so I said, "This *maresciallo* here, together with two thieves, is the author of the crime. They were in league together, I have proof, witnesses." The

16

*maresciallo* kept his mouth shut, and that proved his guilt. Finally, as we weren't getting anywhere, just shuffling backwards and forwards, I killed the *maresciallo* without mercy, because he was guilty of the crime for which I had been treacherously arrested. Then I told Luciano to pick up the cartridges and hand them over to the *brigadiere* and the mayor.

'When I handed over the tommy-gun they arrested me immediately, without taking into account the fact that I had carried out an act of justice, and they forced me to write a confession stating that I had killed the *maresciallo* because of a personal vendetta.

'For this act of bravado I was put inside again, even though the judge acknowledged the *maresciallo*'s guilt, and admitted that he and the two thieves had planned and committed the crime. Now I'm in Reggio Emilia prison, the worst place on earth, the viciousness of the wretched and degraded cons here is even worse than at Porto Azzurro. If you can, send me something to eat and something to wear. I am always hungry, and it's difficult for me to chew as my teeth are rotten, so send fruit, biscuits, tinned stew, soft things like that. I beg you to visit me as soon as you get out and bring Orlandino with you. After all, I am his father and I miss him, he is always far away from me. Now I must end this letter, but remember that my love for you will never end. Hugs and kisses to you, lots of kisses, especially to my dear little Orlandino. Yours ever, Orlando.'

Before I took his son to see him, however, I waited until he was in better health. He would have had a fit if he'd seen the child in that run-down condition. I gave him penicillin and powdered cortisone and it seemed that at last the pustules were drying up, thanks to the cortisone. The bad skin flaked off leaving a beautiful new skin underneath.

Meanwhile I was looking for a way to make some money, because I couldn't go on living at La Spagnola's expense; she had me and Orlando on her back. Out of desperation, and finding nothing else, I started up again with the travellers' cheques. But this time I was more cautious, I didn't want to go inside again. I decided to work alone, without accomplices.

At one time, in the Bar Bengasi, I had known a man who was a waiter in a hotel on the via Nazionale. His name was Vito; he was thin, balding, distinguished-looking, nobody would ever suspect him, and he spoke French like a Frenchman.

I remembered that he had once put a proposition to me and I went to look him up. I told him that I was on the game, that I went with Americans and they often paid me in travellers' cheques and I didn't know where to change them. He said to me, 'Bring them here if you like, I'll change them for you.'

This Vito had won the confidence of the manager of the hotel and was on good terms with everybody there, including the cashier, for there was a bank right inside the hotel. It's not a luxurious place, more of a commercial hotel, with lots of tourists from all over the world and businessmen who come there regularly.

So I bought travellers' cheques in the Campo dei Fiori, dealing with two bag-snatcher friends of mine, or else I went to Trastevere, to Aldina Bandy-Legs or to Luigi, the fellow known as the Beak.

The price varied from day to day, sometimes more, sometimes less, but it was usually 20,000 lire for 100 dollars' worth. Each cheque was worth 30, 50 or 100 dollars.

Quite often Bandy-Legs said to me, 'Here, Teresa, I'll let you have these cheques cheap, give me 10,000 and take them. They've been in my pocket for a week, they're beginning to burn a hole.'

I took these cheques, 200 or 300 dollars at a time, to Vito. Immediately whoosh! he was off like a rocket to change them in the internal bank. I put 20,000 to 30,000 lire in his hand, according to how much he'd changed for me.

'Doing all right?' he said to me.

'Yes, last night I hooked an American, he was blind drunk, and he gave me all these travellers' cheques.'

'Aha! You're smart,' he said, 'you know how to handle these Americans, you did the right thing. Those turds are loaded with money, the only way to treat them is to empty their pockets for them!'

He changed all these stolen cheques for me, although the thefts had been reported. Maybe he guessed, maybe he realised they were hot, but he pretended not to know. We carried out our transactions smoothly: I went in, he changed them for me, I put the money in my pocket and sailed out.

I bought meat and ham for La Spagnola, I even bought her a television set for her birthday. I fed Orlandino well, fattened him up. I took parcels to Ercoletto, who had meanwhile been transferred to Cassino, and parcels to my brother Orlando in Reggio Emilia.

Then I decided to take a room of my own and I moved in with this old landlady. She was eighty, ugly as the plague, but she still thought about men. She wanted to marry a fellow who had a fruit stall in the market; his name was Giomberto. I don't know whether he ever married her on not. He was quite keen to marry her just to get his hands on the money she had tucked away in the bank. They said she had half a million. Everybody said he was only after her money, somebody even said as much to the old girl, but she wouldn't listen. 'They're all jealous, just jealous,' she said. 'Teresa, my dear, if you don't watch out, they'll pull the very chair from under you. Have you seen how handsome Giomberto is? And how much he loves me? Every evening he brings me a beautiful muscatel pear to eat.'

I paid the old woman 20,000 a month for a room with use of kitchen and bath. There was no hot water, the room was no bigger than a cupboard, you could barely get a camp bed in. The kitchen was a pig-sty festooned with strings of garlic and onions that gave off a sharp, noxious odour. I made the best of it, it wasn't too bad and it wasn't too good, either. There were times when I made quite a bit of bread and times when I made very little. But I didn't stick my neck out, because I was scared of going to prison again.

One day, when I was walking back from Porta Portese with Orlandino – I'd gone there to buy a blanket – I felt a sudden longing to see my son, Maceo. It was such an overpowering nostalgia for him that my feet automatically, of their own accord, turned and walked toward viale Marconi. With aching feet, carrying the child in my arms, I walked all the way to my son's house.

In front of it was a shabby little garden where the dogs went to do their business. There were two mangy trees and four flower-beds with sickly yellow bushes. There were also two green benches, gleaming with new paint. I sat down on one of them, facing the house, and waited for him to come out.

I waited and waited, but that son of mine never appeared. The longer I sat there, the more I desired to see him. I thought: If he comes out, I'll pretend I'm just walking here with the baby, by chance, that I didn't know he lived here, then it'll be all right.

I walked up and down, up and down. No sign of Maceo. I

waited till evening, I waited till my eyes ached with peering at that wretched doorway where so many people went in and out, but never the one I waited for so longingly.

I couldn't go up to the apartment because they had told me that, as far as he was concerned, his mamma was dead. He had said it himself, so they told me, some years ago, after his aunts, my mortal enemies, had set him against me. They told him I was a bad mother, a criminal without a shred of honour or morality.

They said to him, 'Your mother's always in prison, she goes with all the crooks and whores, she's an outlaw, an enemy of the family, you must repudiate her!' And so he did.

He said, 'From this day on, I no longer have a mother. For me, she is as good as dead.'

He's got a good job at Pirelli's. He is married, and they live there on viale Marconi with the mother-in-law. She's a good woman, very understanding.

Before he did his military service he used to come and see me, even though he was still living with his aunts. He had made friends with Ercoletto; we ate pizza and went to the cinema together. But after his time in the army he changed. He got engaged, started giving himself airs like a gentleman. He got this job at Pirelli's and he didn't want to know me any more. He said, 'My mother has a lover, they live together without being married; an employee of Pirelli's can't have a mother like that, it's not the thing at all.'

He's a good-looking boy, my son. Not because he's my son but he really is stunning. He's six foot tall. He has a sweet face. Physically, around the eyes, he resembles me. His character is like his father's: he is of his father's stock. He's not bad, he's sensitive, a good boy. But he lets other people influence him, lead him by the nose.

It was mainly my sister-in-law Ines who turned him against me. I had written to him from prison, telling him I was alone, hungry, begging him to visit me. And she said to him, 'Are you crazy? Prison? For heaven's sake don't go and see that wretched mother of yours!' As if setting foot in the place for half and hour would contaminate him! In fact, he never came, he never even sent me a postcard.

When I was out, he often came to my place; he and Ercoletto played cards together and drank beer. Sometimes my son read me a sermon. 'Mamma!' he would say, 'look what you've done, look what a mess you've made of your life! You live in the clouds, full of dreams and fancies, but you always end up in clink! Your women friends have grown rich, your brothers live decent lives, they're successful, and here you are, a beggar! You know only thieves and whores.'

He was repeating his aunt's own words. I said, 'Well, just kid yourself these thieves are earls and princes – what's it to you? If the people I mix with had money, you would treat them with respect. Pretend they're rich, immensely rich, fabulously rich, and bow down before them!'

The final blow was struck by the girl he married, because she's a haughty, stuck-up piece. Her name's Mimma, she's an Abruzzese and there's bile and bitter gall in her blood. She wants to be put on a pedestal and worshipped, she thinks she's a little plaster saint. She's quite hopeless in the house, can't do a thing. She should thank the good Lord who made her that she's got a domesticated mother who does it all for her: cleans, washes, cooks, the lot. The daughter never raises her little finger in the house, she's afraid of spoiling her hands. She wears her nails very long, and when they break she sticks them on with adhesive tape. As far as brains go, she's a donkey. But she's crafty, all right. As soon as she laid eyes on my son she started dominating him: 'If you don't pass your exams, I won't get engaged to you.' Then: 'If you don't get a good job, I won't marry you.'

And my son passed his exams, got his job at Pirelli's. He had to sweat blood to do it, he had to humble himself, beg favours, fawn. He had taken a tremendous fancy to this Mimma. He was madly in love.

Her face is no oil painting: she has a pug nose, thin lips, goggle eyes. My son likes her, I don't. She's of average height. She hasn't got much hair, she's slightly bald. I wouldn't call her a raving beauty.

In my opinion, my son is too good for this Mimma, she can't hold a candle to him. Everybody says so. Not because he's my son, but he's got a fine, stalwart figure, he stands as proud as a statue. Besides, he's a gay spark, he likes to have fun, whereas she is sulky and dour. She wouldn't give you the time of day. She keeps him under her thumb and makes him work, because she wants a luxurious motor-car, she wants a beaver lamb coat, she wants to eat off silver plates, she's greedy.

She's for ever standing in front of the mirror, brushing those few hairs. 'Maceo has neither father nor mother,' she says. 'The father is dead, the mother lives in sin with a man – it's not respectable.'

Then she gets out her nail varnish, a sticky-looking pink, and starts painting her nails, first her toes, then her hands, and while she's painting she's complaining: 'This is respectable . . . that is not respectable . . . this is the done thing . . . that is not the done thing.' She's worse than the judge at a trial.

# 36

I used to go to the hotel on via Nazionale about noon, when Vito knocked off. I dressed very smartly, in a light brown coat with a fur collar, a beautiful yellow blouse and a bracelet here and there. My hair was always newly-washed and set. I put on this act, playing the high-class whore, for Vito, so that he would believe I had come by the travellers' cheques honestly. To keep him unsuspecting I invented stories.

'It went well last night,' I'd say. 'I cottoned on to a really rich American and I made him give me 100 dollars. Then I met a friend of this first one – he was all bloated and his face was puffy.'

'Good, Teresa,' he would say, 'do the bastards, rob them! They're an ignorant rabble and they think they're somebody just because they've got money, they treat you like dirt because you're a waiter, or a whore. Get all you can off them, strip them, skin them alive!'

I said, 'This American's called Gionni, he's very possessive, he wants me all to himself. He wants to marry me and take me to America, you know. His wife's dead and now he wants to marry me.'

Vito replied, 'Great! Marry him, then ditch him, but get every last cent off him first.'

I told him this tale because next day I wanted to change 500 dollars, and I would be able to say Gionni had given them to me. This Vito was a bit of a twit, he never even noticed that the cheques were signed by all sorts of different people – there were women's names on them, Italian names even.

He said, 'Come on, Teresa, I'll buy you a coffee.' We went to a bar nearby and he bought me a coffee with cream. As long as I spoke ill of the Americans, he was happy. It was an obsession with him.

'What's he like this fellow who wants to marry you?' he asked.

I said, 'He's six foot six, and he must be seventy years old. His hair is light chestnut, I don't know whether he dyes it. He wears his trousers up to his armpits and keeps them up with two red braces with the word "Victory" embroidered on them.'

My imagination was running away with me. It was true I had known an American like that, but many years ago. This fellow wanted to marry Dina, and his name really was Gionni. He never even noticed me, he was mad about Dina. He was seventy, but looked a bit older.

'Good girl!' said Vito, 'pluck the old cock, truss him and roast him!' and he beat his hands on his thighs. He drank one coffee, then another, always with whipped cream on top. He put in four or five spoonfuls of sugar, then piled the cream on top. He had a sweet tooth and was greedy for sweet things. As a result his teeth were all rotten and decayed.

He said, 'Then what did you do?'

'I took him to a pensione, undressed him, got him all steamed up and then said, "Give me a hundred dollars at once or I'll walk out and leave you flat." He coughed up immediately.'

So I bragged to him, and he laughed, showing those rotten teeth of his. He offered me another coffee and slapped his thighs with his hands. He was quite a likeable fellow, but he had this fixation, this phobia about Americans.

'Go on!' he said, 'tell me some more.' My imagination took flight like a bird; I became a story-teller, a liar. Oh, the yarns I spun him!

One day, when I went to my appointment with this Vito, he wasn't there. I asked for him and they said, 'Please, signorina, don't set foot in here again or the manager will have you turned out.'

I said, 'Why? What ever for?' I showed my claws at once, so that they wouldn't get the better of me. At the same time I was looking round for a hasty exit.

Then a waiter came along, a certain Vincenzino, a friend of Vito's, and he said, 'You know, Vito was called in to the manager's office. They asked him who gave him the travellers' cheques.

He told the manager the Americans gave them to him as tips, but the manager said, "Who are you trying to fool? Hundred-dollar tips?" Then Vito replied, "Well, actually, I get them from a young lady who goes with all these Americans. They pay her in travellers' cheques." '

The manager told him that all the cheques were stolen and the owners had reported the thefts. 'But I won't send you to jail,' he added, 'because it is partly my own responsibility, and if we don't hush the whole thing up I shall lose my job as well as you.'

So, rather than lose his position, the manager resigned himself to paying 2,007,000 lire, the value of the stolen cheques. He would pay it all back in instalments, so much per month.

I was relieved when I heard this. I was afraid Vito had been arrested and I could feel the handcuffs on my wrists already. 'Now,' they said, 'go away, signorina, and don't show your face here again, because the manager is furious with you.'

And that is how that fountain of plenty dried up. I didn't see Vito any more. After that I started dealing in oil and household linen again. I don't earn so much, but it's less risky and the work is steady.

Then one day a friend says to me, 'Listen, Teresa, would you change this cheque for me, then we'll go fifty-fifty on it?'

'If it's false,' I say, 'the answer is no. I'm not sticking my neck out for 80,000 lire.'

'No, it's good,' she says, 'I guarantee it.'

'All right, then, I'll go to the bank tomorrow morning and cash it for you. But why can't you go?'

'I haven't got any documents,' she says, 'besides, the fuzz are looking for me.'

As I walk up to the counter I find the police there waiting for me. It's a dud cheque, stolen, and that bitch has dropped me in the shit!

So, inside I go again, after acting in good faith, and for a mere 80,000 lire! I find all my old friends and acquaintances.

'Hallo!' they say, 'back again?'

'Leave me alone, for Christ's sake!' I say.

I ask to be put to work and they send me to the kitchen garden. I have a spade, I have to dig, get out the weeds, water and sow. To start with there's a certain Antonia working with me, a chatterbox who never stops talking. She even manages to talk while she's digging, God knows how, she must be an acrobat.

Part of our task is to feed the hens. There's a coop with some twenty chickens in it. They're plump, well-fed, vicious. If you go in they peck your feet, and if you don't give them enough to eat they shriek at you and, out of revenge, go for your legs.

Every now and then one of these chickens disappears. I ask Sister Carmina: 'Who's taken the red hen?'

She says, 'Ssh! Shut up and mind your own business!'

'Well, I don't want to get the blame,' I say.

'Don't worry,' she says, 'there aren't any thieves round here.'

Antonia starts to laugh. The nun gets angry. She says, 'What are you cackling at, you idiot?'

Antonia puts her hand over her mouth and goes on laughing.

'Go to work!' says the nun, 'and put your backs into it!'

Only yesterday, talking to the gardener, I found out where these carefully fattened-up hens go to. He says, 'Teresa, you'd better feed them well, because they end up in Judge Giglio's oven.'

For this work they pay me 8000 lire a month, including the superannuation contributions and the stamps.

Antonio is pregnant, she told me the other day. 'But who is it?' I say, and she starts to laugh.

She says, 'The nun, of course!'

'What!' I say, 'is one of the nuns a transvestite now?'

She says, 'No, the nun is just a blind, the real father is called Serpente.'

'Aha! So that snake in the grass has popped up again, has he? But where is he? I'll give him a flea in his ear.'

'He's at the other prison, the one I was transferred from,' she replies.

The day after this discussion Antonia didn't come down to the kitchen garden, nor the next day. I asked Sister where she was.

'In the infirmary,' she says.

'What's wrong with her?'

'Nothing, you keep your nose out of it.'

I was curious. The baby couldn't be born yet because she had told me she was in her fifth month. Then, at supper time, I heard from a friend that she had tried to abort herself with a kitchen knife and had cut her womb in half. Now she was in the infirmary and nobody knew whether she would live or die.

Thank the Lord my ovaries are frozen, there's no danger of

my getting pregnant. I tried to visit Antonia but they wouldn't let me into the infirmary. They said she had lost gallons of blood. But where did she keep all that blood? A skinny little woman, a chatterbox, rather sweet, pale-faced, you'd think she had sugar and water in her veins instead of blood.

What makes me mad is that I had to leave Orlandino with his mother, the dwarf, and she packed him straight off to boarding-school. That woman has no patience with children. She's got no money and no initiative to go out and make some. She lives in a hut by the sea, with no heating, no light, no bed. She sleeps on a mattress on the floor, goes out to scrub floors, earns 30,000 lire a month and lives like that, happy as a pig in shit. Every time she has a child, she pops him off to boarding-school, to the orphan-age, where the kids grow up half-dotty, tubercular and back-ward.

Ercoletto is still inside too. He doesn't write often, but he writes. He says that, in Cassino, there's a sadistic *maresciallo* who gives the cons hell. When Ercoletto said, 'I could just do with a nice plate of spaghetti now!' the other replied: 'I'll eat the pasta, you eat potatoes!' and, as Ercoletto answered back, he shut him up in the punishment cell for ten days. On the other hand, the governor is as soft as butter. But he's not the boss, because he's a civilian; the boss is the one who wears the shoulder-pips, that is, the *maresciallo* of *carabinieri*.

When the governor heard about it he sent for the *maresciallo* and said to him, 'My dear *maresciallo*, I'll have you thrown out of here, *ipso facto*.' And the *maresciallo* replied, 'My dear gover-nor, just you try it!'

In fact, he didn't succeed in throwing him out, nor did he make him mend his ways. They are always at it hammer-and-tongs, but there they are, the two of them, and the one who wears the uniform is the real boss. That's what Ercoletto writes to me from prison.

I shall be out before him, in ten months. I'm saving up money for that day, because, as usual, I have no home, no furniture, nothing. I left a trunk full of stuff in store at a cobbler's shop in via San Giovanni in Laterano, but God knows if I'll ever see it again; the cobbler is half-witted, they pinch shoes from under his very nose, he puts honey on instead of glue and chews bits of leather all day long – he's soft in the head.

The thing is, when I come out I don't want to be a thief any more. I want to find work as a dressmaker, even though I don't know how to sew . . . well, what the hell, I'll manage somehow. I'll buy materials on the never-never and after the first payment I'll change my address. All I want is to set up home with Ercoletto and Orlandino, calmly, quietly, in some nice peaceful place. I don't want to go back to prison any more.

# LORD PETER VIEWS THE BODY

## Dorothy L. Sayers

Written in the inimitable style of her best novels, here is another collection of Lord Peter Wimsey stories, equalling the STRIDING FOLLY volume.

Lord Peter here puzzles his way through such mysteries as 'The Abominable History of the Man with Copper Fingers' and 'The Fantastic Horror of the Cat in the Bag', besides many others.

Without doubt Lord Peter Wimsey is one of the greatest fiction detectives of this century, and this fascinating collection only further demonstrates the fact. This book is a necessity for both established readers, and newcomers.

NEW ENGLISH LIBRARY

# NEL BESTSELLERS

| T011 631 | MASTER MIND OF MARS | Edgar Rice Burroughs | 30p |
| T015 564 | LOST ON VENUS | Edgar Rice Burroughs | 35p |
| T010 333 | REVOLT IN 2100 | Robert Heinlein | 40p |
| T021 602 | THE MAN WHO SOLD THE MOON | Robert Heinlein | 40p |
| T016 900 | STRANGER IN A STRANGE LAND | Robert Heinlein | 75p |
| T022 862 | DUNE | Frank Herbert | 80p |
| T012 298 | DUNE MESSIAH | Frank Herbert | 40p |
| T015 211 | THE GREEN BRAIN | Frank Herbert | 30p |

**War**

| T013 367 | DEVIL'S GUARD | Robert Elford | 50p |
| T020 584 | THE GOOD SHEPHERD | C. S. Forester | 40p |
| T011 755 | TRAWLERS GO TO WAR | Lund & Ludlam | 40p |
| T012 999 | P.Q.17 – CONVOY TO HELL | Lund & Ludlam | 30p |
| T014 215 | THE GIANT KILLERS | Kenneth Poolman | 40p |
| T022 528 | THE LAST VOYAGE OF GRAF SPEE | Michael Powell | 35p |

**Western**

| T016 994 | No. 1 EDGE – THE LONER | George G. Gilman | 30p |
| T016 986 | No. 2 EDGE – TEN THOUSAND DOLLAR AMERICAN | | |
| | | George G. Gilman | 30p |
| T017 613 | No. 3 EDGE – APACHE DEATH | George G. Gilman | 30p |
| T017 001 | No. 4 EDGE – KILLER'S BREED | George G. Gilman | 30p |
| T016 536 | No. 5 EDGE – BLOOD ON SILVER | George G. Gilman | 30p |
| T017 621 | No. 6 EDGE – THE BLUE, THE GREY AND THE RED | | |
| | | George G. Gilman | 30p |
| T014 479 | No. 7 EDGE – CALIFORNIA KILLING | George G. Gilman | 30p |
| T015 254 | No. 8 EDGE – SEVEN OUT OF HELL | George G. Gilman | 30p |
| T015 475 | No. 9 EDGE – BLOODY SUMMER | George G. Gilman | 30p |
| T015 769 | No. 10 EDGE – VENGEANCE IS BLACK | George G. Gilman | 30p |
| T017 184 | No. 11 EDGE – SIOUX UPRISING | George G. Gilman | 30p |
| T017 893 | No. 12 EDGE – THE BIGGEST BOUNTY | George G. Gilman | 30p |
| T018 253 | No. 13 EDGE – A TOWN CALLED HATE | George G. Gilman | 30p |
| T020 754 | No. 14 EDGE – THE BIG GOLD | George G. Gilman | 30p |

**General**

| T021 009 | SEX MANNERS FOR MEN | Robert Chartham | 35p |
| T019 403 | SEX MANNERS FOR ADVANCED LOVERS | Robert Chartham | 30p |
| W002 835 | SEX AND THE OVER FORTIES | Robert Chartham | 30p |
| T010 732 | THE SENSUOUS COUPLE | Dr. 'C' | 25p |

**Mad**

| S004 892 | MAD MORALITY | | 40p |
| S005 172 | MY FRIEND GOD | | 40p |
| S005 069 | MAD FOR BETTER OR VERSE | | 30p |

---

NEL, P.O. BOX 11, FALMOUTH, TR10 9EN, CORNWALL
  Please send cheque or postal order. Allow 10p to cover postage and packing on one book plus 5p for each additional book.

Name ....................................................................................................................

Address..................................................................................................................

       ....................................................................................................................

Title ....................................................................................................................
(NOVEMBER)